D1116095

Sexual Detours

Infidelity

and Intimacy

at the Crossroads

Dr. Holly Hein

St. Martin's Press   New York

SOMERSET CO. LIBRARY
BRIDGEWATER, N.J. 08807

SEXUAL DETOURS. Copyright © 2000 by Dr. Holly Hein. All rights reserved. Printed in the United States of America. No part of this book may be used or reproduced in any manner whatsoever without written permission except in the case of brief quotations embodied in critical articles or reviews. For information, address St. Martin's Press, 175 Fifth Avenue, New York, N.Y. 10010.

Book design by Donna Sinisgalli

Library of Congress Cataloging-in-Publication Data

Hein, Holly.

Sexual detours : infidelity and intimacy at the crossroads / Holly Hein.—1st. ed.

    p. cm.

Includes bibliographical references.

ISBN 0-312-25335-4

1. Adultery—United States—Psychological aspects. I. Title.

HQ806.H45 2000

306.73'6—dc21   00-023902

First Edition: April 2000

10   9   8   7   6   5   4   3   2   1

To my precious, challenging,

and ever-affirming children,

Noëlle and Nicolas—

I dedicate this book.

Contents

Acknowledgments   ix

PART ONE
Prelude

1.	The Voice of an Affair	3
2.	The Self	23
3.	Romantic Love	35
4.	Marriage	46

PART TWO
Intermezzo

5.	The Triangle	67
6.	Sexual Detours	77
7.	Marsha: A Search for Identity	87
8.	Norma: An Avoidance of a Life Issue	97
9.	Luke and Travis: An Escape from Anxiety	105
10.	Shawn: A Substitute for Intimacy	120
11.	Neil: In Search of Self-Esteem	136
12.	Amanda: A Source of Power	147
13.	Lois and Tom: A Way of Sustaining the Status Quo	159

PART THREE

Finale

14. The Aftermath   175

15. Endings   195

16. Beginnings   212

17. Growing Whole   229

Bibliography   *255*
About the Author   *259*

Acknowledgments

This could be a very long story because there are so many people I wish to acknowledge. All of these people contributed in no small way to this book.

One sunny August afternoon three years ago, I stood in my friends Ken and Patti's kitchen. We started talking about a book I wanted to write. Several topics piqued my interest. I chose sex. Little did I know that fate was pulling the strings, and that sex with all its illicit excitement and humiliating revelations would even make its way into the hallowed halls of our government in its unexpurgated version.

Many of my patients, both single and married, who were in a relationship or were craving one, had distorted views of sex and marriage. They lived together and slept together, but they knew very little about each other. I wanted to write about the subject of sex and infidelity in order to teach people how to forge stronger, more grounded, and more intimate relationships. I wanted to teach people to understand that in order to make choices that would fulfill their physical, emotional, and spiritual selves, they need to grow whole—whole enough to separate fact from fantasy and love from lust, and to rework all of this into an intimate bond. It is amazing to me that so much is known about sex, but so little is understood on a deep emotional level. Hence, the name of the book: *Sexual Detours*.

I wish to thank Leslie, who is my good friend and right hand. She helped me stay motivated throughout the proposal and first two chapters. Enter David Codikow, who so generously gave me his legal counsel and heartfelt advice. He led me to my wonderful agent, Kim With-erspoon. She took a chance on a nonpublished writer and sold the book to Laura Yorke, whom I consider a person of fine professional substance and stamina who stayed with me throughout the process. They have both become good and valued friends. The publishing busi-ness, being what it is, led me to Lara Asher, whose fine editing brought the book you see before you to completion.

I would like to acknowledge many of my other good friends who know what they've done along the way: Ron, who always felt my voice was worth being heard; Caroline, who years ago wanted me to write a book (but as a single mom with two kids to raise, a full practice, and the completion of a doctorate, I couldn't have done it any sooner); Holly and Ava, my soul sisters; John; Ami; Stuart; Afton; Bill; my brother Orrin; Nick M.; Lynette; Irma; Reba; Edna Mae, who took care of those whom I loved; Bill S.; Marshall; Keith; Dan; Michael and Janet; Peter and Nicole; sweet Maryam; dear, dear Tarquin; and Samoan Barish.

In Nature there is sound and silence.
In love it is the same. Listen . . .

Sexual
Detours

PART ONE

Prelude

Chapter One

❦

The Voice of an Affair

> In the middle of the road of life
> I found myself in a dark wood
> Having strayed from the straight path.
>
> —DANTE, *THE DIVINE COMEDY: INFERNO*

Affair. The word breathes. It's palpable. It evokes emotions that swamp the senses. For those caught up in the whirlwind, love beckons. Lust and longing rule. Passion is awakened. We are filled with yearning, desire, exhilaration, and freedom. Alive. For others, the word *affair* strikes at gut level. Jealousy and rage. Loss and abandonment. The horror of betrayal vies with the chill of fear. The calamity shakes our soul to the very core.

I believe that *everyone* involved in an affair suffers deeply, for an affair is an assault upon the rock of fidelity. Fidelity is the hearthstone upon which we build our homes and families. Fidelity is where we invest our hopes and dreams. Fidelity is the last bastion for us all. When a partner takes a sexual detour from marriage vows—whether vows were echoed in vaulted cathedrals or whispered in secret—silence falls. A world shatters. And it is to those who live in these shattered worlds that I try to bring a semblance of understanding and growth, helping them heal and grow whole again.

In this book, I want to clarify that at its deepest level, an affair is a betrayal of the self. An affair tells us the story of a shadowed self, a part of ourselves about which we feel uncertain, a self that is not whole or authentic. Self is that combination of feelings, thoughts, and actions unique to each one of us. There are parts of ourselves that we do not allow ourselves to feel or to know, and often the first symptom of this lack of an intimate connection with ourselves is an affair.

An affair, or a sexual detour as I prefer to call it, is an avoidance. A path around a bruised or damaged part of ourselves, not only a sexual detour around the marriage. An affair is an immediate reaction to a present circumstance and lets us avoid dealing with conflict by providing an alternate choice. The underlying issues have roots that reach far into the past. An affair is a cover story, a curtain, a shadow play for a story begun long ago, buried in the unconscious, that is being replayed in the present. This drama takes place offstage, in the wounded, hidden aspects of the self that remain unknown. Because unconscious reasons are out of our awareness, we give ourselves rationales for an affair that often have nothing to do with the real drama within.

All of us who have been in any way touched by an affair seek answers. To my patients, no matter on which side of an affair they find themselves, I repeat the same litany: A sexual detour has little to do with sexual chemistry and a lot to do with the chemistry of escape. It has little to do with the ability to have great sex and a lot to do with the inability to communicate on an intimate level. The truth is that an affair is more about who we are, what we are afraid of, how we handle our conflicts—both within ourselves and in our marriage—than about the third party in the triangle.

In an affair, the betrayed marriage partner usually symbolizes the anxiety or conflict from which we seek to escape, and our fantasies center around the new sexual partner who promises a ticket to freedom. A marriage partner is often the one whom we blame for our problems. The reason for this is simple: Happily, a marriage partner usually means that we have found someone in whom to invest all our hopes and dreams. Unhappily, this means that he or she becomes heir to the impossible task of fulfilling them. No one can accomplish this herculean task. No one can fulfill our unspoken longings and heal all the wounds within. In marriage, if we lay the unfinished task of growing up and growing whole at the feet of our marital partner, he or she may begin to represent what we want to avoid.

The Meaning Behind a Sexual Detour

Our childhood experiences are replayed in our intimate adult relationships. Wounds sustained in childhood shape the wishes we hold for our adulthood and the nature of our adult interaction. When our adult reality does not match those unfulfilled childhood wishes, we *react*. The most common reaction is flight. When we escape from a current conflict by engaging in the flight to a sexual affair, we may believe that new wounds in the present have triggered our behavior. The truth, however, is that past experiences fuel both the nature of the issues and the manner in which we choose to address or to escape those issues. In this way the drama of our early lives is replayed in the present.

Escape from intimacy with a marital partner via the route of a sexual detour allows us to avoid confronting conflicts from these earlier relationships. Shying away from acknowledging or revealing these vulnerable parts of ourselves prevents us from attaining true intimacy, because we express our unresolved conflicts in behavior that harms our relationships and avoids resolution. We seek escape instead of confrontation and insightful solutions.

I tell my patients—especially the ones who do not want to hear it—that, in the deepest sense, a sexual detour has nothing to do with another person. It's about our inability to build intimacy into the marital relationship—indeed, into *any* intimate relationship. It is about who we are and how we feel at the center of our being. It is about what we want. What we fear. What we are afraid to feel. What we cannot allow ourselves to have or to be. It is about what is unknown. Unattended. Unfulfilled. In search of this fulfillment, we sometimes wander alone, lost on a sexual detour.

The desire for more sex is rarely the reason behind the affair, even when sexuality is a major component of the affair. The driving force of sexuality in an affair may simply provide a feel-good escape. Despite the physical intimacy of a sexual affair, sexual detours represent an escape from intimacy. The task of creating marital intimacy requires dealing with frustrations, problems, anxieties. Infidelity, which isolates us from our own pain, offers distance from the problems, not solutions. An affair is about emotional alienation. An affair is not about what we find with somebody else. It's about us. It's about what we cannot find in ourselves.

Intimacy and the Self

Intimacy is something we all want. And why not? Intimacy offers some great benefits. Intimacy with our inner self bestows upon us a sense of confidence and security. When we develop a good sense of ourselves—intimacy with what is within—we are able to express ourselves creatively, bond with others, and risk being genuinely vulnerable. We can have our needs met if only for the simple reason that we know what they are. Intimacy lends hope and infuses us with a sense of well-being.

In order to become intimate with another, we first have to be able to be intimate with ourselves. A sexual detour sends us farther down the road from dealing with the problems within. We may substitute sex, and even marriage, for the self-knowledge necessary for true intimacy. It is only in the discovery of deep personal truths that we emerge as whole, authentic, and capable of achieving true and lasting intimacy.

Intimacy is a catchword for a host of feelings we all want. But at its heart, what does it mean? Intimacy is revealing to ourselves, then to a partner, all our fears, wishes, hopes, and dreams. Who we are inside. Knowing ourselves is one task of adulthood, and communicating that knowledge is the task of forming a relationship. When we each have the freedom and ability to reveal who we are and are accepted, we will be *heard and seen* in the relationship and will have established an intimate connection.

Being heard has nothing to do with hearing, and *being seen* has nothing to do with vision, but they both have everything to do with having emotional needs met. Being heard and seen for who we are gives us the sense of being valued, approved, accepted. Having needs met is a crucial state in infancy when survival is at stake. This translates to emotional survival in adulthood.

Many fears interfere with our ability to be intimate with ourselves or another. Feeling what is inside may simply be too painful or anxiety-provoking for us to face. The fears, anxieties, and wounds covered up by an affair are mainly unconscious ones of which we are unaware. We may be afraid to endure the pain of growth. We may suffer fear of disapproval. Fear that we cannot compete or achieve. Fear of making a choice or taking responsibility. Fear of consequence. Fear of no consequence. With fear couching our every move, we escape to a sexual detour instead and bury there what we cannot handle in reality.

Intimacy with Another

Intimacy with another requires us to be comfortable enough with who we are and have a good enough sense of self-worth to achieve closeness and union without feeling overwhelmed by fear of abandonment or fear of control. The fear of abandonment, and of control, interfere with the development of intimacy. When these fears operate in a relationship, they create distance instead of an intimate exchange. These fears are caused by our very early mothering experiences, which were interpreted at the infantile and childish levels at which they occurred. In the intimate relationships of adulthood, these experiences continue to color our relationships with highly charged emotions.

Building intimacy into a relationship requires learning how to deal with the feelings that provoke a fear of intimacy, instead of running from them. I often tell my patients that their fears of loss and abandonment, or fears of control, no longer represent the same things they experienced as infants and children, even if the feelings remain the same. Feelings aren't facts. As adults we can learn to handle those feelings that interfere with intimacy instead of allowing them to provoke us into flight from intimacy. They don't believe me at first, of course, but sooner or later they do.

A common understanding among therapists is that the lower the quality of marital emotional intimacy, as reflected by our ability to communicate and solve problems, the more likely we are to have an affair. We often make the mistake of believing that the act of being married will provide intimacy and prevent infidelity. Marriage does not carry a guarantee of intimacy, nor does it prevent affairs. Marriage is only a container, an arena wherein intimacy can—if we allow it—occur. Relationships carry risk. Potential. Washing machines carry guarantees.

Intimacy and Sexual Detours

A sexual detour need not be catastrophic, either for ourselves or our marriages. An affair is not a cardinal sin. It is not even a dream come true. But even just a brief fling is something to which we must pay attention, something we must try to understand. A sexual detour presents us with a crisis of opportunity. Sexual detours can motivate us to look into ourselves and finally see who we really are—or want to be. If properly decoded, a sexual detour can lead us toward a path of self-knowledge, growth, and authenticity— toward intimacy. If we understand the hidden meaning, we can empower ourselves and enrich our lives. We must recognize a sexual detour as a sign. A signal. A flag.

It seems easy enough, this business of intimacy, of knowing ourselves. But in truth, understanding ourselves and feeling vulnerable are difficult. We run the other way as fast as we can. Why? Because we're human. We avoid reflection and the intimacy that inner knowledge offers because of the anxiety this process generates. We refrain from introspection because we've been taught an easier route, one that passes for the real thing. We have not been well schooled in the hard work of attaining a whole, integrated self or in the art of forging an intimate connection. Literally and figuratively, we live in an unconscious world. Our culture promotes quick fixes and easy escape. Give me. Get me. Buy me. Illicit dust colors the landscape of love. Sex sells.

The scent of sexual allure, the fragrance of seduction, carries names like Obsession, Jealousy, Joy, Passion. Conversely, survival depends on institutions with names like Fidelity, Trust, Vanguard. We are expected to make our lives cohesive with elements as disparate as oil and water. Lust. Longing. Fantasy. Denial. We are largely taught an ethic that undermines lasting intimacy. We've inherited a paradox.

One of my first cases exemplified this cultural legacy of ours to an extreme degree. Irene and Zachary were as green in the business of relationships as I was in treating them. They were in desperate straits. Irene felt disillusioned, confused, helpless, and hopeless. Her self-esteem drained out of her with every drop of new beauty lotion. Zachary, her husband of two years, was equally beside himself about the marriage and even less intact. The marriage was in a downward spiral. They dangled on the brink of a divorce. Or an affair. Whichever came first. Fortunately, I did.

Since their marriage, Irene had presented herself every evening fully made up and glamorously decked out. If they didn't have sex, she felt rejected and unloved. Zachary, for his part, felt inadequate and anxious. The only reaffirmation of self-worth for either of them depended on her successful seduction. Sexual encounters were tense. All of them were silent. The diamond of their marriage held no facets. Certainly no intimacy. Not a shred of communication. Sexual allure was the key. The crucial element was arousal. I was dumbfounded when I realized that Irene meant to keep love alive with perfume. Worse, if that didn't work, her next ploy was to keep Zachary off guard by flaunting the attention of other men. She would make him jealous.

Luckily, I had learned a thing or two about what keeps people together and knew it had nothing to do with what fragrance she wore or how much she shredded his sense of self-esteem. Elements that hold people together vary in degree. Shared values and goals, the integrity of the family unit, even a dysfunctional one, keep people together. The common denominator of what makes a relationship last is the ability to communicate inner wishes and fears to a responsive partner. In short, not sexual chemistry, but the ability to be intimate.

Historical Perspective on Sexual Detours

A look at history may teach us how the past colors our current attitudes and expectations of love, marriage, and fidelity. In the beginning, sexual detours were not an issue. Cave dwellers didn't hold seminars on strengthening their marriages.

In the history of mankind, sexual intimacy did not begin with fidelity. Male and female met, mated, and separated in the same manner as almost all other animals. Among cave-dwelling humans, monogamy for life did not occur. While sexual activity did not include fidelity, it contained something much more profound: With impregnation of the female, sex left attachment in its wake. Not between lovers, but something much more instinctual: the passionate attachment between mother and child. This attachment, as much a biological imperative as procreation, ensured survival of the species.

In the book *Passionate Attachments*, Willard Gaylin observes that the human infant is born in a state of helplessness unparalleled in the animal kingdom. Babies remain in a state of incapacity, unable to survive, longer than any other creature. The human infant can neither clutch nor cling, nor is it capable of fight or flight. A loving adult must care for it. Imagine that: *must*. Otherwise a baby will soon die.

The need for attachment stems from our upright posture. Our brains are massive, but the pelvis—because it is structured to an upright state—cannot give birth to a fully formed head. We are born prematurely. The first year of life is an extrauterine fetal year. The attachment between mother and child gives the infant the best chance to survive not only this premature birth but also the many years ahead.

With the evolution of humans, females of the species gathered together in groups in order to better ensure the survival of their young. The group effort resulted in the evolution of cultivation and storage. Females clustered in shelters that males would visit, then leave. Sex would attract the men. Motherhood would hold the women. It still does.

When agriculture took root, men began to spend more time around these clusters, and groups evolved in which males played a more permanent part. As primitive clans were established, incest taboos developed, but indiscriminate mating remained necessary for survival of the species.

Males and females eventually learned that their family unit increased their ability to survive. Only then did marriage evolve. Marriage existed in the context of procreation. Children were needed to help with the labor that ensured the family's survival. Ages passed where marriage laws and customs were a simple civil ceremony. Only when the Holy Roman Empire and canonical law were at their peak did marriage become a holy sacrament. This enabled families to more securely transfer land and inherit wealth. Marriage choices were largely made on the basis of the wealth the partner could bring into the new family unit. Companionship, happiness, and contentment were held in high regard, but they all existed as lesser considerations. Marriages were an economic matter, an orderly, *arranged* affair.

The Emergence of Courtly Love

Love, however, was another story. In human history, love had been loosely defined either as eros—sexual desire—or as spiritual love. The Greeks considered friendship the purest form of love. Eastern cultures did not burden their relationships, which often showed great warmth, stability, and devotion, with the notion of romantic love. Sexual desire was separate from the notion of love. Love in the context of romantic love did not enter society's vocabulary until the twelfth century. Our Western romantic-love-before-marriage premise is a holdover from the Middle Ages when crusades and troubadours were in full session. During that period in time, the concept of romantic love blossomed, and afterward it became fashionable to marry for *love*.

Courtly love swept through the feudal courts of medieval Europe in a tidal wave of poetry, songs, and love stories that ignited the imagination of the Western world. Its fire, aided in the later eighteenth century by the rise of the pulp novel, blazed a trail into myths that have carried the notion straight down into our present-day hearts. Romantic love—from the Song of Solomon to Shakespeare—became epidemic. Courtly love caught the romantic imagination and filled inner needs to the extent that it has remained a driving force of our present-day relationships. We drink romance as old wine in new glasses.

THE CONNECTION BETWEEN
COURTLY LOVE AND ADULTERY

For hundreds of years, "falling in love" was presented as a rupture of the conjugal couple—adultery. History celebrates adultery. In literature and myth, some of the most passionate love affairs occurred when one or both of the lovers were married. Paris and Helen, Tristan and Iseult, Lancelot and Guinevere, Paolo and Francesca, Don Quixote and Dulcinea, Dante and Beatrice, Anthony and Cleopatra.

The phenomenon of romance and courtly love was not left to the imagination. The ladies of the Middle Ages gathered into groups called courts of love. Their purpose was to define the rules and traditions of love. According to *A Short History of Women* by John Langdon-Davies, such a court, led by the Countess of Champagne in May 1174, created a list of thirty-one rules that explicitly defined the rules of romance. A sampling:

> *Marriage is no good excuse against loving.*
> *Whoever cannot conceal a thing, cannot love.*
> *Love must always grow greater or grow less.*
> *Love that is known publicly rarely lasts.*
> *Every lover turns pale in the sight of the co-lover.*
> *A new lover makes one quit the old.*
> *Real jealousy always increases the worth of love.*
> *The true lover is haunted by the co-lover's image unceasingly.*

Extramarital passion was love. Love was yearning. Love was lust. Love was infidelity. We still seek to emulate in an institution of reality—namely, marriage—the forbidden romantic love that existed only in myth.

This then is our legacy: an animal heritage of biological givens that embraces both indiscriminate mating and an instinct for attachment, marriage as an economic survival tool that is no longer necessary, and an eight-hundred-year-old romantic code of love that has little to do with either.

The Contemporary Nature of Sexual Detours

Just as a look at history provides a glimmer of understanding for our present-day attitudes and expectations about love and marriage, a glance at our present-day lives shows us how those past romantic love ideals provide fertile ground for adultery. Romantic love continues to be a loose cannon on the deck of marriage. We only have to look at the growing divorce rate to prove this claim. Affairs are commonplace. Half of marriages end in divorce. More children are raised in shattered families than united ones.

Affairs are present to a great degree in marriages that end in divorce. Affairs are reflections of how we isolate ourselves from our marriage partner. This desire for isolation may stem from the unrealistic expectations we have of our partner, which can result in unspoken resentments, anger, even despair. Given the degree to which affairs contribute to the isolation of marital partners, it is easy to see why a host of misconceptions have accumulated about affairs.

Four Misconceptions About Affairs

1. *In every affair there is a saint and a sinner; the victim is a saint and the betrayer a sinner.* It is not as simple as that. An affair is not something that happens *to* people. It happens *between* two people, even though one may have been betrayed.

   Notwithstanding cruelty and abuse, both marital partners have a piece of the pie of responsibility when one partner chooses a sexual detour. We may or may not have acknowledged our role consciously, but there are no victims, only volunteers. Sadly, affairs turn love into alienation more often than enduring friendship, and moral judgments have no constructive force. They do not heal wounds or shattered families.

2. *The marriage is over.* Clearly, that is not the case. An affair is not something that ends marriages. Period. I'll say it again: An affair is the cover story. The real drama lies in the underlying factors within ourselves and how they manifest in a relationship. It takes two people to form a marital relationship. Or fail at forming one.

   An affair, if understood at its deepest level, can help a marriage. A marriage where one or both of the partners have unexpressed and unmet needs is not a marriage where intimacy exists. What we learn about ourselves on a sexual detour and are able to integrate into our lives may enrich and strengthen our marriage. When an affair ends, a real marriage may actually begin.

Many marriages begin with intimacy but lose it somewhere along the way. In an attempt to find it again, we may look for intimacy in an affair. Intimacy, however, is not baggage we transfer from one place to another or one relationship to another. It is built step by step. In forgoing an attempt to rebuild intimacy within a marriage by looking for it in an affair, we forgo the potential intimacy that marriage may have to offer.

3. *Sex in the marriage has failed and is over.*

> Sex does not fail, communication does.
> Sex in affairs can exist without love.
> Sex is not intimacy.
> Sex cannot resolve and heal the past.
> Sex is not a substitute for low self-esteem.
> Sex can be restored.

We are sexual beings capable of having multiple sexual partners. Intimacy is another story. We rarely have several intimate relationships. Intimate relationships are not easily substituted. A marriage that has undergone the challenge of surviving a sexual detour can be successful in every way. Intimacy can be established. Sex can become an expression of the intimacy the relationship did not have before.

4. *An affair means we no longer love our spouse.* An affair does not reflect on love as much as it does on our ability to understand ourselves or communicate with another. Affairs mean different things to different people.

In order to shatter myths, it is easier to recognize what an affair is *not*:

> An affair is not the end of the world.
> Nor is it the beginning.
> An affair is not something to be afraid of.
> An affair is not about receiving a new lease on life.
> An affair is not the answer to our prayers.
> And contrary to how those of us caught up in the rapture may feel, it's not even the realization of our wildest dreams.
> An affair has nothing to do with more, or better, sex.
> An affair is not even a
> Certainly not sin.
> An affair has nothing
> An affair is not abc
> looking face.
> It has nothing to do
> or great legs.
> Most important, ai
> body else. It h
> your arms. It
> inside.

www.primals.org

An affair is an urgent i going on inside of us. As an example, let's use Jake.

Jake has been married for thirteen years. Jake is a hardworking, earnest man, with a rich creative streak that has been buried under the everydayness of his life and the demands of his career. He adores his children and loves his wife. But. He becomes animated when he talks about the woman with whom he has begun an affair. He can hardly contain his enthusiasm as he describes her. Her eyebrows are gorgeous. They arch. He sighs with adoration. He rhapsodizes. He enthuses about her hair. It lifts off her head. It bounces. Another poignant sigh.

"That's only hair!" I want to bellow at him. And I do. Usually I'm more gentle in translating the bulletins from within. I'm in on what's underneath all the nonsense about the hair. I am the observer, the therapist, and as such, I don't need to fool myself. Jake does. He is defending himself against the pain, fear, and unfulfilled longings of the primitive emotions within his inner world. It's too painful for Jake to see his lost dreams. It's easier to find new ones in someone else's image, someone else's hair, than to undertake the work of making real life better. It is hard for anyone to acknowledge the emptiness inside and bear the terrible isolation of not having a part of one's inner self connected to life.

The truth is that the bounce, the youthfulness of that bounce, brings out something in Jake. Something alive, creative, and vibrant that he doesn't give himself permission to express otherwise. He needs to confront his buried youth, his hopes, his dreams, not her hair. It's never the hair. Or the bounce. Or anything. It's never about somebody else. It's always about ourselves.

The emotions lent by an affair are never given for keeps. Eventually, the bounce will become meaningless. We can continue changing partners all we want—an endless list—given our biological heritage of scouting eyes and vagrant heart. But the problems never change. Only by discovering and feeling what is in our inner

world can we achieve the intimacy we crave. Without this understanding, we will unknowingly be driven toward a sexual detour.

About This Book

In the effort to embolden my patients to take real constructive
action, instead of hiding in denial and wasting their life on mean-
dering detours, I guide them on a voyage of discovery. I encourage
them to pay attention to the region of themselves that lies silent but
that fuels some of the most dramatic choices of our lives. I repair
cables of communication and translate the language of an inner
world so that my patients can become intimate with themselves.
This self-intimacy helps them to emerge integrated and whole, find
who they truly are, and grow empowered to shape the future in a
direct and straightforward manner.

For this reason, I welcome the siren call of a sexual detour. I
implore, beg, and otherwise harangue those patients of mine connected to an affair to harken to its sound, for an affair has a voice all its
own. Unmistakably loud and clear. A voice from within. It is an emotional narrative about ourselves, not just about our marriages. It is a
plea beseeching us to discover our true self and the untapped potential of who we are.

I have tried to put this endeavor into the pages of this book.
This book is of interest to *anyone* connected to a sexual detour:

> Those of us enchanted by the beginning of an affair.
> Those who are in the full throes of an affair.
> Those entangled in an ongoing affair they don't know
>   how to end.

Some may want to renew and strengthen an existing marriage.

Others may have come to the painful recognition that an affair means their marriage has come to an end.

Those facing the task of remarriage with the partner in an affair.

Still more meeting the challenge of rebuilding an independent life, without the partner in the affair *or* in the marriage.

And there are those recovering from devastation and injury, living with feelings of betrayal, loss, and abandonment.

This book examines the intrapsychic and interpersonal complexities that lead to a sexual detour, detail what occurs when a sexual detour takes place, and sift through the aftermath to lead you toward recovery. The progression follows the stories of various sexual detours that illustrate how the fantasy and illusion of affairs cover up the real issues we have to recognize in order to make our lives and marriages more rewarding.

Through understanding what a sexual detour means in a very personal way, we can gain a more authentic self. Self-authenticity empowers us with confidence and self-esteem and enables us to express ourselves more easily, bond with others, and risk being vulnerable. Being authentic, we are capable of intimacy, the most positive result of which may be to enrich and strengthen an existing good marriage, end a bad one, or provide for an intimate and lasting relationship with another.

For both men and women, to look inward honestly, to face the inner self intrapsychically and interpersonally, is a heroic journey. Olympian. To know who we really are, to be intimate, takes courage. Joseph Campbell believed that a hero's journey was not contained in a single courageous act but in a life lived in self-discovery. With this book I offer my hand both symbolically and literally to help you embark on your journey within. Because, yes, there is more than a detour to follow.

So, this book contains what I see. It's about what I do. Every day. I bring sight and sound to my patients by guiding them on a voyage of self-discovery. I help them grow whole and become everything they can become. And now I attempt to do the same for you. If I am successful you will be introduced to someone with whom you can become truly intimate: yourself.

So let's get down to business and take a look at ourselves. A good look.

Chapter Two

❧❦

The Self

Know Thyself

—TEMPLE AT DELPHI

"Know thyself?" If I knew myself, I'd run away.

—GOETHE

❧ Some of my patients would swear that I couldn't care less about what they think. They know it's because so much of what they think is designed to bury and deny what they *feel*.

In my office, I tend to use volume. I love to see feelings. I'm desperate for passion. Sadly, I see pain. I see anguish and the terrible isolation people feel because they cannot connect on an inner level with who they really are. So I like it when I see feelings, when my patients know something on a gut level, because it's the inside breaking out. It's the fragile yet indomitable inner self breaking through the eggshell of who we think we are, or who we may even pretend to be.

There's a lot of language floating around trying to explain the self in esoteric, inexplicable terms. But let me make it simple. Who and what are we talking about when we use the term *self*? We are who we think we are and feel we are. We are our attitudes and experiences. We are how others experience us. We are a combination of our thoughts, feelings, and actions. We are a psychological fingerprint of hopes and longings, wishes and fears, that mingle with our DNA heritage of chemicals and physical and hormonal circuitry.

From the moment of conception, our psychic landscape is colored in an endless array of hues. With the genetic wiring in place, this landscape is brought to life at birth, then subjected to the nurturing process. Our psyche gets woven into the tapestry of who we are and who we become with a combination of nature and nurture.

The Unconscious

In thinking about ourselves, it may help to use the example of a building. Imagine that we exist as the structure of a building. This building fills up with the content of who we are. The content is a combination of cognitive thoughts, moods and feelings, actions and behavior, all influenced by chemicals, genetics, and nurturing.

As in most structures, the basement is the most neglected part. It seems the least important is left the most unattended. No one pays attention to it, or wants to visit, let alone live there. The basement houses the equipment that keeps the building running. What goes on in the basement keeps us functioning: passionate, creative, alive.

This basement is our unconscious—a storehouse of unremembered frustrations and feelings and events. The thousand and one acts, events, attitudes, and incidents that we as children experience.

These experiences either helped build and create a good sense of self, or left us fragile and sometimes shattered. These events are put out of our awareness, tucked neatly into the basement.

The basement houses what we record—which is everything. We sift through it in a creative way, submerging pain and anxiety below awareness and allowing only certain feelings to surface. How we feel about ourselves is influenced by that part of ourselves of which we are unaware—the unconscious.

Everything that enters the unconscious during our developmental years stays there. Forever. The unconscious knows no passage of time. The unconscious cannot be taught. It cannot be changed. What is unconscious is an imprint that stays with us. The unconscious part of ourselves never forgets. The unconscious will not be tricked into revealing what lies there. It surfaces in dreams and in our behavior but is often disguised.

UNCONSCIOUS DIMENSIONS OF THE SELF

One of my patients looked and behaved like a physical metaphor for the unconscious. She was an iceberg. She was majestic and cold. Her haughty arctic beauty froze any human contact. She floated above her inner world in a cool and otherworldly fashion. What she revealed, both to herself and to me, was only the tip of the iceberg. Her icy demeanor and cold control over a tiny and visible portion of herself swam above a submerged continent—a self of which she was unaware. I had the sense that if she didn't map her subterranean depths, she would collide with the forces in the continent and fracture just like ice.

At that time in my practice, I was operating under the impatience of youth, and rather than allow the patient to come to her own conclusions, I impetuously barged ahead. I still operate in this rather charged, headlong fashion because life is too precious to waste one moment in self-absorption rather than self-discovery. Discovery, as I know it, is done by traveling. Movement. In this vein, I bombarded her defenses, feeling that if she was going to crack it might as well be in my office. The rewards were surprising and heartwarming.

She blossomed before my eyes. As it turned out, her ability to recognize and access the hidden parts of herself prevented emotional catastrophe. Instead, she was a natural-born traveler of inner space. The reflection of her inner world began to cast light and color like a prism, an emotional aurora borealis that took one's breath away. She became so much more than an iceberg, as the unconscious dimensions of herself were understood.

UNCONSCIOUS CHOICE

We're all icebergs. A portion of who we are rises above the water-line of conscious sight, but more accumulates below. Knowledge of our depths is vital. The dimensions of what composes that hidden, unknown part of ourselves can rule the day. The importance doesn't lie in the tip. What happens below the surface gives us the power of choice and action, to shape and influence the course of our lives.

What fills our thoughts every day is conscious. If asked, we wax eloquently about who we are. We can be accurate and articulate about ourselves. We have rational explanations of our identity, especially of our behavior, no matter how irrational it may be. However, unless we delve into ourselves and try to understand the motives for our behavior, we will be subject to the influence of events we have suppressed from early in childhood. We will not have the free choice of action in our adulthood.

UNDERSTANDING THE UNCONSCIOUS

Historically, the only way to see into the unconscious has been through free association. It is a wonderful luxury to allow the mind to roam free, unrestrained by structured conscious thought. Einstein discovered the Theory of Relativity using this technique. In free association, or self-association as I like to call it, we do not defend ourselves against the unconscious terror or anxiety within. We are free to see ourselves through the oblique angle of self-interpretation, which, while deadly accurate, is not dead-on.

In interpreting the unconscious dimension of ourselves, we must use intuition, perception, imagination, and metaphor as a way of seeing and understanding. The unconscious refuses to discuss anything in plain English. Symbolic interpretation, for instance, is what we do in order to understand our dreams.

If we view ourselves through the prism of the unconscious, we catch a glimpse of who we are and what we need. This insight gives us freedom to choose what we do on a conscious level, instead of being driven by unconscious forces.

When we are able to see aspects of our unconsciously motivated behavior or feelings, the revelation is, quite simply, surprising. Emotional vision can engender profound epiphanies. Illumination, however, does not need to be earth-shattering at all. Take something as simple as the phenomenon of sudden knowledge. We feel blue, then it strikes us that it's the anniversary of something powerful, like a parent's death or the end of our marriage. The unconscious timetable is never late. These are times of our lives that we buried, but our mood doesn't forget. These events are indelible imprints on our soul. These little lightbulbs are only the daily change of the unconscious part of ourselves. They give us, if we want to accept them, small gifts of self-knowledge. Tokens for the ride.

THE UNCONSCIOUS AT WORK

We all have the habit of avoiding our unconscious subterranean depths and concentrating only on the tip of the iceberg. Something much more fundamental is at work down below, but it's far easier to take the cover story at face value. Take, as an example, this prelude to an affair.

Sam was flirting. He denied it, of course. But he was lunching. A lot. What he was hung up on, what he wanted to resolve in his treatment with me was his dissatisfaction about his wife's looks. Her nose, to be exact. He was stuck on that nose. Why wouldn't she have her nose fixed? She wouldn't listen to him. He tried to persuade, cajole, and plead. If she fixed her nose, everything would be perfect. She would be perfect. He'd even give up lunching.

The nose was nonsense, just like the hair a few pages ago. It wasn't the nose. It's never the nose. One day Sam and I spoke at length about what his feelings about her nose engendered in him and tried to discover if it reminded him of anything significant in his early life. When he connected his wife's nose to his past, he bolted upright, as if struck by lightning. The more he talked about his feelings as the son of a critical, selfish, disapproving father—a dad who didn't seem to care how he felt, who never gave the little kid or gawky adolescent enough approval to feel good about himself—the less his wife's looks mattered. The more he talked about how bad he felt about himself, the better he felt about his wife's nose.

Soon the nose lay by the wayside. A pretty nose became unimportant in the context of why his wife's looks were so important to him. It became clear that he was fixated on his wife's looks, but his unconscious was fixed on his father's disapproval. Her looks had been carrying the burden of his self-esteem, serving the function of receiving approval from the world and from his father. A big job for one imperfect nose.

Trying to escape from feeling a certain way about himself, as his father's son, via the detour of his wife's fixed nose—or an affair with someone more attractive—would have been a dead end for Sam. Sam could have obsessed over appearances all he wanted. Plastic surgery on his wife's nose wouldn't ever change how he felt about himself. He would have bounced from nose to legs, from stomach to breasts; from lunch to dinner. There's no end in sight. Only the recognition of what lurked beneath the surface would ever have given Sam, or his wife, a breather. It's backbreaking work trying to shore up unconscious issues of self-esteem by fixing someone else's nose.

We can change ourselves. What we cannot do is change the past or someone else. It's never about someone else. It's always about ourselves. My point is that if we concentrate on the cover story of an affair, we do so at our own peril. We allow the real drama to go unrecognized. These dramas are internal issues from an earlier day, stored in the basement of the self, that may motivate us to go on a sexual detour without even knowing the real reason why.

Nurturing and Self-Esteem

Growing up is hardly a benign process. None of us escapes the glory or the heartbreak inherent in childhood. Indeed, our sense of ourselves and self-worth is always well-trodden ground. We all sustain the footprints of those who have stomped, unwittingly and usually lovingly, on the garden of our budding self (and there are many of us blighted blossoms floating around the world). The inevitable stampede of parenting guarantees that we will sustain bruises.

The painful events of childhood become a tender spot we avoid by suppression or denial. The area of conflict—the bruise—camouflages pain in much the same way a bump develops a black-and-blue shield. We literally drop painful events into the unconscious, where they remain out of our awareness. These become our unmet, unconscious needs and to our knowledge don't exist. But they do exist—in the way they are expressed in adult relationships. With our intimate adult partners, we seek to have these wounds healed and, in doing so, inadvertently create more conflict because our unconscious expectations are supremely unrealistic.

We develop good self-esteem from a mothering experience that recognizes our true wishes and shows us approval, not rejection. The nurturing process of childhood can enhance or diminish how we feel about who we are. While our physical bodies depend upon physical nurturing, our identity develops through intimate personal nurturing with our mothering figure. With a nurturing mother, who can accept us for who we are, a whole sense of ourselves flourishes. We grow into authentic, creative, confident adults, capable of intimacy. Sounds easy. It's not. Parents, too, are flawed human beings.

Sometimes, our sense of ourselves is compromised because our emotional needs were not met. If the handling is a bit rough, we do not develop an authentic, whole sense of who we are. We may even develop a false self. This is our camouflaged representation to the world of how we had to be seen as a child. When we have had the kind of mothering that does not reflect our true emotional state, does not approve of it, or overrules it in an effort to fill our mother's own needs, we learn to reject ourselves. Our experience with another parenting figure, like the father, can mitigate a negative effect, but the younger we are, the more indelible this imprint of disapproval from the mothering figure. Our self-esteem is at the mercy of our first romance.

OUR FIRST ROMANCE

What takes place during the nurturing process, during our first romance, is crucial to our adult relationships because there is a direct connection between this experience and a later capacity for intimacy and love. The first romance predicts the nature of every other romance. Fathers, siblings, life experiences, too, all color and impact the building of the concept of ourselves, but when our first relationship is traumatic it will leave a slight fissure in our self-esteem. Consequently, problems with how we feel about ourselves come forward later in life and hinder developing an intimate relationship in adulthood.

One of the deepest needs, beginning with infancy, is for acceptance and approval. But somewhere along the road, some of us learn that if we share something truly important to us, it is devalued, taken away, or not even noticed. We feel frustrated, misunderstood, and invalidated. If we are known for who we are and still gain approval, we develop an authentic sense of self. If not, we are compromised and wounded, and the repair job is left to us in our adulthood. This is the repair job we may mistakenly and unknowingly seek by going on a sexual detour. This is the drama we conceal with the cover story of an affair.

The Development of Sexuality

The development of sexuality is a further extension of childhood self-esteem issues. The integration of ourselves as sexual beings begins in infancy with a bath of physical sensations that are crucial to survival. In infancy, physical and emotional bliss merge. We seek to reexperience this union in an adult sexual relationship. The adult wish to have a partner who kisses, smiles, and holds the same way we experienced in infancy is built on familiarity. It is what we have stored in our unconscious memory. When the kind of touch we received as infants is not congruent with the kind of touch we receive in our adult relationships, some adjusting is required. For example, a lack of touch in infancy might lead to a greater need in adulthood, but it may be a need we find difficulty expressing because we've never had the experience to duplicate. Conversely, a physically affectionate mothering experience might leave us unfulfilled with a less demonstrative mate in adulthood.

The relationship between intimate sexual adults can be compared, in its intensity, only to the love between mothers and babies. The baby relates to the mother using her body as well as its own. The reason our adolescent and adult relationships are so intense is that they reawaken in our unconscious world the first passionate attachment of our first romance.

Sexuality is the adult physical expression of all we have experienced before. Sex can soothe and bring many sources of anxiety under control, as did a mother's holding, stroking, soothing, and comforting. Aside from the instinctual biological urge, sexual union provides a mutual sense of caring for the adult just as nurturing in early infancy did for the infant.

THE WORLD OF SEXUAL MATURITY

We make giant strides from the sexuality of infancy and childhood to the sexual maturity of adulthood. We move at lightning speed. The baby moves from playing with the mother to playing with himself. We crawl toward a separate physical self, all the while building closer emotional ties to help weather the psychic journey ahead. Our early growth is a precursor of the seeming paradox of adult relationships, where intimacy requires that we are separate and connected at the same time.

So it goes that after the intimacy and bliss of infancy and childhood, we're treated to what may appear to be a handful of relatively calm years in an innocent, latent childhood, where we are sane, manageable short people. This theater of operations is a staging ground for adolescence, where the needs that are later expressed in sexuality mull around, preparing for the real invasion. When puberty bursts upon the scene, it hits us with a tidal wave of hormones. Flooded by growth, and sexual capabilities, we are catapulted into the adult world, sexual organs leading the way.

The sexual maturity of adolescence thrusts upon us the complex world of adult sexual relationships before we are emotionally ready. We emerge from adolescence lustful creatures full of insane desire, longing for the reunion and passionate attachment of our first romance. And before we know it, we're there. From mother's arms to lover's arms. We sail on wings woven in an earlier time, sustained in flight by cloth spun of unconscious longings and dreams. Hopefully, we're well on our way toward being a whole, integrated, and authentic self. Usually we're not. But we're in the thick of it. And how do we try to recapture that first romance and replay our earliest drama? We do it, of course, by falling in love.

Chapter Three

❧❧

Romantic Love

Lovers come. And lovers go. Over the sands of time
they go. And they know all there is to know.
Lovers know.

—KORAN

Love looks not with the eyes, but with the mind,
And therefore is winged Cupid painted blind.

—SHAKESPEARE,

A MIDSUMMER NIGHT'S DREAM

❧ *It had to be you . . . In this world of ordinary people . . . Some enchanted evening . . .* Anyone who remembers Broadway musicals, or has been entranced by the golden era of movies, knows about romantic love. Knows it by sight, by sound, and by heart. We all have the same expectations of romantic love. It will be intense and rapturous, and last forever.

Freud taught that all love is a refinding. Psychology abounds with the theme that in romantic love we attempt to re-create the bliss and union of infancy. Perhaps even more than the recapturing, we want to make it last. Romantic love, at its deepest level, is about hope. It is a wish for the reunion of that first romance. Nothing demonstrates more poignantly the intensity of that inner longing for reunion than love at first sight. And it happens. It really does. And forgive me for being the messenger, but romantic love dies. If we are to have forever after, and all that the hope in romantic love wants to achieve, we have to learn how to find it by creating intimacy, but we won't have it with romantic love. I'll say it again: Romantic love fades. And here's why.

Romantic love is a complexity of unconscious, involuntary feelings, attitudes, and expectations about love. "In lust" happens at first sight, and we call it love. We idealize. The passion of romance is always directed at our own expectations, our own fantasies. To fall in love, according to Stendhal, one must first admire, then fantasize, receive a shred of hope followed by a dollop of doubt. The doubt creates a line of tension that gives us both pleasure and anxiety.

Romantic Love Is Our Idealization

Let's get something straight: As pure, innocent, sweet, and cherishable as it is, romantic love is blind. Deaf and dumb as well. This is another thing I hound my patients about. They protect their beloved from my prying eyes because they know what I will see. I will not see the same person they do—the person they wish existed. This can work conversely; sometimes what I see is a lot rosier than what out-of-love jaundiced eyes see. But I press my point even to deaf, love-struck ears.

LOVE AT FIRST SIGHT

In love at first sight, the other person doesn't even have to be there. Whom we see, whom we meet, even whom we fall in love with has little to do with the other person. Even the one standing right in front of us. People "fall in love" with images. Lovers are replications of pictures tucked way back in the realm of unconscious memory. We all yearn and seek, find and re-create. We idealize people as we did the parents of our childhood. The image of the parent stamped upon our souls is never far from romantic love's eyes. The complication is that the same trigger that generates romantic love also conjures up memories of disappointment, separation, loss, and abandonment. Sooner or later this ambivalent mixture of love and disappointment surfaces. There are always two sides to every coin.

Love at first sight is triggered by the unconscious memory of something overwhelmingly positive and familiar. In what has been called the recognition of love, we hear a haunting melody, something we once knew. One trait or another in the desired person sets off an instant regeneration of the primary parent. It could be the shadow of a smile, but it's enough to set the wheels in motion. That flash of recognition triggers our imagination and creates our ideal. Consequently, what we see in the beloved is deadly accurate. Those rose-colored glasses are prescription lenses geared for the wearer.

LOVE AS THE WISH FOR SYMBOLIC UNION

Falling in love is a longing. Everyone knows that, above all else, lovers want to be together. The earliest myths spoke directly of union and reunion. Plato comprehended the nature of romantic love. In Aristophanes' myth, as portrayed in Plato's *Symposium,* primordial man was round with four hands and four feet. He had a single head with two faces on a swivel neck. When the creature dared challenge the gods, Zeus punished him by cutting him in two. But once man was split, each half yearned for the other. Zeus, in pity, moved their reproductive organs in order that they could periodically fit together.

> For the intense yearning which each of them has towards the other does not appear to be the desire of lover's intercourse, but of something else which the soul of either evidently desires but cannot tell, and of which she has only a dark and doubtful presentiment. Suppose Hephaestus, with his instruments, to come to the pair who are lying side by side and to say to them . . . "Do you desire to be wholly one, always day and night to be in one another's company? For if this is what you desire I am ready to melt you into one and let you grow together.". . .There is not a man of them who when he heard the proposal would deny . . . that this meeting and melting into one another, this becoming one instead of two, was the very expression of his ancient need.*

Two and a half millennia have passed since this was written. With the emergence of psychology, we have gained insight into the intensity of the mother-infant relationship and now more fully understand what Plato meant by "ancient need."

---

* Plato, *The Symposium: The Benjamin Jowett Translation* (New York: Modern Library, 1996).

The Evolution of Romantic Love

The notion of romance as we know it today burst into Western society during the Middle Ages with a tale of love and death. Romance made its debut with two of the most famous lovers of all time, Tristan and Iseult. Adulterous lovers. Their story, as in all romantic love, carries a theme of separation and longing for reunion. The moving, epic tale of the star-crossed lovers' saga imprinted itself upon the entire Western world a mere eight hundred years ago and created the tide of romanticism upon which we still ride today.

I have paraphrased here the story of Tristan and Iseult, so magnificently retold and explored by Robert A. Johnson in his book *We: Understanding the Psychology of Romantic Love,* in order to illustrate romantic love and how it still colors our emotional lives today.

Tristan was destined to become a great Knight. Iseult, the Fair Daughter of Sorcery, had the gift of healing. She was beautiful and desirable beyond measure. She was destined to become a Queen.

When Tristan is wounded in a battle, only Iseult can save him. Tristan is taken to Iseult for healing and, upon recovery, returns to serve the King. A bird drops a strand of golden hair. The King, taken by the bright gold hair, vows to wed the woman to whom the strand belongs. Tristan offers to find her, for he had recognized the strand of hair as belonging to Iseult.

Tristan finds Iseult and takes her to his King. Iseult's mother gives Iseult a wedding night love potion designed to cast a magic spell on Iseult and the King. Iseult and Tristan mistakenly drink this potion on the voyage. Drunk with the magical spell of the love potion, Tristan and Iseult spend one night together. When they reach the King's land, Iseult marries the King and becomes Queen. The lovers, still under the spell of the love potion, are miserable apart. They come together in an enchanted orchard, outside of time and reality, and live there together. After a period of years, filled with honorable intentions to serve the King, Tristan and Iseult separate and return to reality.

Tristan, despite marrying another, remains possessed by Iseult. Iseult longs for Tristan. Tortured by separation, Tristan vows to return. When Tristan's wife learns of her husband's longing for Iseult and his plan to reunite with her, she takes vengeance upon him by deceiving him into thinking that Iseult has died. Believing his beloved Iseult dead, Tristan dies of grief. Iseult, upon finding him so, dies from sorrow by his side.

Oh, my. Who doesn't love lovers? The whole world loves lovers. And who doesn't want what they have? We all do. Only it's easier to have in myth than in reality. Friendship can live. Love can grow. Sex can get better. Mature love can endure. Intimacy can last. But romantic love dies because we outlive the idealistic state of the enchanted orchard.

THE THREE CHARACTERISTICS OF ROMANTIC LOVE

The early notions of romantic love, and the falling-in-love state that characterized courtly love, exhibited three characteristics all designed to fan the flames of desire and keep romantic love alive.

1. Because romantic love began as a taboo, the first requirement was that the lovers were not sexually involved. This
   was eventually modified.
2. The second requirement was that the lovers were married to others.
3. The third requirement encouraged the lovers to suffer
   from intense desire.

In order to sustain this intensity, passion was never exposed to
the everydayness of marriage. Separation heightened passion.
Contact and confrontation were thought to unravel illusion. Ardor
was kept alive by being stoked, not slaked. Beyond illusion, passion relied on another key ingredient: mystery. Romantic love was
more akin to idealization and worship.

In myth, intense romantic love is short-lived. It often ends,
tragically, in death. We've mixed a good deal of this romantic love
into sex, into marriage, and into "forever after." We've re-created
what Tristan and Iseult had for a scant few years but try to stretch it
into lasting forever. We still hold the medieval belief that true love
is the ecstatic adoration of an image of perfection. Only in our
imagination can such an ideal exist. In myth, romantic love is
clearly defined. In real life, love, sex, marriage, and intimacy are far
more complicated and confusing.

We must draw a line between the euphoria of romantic love
and the reality of creating intimacy. Romantic love actually inhibits
intimacy because romance is based on illusion, and intimacy is
founded on reality. Marriage helps create intimacy but inhibits
romance. Familiarity, certainty, predictability, and repetition
destroy the illusion of romantic love, but these characteristics help
us build an enduring and enriching life. Intimacy can follow roman-

tic love but should not be confused with it. If we believe that only romantic love will provide intimacy, we delude and shortchange ourselves. Intimacy alone can fulfill what that longing for romantic union represents.

The Chemistry of Love

So romantic love walks in, and what do we have? First, a flash of memory. A primitive unconscious recognition that triggers the creative genius of our imagination. The creative imagination has immense power. Romantic love eludes conscious directives primarily because it is such an unconsciously driven state. The phenomenon releases a storm of chemicals and hormones that nothing on earth can stop. These chemicals, in league with the unconscious, are invincible. Romantic love is a concoction of attraction and attachment dependent upon the potent mix of chemicals.

Romantic love has two stages: attraction and attachment. The eyes serve as portals for attraction. Chemistry, as far as we know, begins visually. The hormones overwhelm us with a hormonal cocktail that results in a physical and emotional state of love and attachment.

ATTRACTION

Conscious—and unconscious—recognition triggers attraction. This releases three hormones—natural amphetamines: phenylethylamine (PEA), dopamine, and norepinephrine. Voilà, we have a love potion.

This heady chemical mix for passion, not unlike the love potion of Tristan and Iseult, is designed to last just about as long, two to three years. That is the life expectancy of romantic love and, interestingly enough, also an affair. Attraction begun visually is a physical state: The chemical basis puts the body on red alert. Joy and excitement mingle with apprehension and anxiety. This feeling resembles fear. Our body finds itself in a state of constant readiness. Our heart beats faster, our mouth gets dry, our palms sweat. The chemicals course through our bodies, giving us a bright-eyed fervor that probably has more to do with survival than love.

The attraction phase coincides with infatuation or what is known as idealization of the love object. When love occurs, we become extraordinary people. The beloved is endowed with power, and the lover basks in the reflected glow. Our self-worth is bound up in the beloved, just as it was in our first romance. Romantic love allows the lover to feel more attractive. Mutual romantic love creates self-validation, a love chorus wherein lovers confirm each other's worth in a timeless duet.

ATTACHMENT

The second part of romantic love is a physical bond of attachment. This begins after the brain stops giving off signals for the love potion. The PEA hormone of the romantic love potion, with its amphetaminelike high, triggers an alarm. After the PEA, the brain sends messages for the endorphins to calm the frenzy. Endorphins are more peaceful, tranquil substances. One of the hormones in this calming phase is oxytocin, produced by the pituitary gland and described as a "cuddle drug." This hormone may be present in higher levels in long-term love. Oxytocin is found in exceptionally high levels in prairie voles, a rodent family known for its rigid monogamy.

When the endorphins take charge, the PEA falls and we settle into the attachment phase of mating so that child rearing can take place. On the evolutionary scale it has rationale. In order to ensure survival of the species, a hormonal mix had to bring about mating, then reduce the desire for sex in order to allow time for the mother to raise the infant. This attachment phase lasts long enough for a toddler to learn to walk. When the mother is free to care for a new baby, the cycle begins again, and the evolutionary engine is jump-started once more. Should our eyes fall on a likely subject, we are once again flooded with PEA and another frenzy of mating can occur. And so the story (and survival of the species) goes.

Romantic Love as an Escape

Adolescents fall in love very easily. The more mature we are, the more difficult it is to fall heedlessly in love. That in and of itself is not a bad thing. Sometimes the highway of romantic love is a detour, in much the same way as a sexual affair. Many people distract themselves from the real growth of adulthood that still lies ahead by the headlong plunge into romantic love. Romantic love can deter us from the challenge of self-development when we submerge our interests and goals and jump into idealized relationships that might not be in our best interest.

In summary, as adults, we try to obtain from our lover what we did not receive from our parents. It is not possible to be in love without reinvoking old conflicts that cause us to re-create an ambivalent relationship. Consequently, we try to resolve past childhood conflicts in a new context with adult partners. The intensity of this relationship represents a window of opportunity for inner knowledge and repair—but we must walk this tightrope carefully. Romantic love can rewrite the drama of our lives and, in many ways, can be a force for change and growth. Or, if we are not aware of its distracting influence, romantic love can deter us from growth and change.

Romantic love makes us terribly vulnerable because we idealize the other and invest him or her with such importance. The refinding of the other, as an adult, becomes so important that we become determined to take possession of what we have recaptured with the ultimate step of commitment.

In this state, shaped by life situations and societal influences, under the influence of unconscious wishes and sustaining the greatest hormonal storm since puberty, we drink of the love potion. Drunk, under the powerful heat of sex, under the sway of the moon and the stars, and with all the hope and yearning romantic love can arouse. You guessed it. We pledge our troth. Like Tristan and Iseult, we vow to forsake all others. In myth, this is where the romance is enshrined in immortality as one or both of the lovers die. In reality, we get married.

Chapter Four

❦❧

Marriage

Man is a knot, a web, a mesh, into which
relationships are tied.

—ANTOINE DE SAINT-EXUPÉRY

❧ Marriage. Rings and things, symbols and celebration. It is a joyous time of life. I cry at weddings. Who doesn't? But why do we cry? Perhaps we cry at the unbearable beauty, the innocence and the fragility of hope. Perhaps we cry because journeys end in lovers meeting. We cry at reunion. Or perhaps we cry because what we find at the end of the journey, the long road home, is so cherished yet so fragile.

All lovers exist in their own private Eden, like Tristan and Iseult, blind to the world around them. But unlike the enchanted orchard of romantic love, marriage is a public affair. Reality is a witness. In the eyes of God, or the State, when we take our lifelong vows, the world watches. We find ourselves down the road from that first romance with an adult version. For better or worse, until death do us part. We find ourselves married.

Embarking on marriage, we all soar, we sail. It is a time of life when emotions run high. Dreams. Expectations. Few of us recognize how fully in marriage we are bound to touch earth. In the midst of euphoria, just below the shimmering surface, swim the undercurrents of fear. Anxiety lurks furtively, like an uninvited guest at the celebration. To one degree or another, we harbor doubts, fears. The future seems to present itself with surprising suddenness. We face the unknown. What lies ahead is new. Terrifyingly new.

We marry, brimming with hope for a future, not even hearing the echoes of the past. But deep within resonates something very old. Inextricably woven in with the new, as yet unknown to us, the past has already been introduced; it has already taken hold. All, or part, of what we have chosen in marriage represents the resurrection of old patterns. We have chosen, in our new life, with a new wife or new husband, something very familiar. In marriage, this fact is revealed to us in surprising ways.

The Wish for Married Bliss

What we unconsciously strive for is someone to help us fill the emptiness. We yearn and long for the feeling of that first romance. Whether we had it and want to recapture it, or never had it and seek to fulfill it, we long for union. For bliss.

Not to disparage the notion, but for many, bliss is synonymous with the kind of union difficult to maintain in the real world. I treated a couple in premarital therapy who believed that, in order to be wedded, they had to be literally joined. The two independent, strong-minded individuals, who had come to me to hash out the decision to marry, were already chafing at the restrictions their expectations had built into their forthcoming marriage. They sat and stared at me, eyes glazed over, and sick smiles pasted on their faces as if their collars had suddenly become too tight. Fortunately, they couldn't convince me that their new favorite word was *we*.

They equated married bliss with an extreme kind of togetherness. They were going to drown each other in their misguided attempt and were submerged in a sea of false expectations. I worried that this would doom them to an early divorce. I released them from their expectations when I balked as one of them was going to accompany the other to the bathroom. I hollered that they could pee together if they wanted to, as long as it wasn't in my office. Bladder functioning notwithstanding, they were eventually able to take delight in the fact that they were two separate people, each respecting and valuing the differences between them as much as their common ground. To this day, twenty-odd years later, they still value and hold this concept dear.

The Sexual Highway

Whom we choose to marry, and why, can be revealed only by the language of the inner self. What we look for in marriage, and what all the legacy of romantic love represents, is a replay of that drama we already know that is tucked away in the unconscious part of the self. All the longings, all the needs, and all the wants left unattended cry out for attention in marriage. A sexual highway forms in the marital relationship that links the past to the present. The sexual marital relationship literally provides a connection from the everyday life of the present to the psychic life of the past. Marriage becomes a two-way street allowing passage for the conflicts from the past to emerge. A free subway ride from the past into the present.

Marriage, as the most intimate relationship we can form in adulthood, forces us to deal with the most formidable issues of our early self. In our marriage, we struggle with issues left over from the development of ourselves in an earlier time. Despite the conflicts marriage presents, it is still the best place for us to try to work out having a lasting, intimate, loving relationship. It's far from easy. As one patient reminded me, any two people can live together as long as they like; only marriage partners face the daunting task of staying together as long as they live.

Intimacy in marriage requires that we have an integrated self. Whole. That we have the ability to move beyond the fantasy, beyond the illusion of romantic love, and form an intimate relationship with another. Besides having realistic expectations, it requires us to have an inner dialogue about who we are and allows us to reveal that self to another. Our issues of the past pursue us from the sexual highway into marriage. If we have a wounded or shattered sense of self, it will interfere with our capacity for intimacy.

There are two main arenas of emotional conflict. The first is the fear of intimacy as represented by two sides of the same emotional coin: abandonment, and control. The second is transference.

FEAR OF INTIMACY

Two seemingly opposite sets of emotions interfere with intimacy: abandonment, and control. At their root, they are the same in that both occur in individuals with a fragile sense of self-esteem, yet at first glance they appear strikingly dissimilar.

Fear of abandonment and fear of control are both sides of the same coin: fear of intimacy. They cannot be felt at the same time. Usually we feel more of one side of the coin than the other. Sometimes we choose a person who expresses the opposite side of this coin for us. I see this in many couples. The adage that opposites attract only means we are similar underneath. I see people with a fear of abandonment pick someone with a fear of control, so one can run and the other can chase. They engage in a duet wherein each person replays past conflicts and expresses fear of intimacy in his or her own unique way.

Fear of Abandonment

A fear of abandonment makes us feel as if we will die or disappear without the other person. As if we will lose ourselves. As infants, this feeling occurred when we lost sight of our mother, because we were not yet able to take care of ourselves and being alone threatened survival. This feeling is so terrible that we may seek to avoid feeling it ever again. Even in adulthood, when being alone does not threaten survival, we may feel as if it does.

When we fear abandonment, we may try to stay glued onto another. We may seek to preserve the illusion of intimacy but, in truth, maintain a distance that prevents us from the vulnerability of intimacy. We may never develop ourselves as independent, whole individuals. Instead of dealing with the fear that we won't be able to survive, we try to avoid the feeling entirely.

Jill's fear of abandonment pushed her to choose men with one foot out the door. She assured me that this was not because she didn't want intimacy. She explained time and again that, most of all, she wanted a commitment. I knew that what she said was true. I also knew that on an unconscious level this wasn't true. She was simply repeating a drama within and avoiding the creation of a new life story for herself.

Unconsciously, Jill chose relationships that created distance and abandonment because that was all she had ever known. Like all of us, she tried to change the past by choosing someone in the present and then trying to change that person so she wouldn't feel the loss and abandonment. Like a broken record, she held onto the past, trying to change history by choosing unavailable men who she hoped would change and become available to her at last. She kept picking all the unavailable men she could find. The more unattainable they were, the more she ran after them, tried to hold them. And, of course, she lost them. She continued to try to change the father of the past by choosing someone like him in the present.

I wanted to convey to Jill that her behavior was designed to maintain distance. She was only repeating unconscious patterns. She would never have to risk being in a relationship if she kept choosing men who would leave. She could continue to be rejected, as she had been by her abandoning father, and keep trying to change the past by repeating it, or she could confront herself and create a new future. In order to do so, she would have to allow herself to feel abandonment and loss and see that she could survive.

I convinced Jill to make a very conscious decision as opposed to following her unconscious pattern. I told her to go against her grain. I suggested that she do an end run around her unconscious compulsion to repeat the past and now pick an available man. A truly available man. Then make it work. She resisted, of course, and thought I was batty, but I badgered until she took a risk and tried, and then tried harder and kept trying. And then of course we both cried at her wedding.

Fear of Control

Fear of control occurs when intimacy feels controlling. Commitment issues are frequent manifestations of this fear because we equate being close to someone with being engulfed by him or her and losing ourselves. We don't want to get too close because something that is frightening or anxiety-producing is associated with closeness. The reason we fear being "smothered" or "swallowed up" by another is that we have a fragile sense of ourselves and perceive the other person as overwhelming and dangerous. The root feeling is—again—that we won't be able to survive.

Paul had a fear of intimacy that manifested itself in an inability to commit. In his early forties, he had never formed a lasting relationship. He stayed in a relationship only as long as he was the one chasing. He thought he fell in love too easily, but I knew the real problem was that he couldn't allow himself to love at all. He fell in love with fantasy, and as soon as the true person and the demands of an actual relationship surfaced, he fell out of love. As soon as real intimacy was offered, he felt threatened.

When Paul was in his chaser syndrome, he would smile at me gleefully, as if to show he had no issue with intimacy. His excuse was always the same. It was his girlfriend who wouldn't hold still and commit to a relationship. I chided him because I knew that he chose people who wouldn't commit because *he* couldn't. As long as they could be blamed, he didn't have to confront himself. He and I both knew he didn't have a snowball's chance in Havana of having a lasting relationship with his current flame. A girl who was halfway out the door was a perfect choice for him. As perfect as the last one had been, and the one before her. Chasing was always a perfect way to avoid the challenge intimacy posed.

As long as the woman was unattainable, Paul loved her. He

didn't want to digest the fact that this was the only way he felt safe enough to move toward a woman. The moment a woman turned toward him, he backed away. They all had to appear aloof, unattainable, in order for Paul to stay and move closer. When the women stopped running, which invariably they did, Paul's chasing would come to a screeching halt and he would run the other way.

Many times Paul has voiced the fear that he would be caught. If it wasn't *caught*, it was *controlled. Strangled. Swallowed*. He worried that he would lose himself if he got married. I helped him see that being in a relationship did not mean regressing into the control of a critical and overpowering mother. But Paul carries his negative mother inside, so he still has a weak sense of himself, avoiding intimacy with another in order to avoid her.

Paul outruns his fears by constantly engaging in go-nowhere affairs because the infantile fear of not being able to survive overwhelms him. It will require Paul's conscious decision to change his behavior if he wants a real relationship. He will have to force himself to stand still and negotiate the delicate act of merging into a relationship with someone. When he does, he may find he can be in a relationship yet still maintain a sense of who he is and survive. But he has to want that for any real change to take place.

THE EMOTIONAL BAGGAGE OF TRANSFERENCE

The biggest trunk of emotional baggage we carry with us into marriage contains transference. Transference carries past conflicts down the sexual highway and thwarts intimacy because it interferes with our being able to perceive our mate as separate and distinct from the people in our developmental past. To achieve intimacy in marriage, it is crucial that we have the ability to perceive our partners as they really are, not as characters in the dramas taking place within us. We each want to be valued for who we really are, not as a figment of someone else's imagination.

The journey that has taken us to the altar is a unique one. Up until this point, we are each distinct. Getting married requires the creation of a new reality. Marriage is a dramatic act in which two perfect strangers come together hoping to find a new world. What they find is a bit more than what meets the eye. First of all, they have to contend with the group. Six or more to a bed, to be exact. Parents, and assorted others, are all thrashing around between the sheets. It has been said that we meet at the altar, virtual strangers, suffering from one or another delusional state, pledging our troth, promising to love, honor, and cherish forever, accompanied by a host of internal ghosts.

What interferes with our ability to see and respect each other as separate and distinct is the fact that we are blinded by the ghosts of the past and our unconscious wishes. We marry someone, then turn that person into a past figure, usually a mother or father, in order to re-create our earlier story. The force behind our choice of a marriage mate, and how we interact with him or her in a marital relationship, lies in the phenomenon we call transference.

Transference takes place in all relationships, but most dramatically comes into play in the marital relationship. A clever trick of the emotional imagination puts someone from the past, usually a parent figure, onto the face of our marital partner in the present. Our unconscious wiring cuts grooves, like a record, and we want to keep playing the same music over and over again. The people we pick for this replay of past history are those with whom we are intensely involved in the present.

Another way to understand the phenomenon of transference,

both positive and negative, is to see it as a mistake. Many psycholo-gists refer to transference as an error in time. We take feelings we had about people in the past and transfer them to people in the present. All of our feelings, the entire drama, have been perfectly preserved in the unconscious. Our feelings toward our parents are always ambivalent. This means that we resurrect in marriage all the old frustrations and hatreds, as well as the positive feelings. What is frequently sought out in a mate, and is then fought out with that mate, is an unresolved drama with our parents. Some of us do this so well that we never really leave home even when our address changes to one a continent away.

Joe and I are having a debate about the wild ride he is currently on. After five years of marriage, the issue for him became sex. Joe is a stud with Carlotta, the woman with whom he is having an affair, but not with Yvonne, his wife. It's not marriage or his wife that denies Joe the freedom to express himself sexually, although that's what he thinks. He feels that marriage, and in particular Yvonne, has inhibited his sexuality. Why? Because he married his mother. Joe's deeply religious and domineering mother took care of his every need, including handpicking his wife.

Joe can be sexual with Carlotta because she exists outside of the marital reality and the unconscious phenomenon of transfer-ence. He has not—yet—cast the mother robes Yvonne currently wears onto Carlotta. Should his wife be removed from the equation, Carlotta would inherit the mantle of Joe's unconscious conflicts about his mother. Yvonne would be free and long gone, and Joe would find himself with old, and new, problems. But that is our ongoing debate. I believe in Joe's sexuality and the ability to enjoy sex within the context of a committed relationship. And if I have it my way, Joe will soon believe that as well and be free to enjoy married sex.

That basement of the self-structure, the unconscious, remembers everything and learns nothing. Once we pull the trigger and transference goes to work, it doesn't matter to whom we are married. All of the past unconscious needs of the self will be layered onto that new person in the present. Our new wife or new husband will do just fine for our purposes, and we will do fine for his or hers. The trouble with this arrangement is that we end up married to the parents we carry around in our heads.

It may seem as if romantic love undergoes a dramatic shift when marriage takes place. What really takes place is that the unconscious feelings are finally free to escape. We have less fear of losing the relationship.

An old adage is that we marry to heal old wounds and settle old scores. All of the unfinished business of our past gets played out with a new partner in the present. There is no way to outfox what psychologists call the repetition compulsion of the unconscious to repeat our past. The unconscious part of the self has simple aspirations. Nothing fancy. The unconscious wants to keep on replaying the same story in an attempt to fix things. As if a switch were left on. Who we are and what we want are bound up in this internal drama. This is the story we must come to know, because it is the driving force behind a sexual detour.

The power of the unconscious lies in our continuing attempt to repeat. The unconscious, as the repository of our past, is the container of the unmet needs of the self. The unconscious uses the present to try to change the past. The unconscious wants to change the past by redoing it in the present. We want to recapture. We want to remake. We want what we had in the past—the bliss part. And we want to redo the pain part, too. We try to change history.

The trouble is that this is futile. We cannot change the past, only try to shape the future.

Knowing the inner self in an intimate way is the only way we can override the repetition compulsion of the unconscious. Self-knowledge doesn't erase the program—transference doesn't disappear—but the power of the unconscious is deflated once it becomes conscious. Consciousness gives us the power of choice. Awareness allows us to create a future instead of just trying to re-create the past.

Stages of Marriage

Most of us marry with unrealistic expectations, unreasonable ideals, and mythological beliefs. We seek safety in marriage and regard it as a harbor, a safe haven in which to live and raise a family. We marry because of tradition, because it is expected, because we cannot fathom life in an unattached state. We marry because of lifestyle, financial support, and appearances. We marry because romantic love and sexual desire swamp us. We marry with variations on a theme, but it is always with the internal wish for the reunion, the refinding of a love object that harkens back to our first passionate connection in life.

When legal marriage takes place, the crucial content of the marriage contract is never revealed. Nothing in the marriage certificate even closely approximates what takes place in our heads. We rarely discuss these assumptions in detail. But the assumptions are there. All of our assumptions about fidelity, discretion, honesty, and how we meet each other's needs is spelled out in clear detail in our unconscious expectations.

The marital agreement we drag around in the unconscious part of our self carries all the specifications of what we expect of our partner. This has nothing to do with our stated objectives or those late-night discussions of what marriage means, of what we expect, or what we intend. Or even of what we are supposed to provide in turn. All our unconscious assumptions were written long, long ago, when the world of the self was very new. Most of the expectations and assumptions begin the same way:

If you loved me, you would . . .
put the lid down.
leave the lid up.
put the cap on.
leave the cap off.
walk the dog.
get rid of the cat.
turn the music up.
turn the music down.
not talk so much.
talk more.
want sex all the time.
not want sex all the time.
never feel angry, hurt, or misunderstood.
never let me feel angry, hurt, or misunderstood.

In other words, *make me feel loved, whole. Be perfect for me. Make me perfect, too.*

Somewhere along the way, sooner or later, we find out that marriage means something far different from what our assumptions thought marriage meant. Moreover, it doesn't mean the same thing to our partner as it does to us. Even within our own adult developmental cycle, what marriage means will change. Marriage is a complex tapestry woven of many threads that go back in time. Moreover, how we change over time causes us to create many marriages out of what began as one. There are broad categories common to most marriages. Close behind Shakespeare's seven stages of man, marriage has six stages, each with piercing characteristics lasting around five years, give or take. Marriage is a difficult process to navigate, and having a road map indicating the bumps and curves telling us what to expect is helpful.

STAGE 1: NEWLY MARRIED

We all know this one. It still glistens. It has the musical score. It's the honeymoon phase. We're madly in love. Lots of eye contact, lots of touching. Lots of sex. You are mine. I am yours. You are perfect. I am perfect. We are perfect. We are one.

We experience this stage of marriage more as an expectation than a relationship. It is filled with desire for fusion and contains assumptions, high hopes. The burden we put on our partner in this stage of a relationship is that he or she will make our lives whole, happy, meaningful, intense, and ecstatic. Forever. We have an underlying anxiety about how to make this stage last.

STAGE 2: RECENTLY MARRIED

We attempt to harmonize our married state as we deal with issues of intimacy. In this stage, partners still want fusion but may experience fear of control or fear of abandonment. We begin to recognize that we are not exactly alike. The demands of reality reveal themselves more clearly than before. We notice differences. Different temperaments. Different needs. Annoying characteristics surface.

This phase ends when we recognize that the other is not perfect. Reluctantly, we give up romantic ideas of fusion and perfection as we start to deal with the issues of compromise and settle for what reality has to offer.

Most affairs and divorces occur during the first and second stages of marriage.

STAGE 3: MARRIED

Reality makes itself more deeply known, and handling ambivalence within the relationship becomes important. This stage sets in when expectations begin to assert themselves. We lay to rest our wishes for fusion and settle for a basic merger. *How much of myself do I have to give up to be in a relationship?* We recognize the need for problem-solving skills and master the art of compromise as the pressure of marriage and career combine with the realities of raising a family. Children bring a new reality. We learn that the train of romantic love must exist on a different timetable and track from the one carrying the kids, for the simple reason that a train can't run on two tracks at the same time.

STAGE 4: REALLY MARRIED

This hallmarks the first real recognition of the passage of time. The dramatic changes that accompany growing children and the added responsibilities of parenthood reflect the deepening realities to which a marital relationship is subjected. The need to maintain one's identity is strongly felt and causes conflict. *Who am I? What do I want? Don't want? What do I need? Don't need? What have I become?* Disenchantment with oneself may travel under the guise of disappointment with the partner in marriage.

Sex in this stage of marriage is a lived-in reality with children and family. The juggling doesn't stop there. We are caught between two worlds. Grown children leave home; the parental generation ages and dies. There is little room left for illusion. The turbulence felt at the end of this stage of marriage heralds the oncoming force of change.

Over a quarter of affairs and divorces occur in marriages of fifteen years or more.

STAGE 5: REMARRIED

This time of life is all about change. Changes abound, and with them, a chance for reconciliation presents itself. When children become young adults and leave the family home, there is a mandate for renewal, and the marital relationship changes.

A renewed thrust is present regarding accomplishment in careers. Second careers begin. We see ourselves more clearly and can recognize our own inner struggles. Along with a need for acceptance of oneself and our aging process comes an acceptance of our partner. There is a wish to experience our lives more fully. The sexual relationship often improves when children are away at school and the marriage partners are alone.

STAGE 6: FINALLY MARRIED

A great deal of warmth, acceptance, affection, and tolerance underscore the late stage of marriage. Maturity allows for the inclusion of flaws. The age in which we live prolongs life, vigor, sexuality, and emotional well-being. Redirected energies are aimed at finding out what lies ahead, before what is left is over. We may face the illness or death of a spouse. There are more memories upon which to draw for strength, in contrast to the wishings and longings of earlier times.

Intimacy and Marriage

Ultimately, marriage is not about romantic love. Marriage is not about longing or wanting. Marriage is about having. About giving. About knowing. About seeing and being seen. About hearing and being heard. Marriage is about developing intimacy, the only thing that gives us what all that longing is really about.

Marriage can help us evolve and become more mature, or it can perpetuate the way we seek to isolate ourselves from intimacy. The way we develop intimacy with our self and our partner, and the way we penetrate the veil of transference, is primarily dependent upon the kind of communication system we have developed.

Great sexual feasts do not provide the intimacy necessary to keep a marriage alive. Steamy sex may not survive reality. Sex in marriage has the power to enhance and hold, to allow a real relationship and true intimacy to develop and flourish. But if there is a problem within, where we avoid ourselves, there is a lack of intimacy in the marriage, and eventually this reflects itself in one way or another.

Marriage can become a way of maintaining distance and perpetuating the way we isolate ourselves from intimacy. Not all relationships can withstand intimacy. For those of us with a fragile sense of self, marriage may include an affair that creates the distance we need. The closer we are to another's vulnerabilities, wishes, and fears, the nearer we are to our own. For some of us, real intimacy proves too dangerous, too overwhelming, and we turn away, toward paths that provide more distance.

In search of the intimacy a marriage has not provided, for any number of reasons, we may seek to fill unmet, unspoken needs with an affair. When we do not know what we need, we have difficulty developing a binding tie. In the absence of intimacy, and with the decline of romantic love, under the stress of the realities imposed by one or another stage of married life, the fracture of fidelity can easily occur.

When marriage disappoints, when what we sought to have and hold eludes our grasp, when our attempt at redoing our first romance fails, a shattered self takes flight and seeks to fill unmet needs in other ways. We make a second pass at recapturing that early first romance. We do it silently, quietly, perhaps unknowingly. Even unintentionally. In search of the self we do not yet know or fully feel, we turn away from marriage toward a sexual detour.

PART TWO

Intermezzo

Chapter Five

❧❧

The Triangle

*So heavy is the chain of wedlock that it needs two
to carry it, and sometimes three.*

—ALEXANDRE DUMAS

❧ Flirtation has endless possibilities. Fantasy and illusion
cavort rather heedlessly on those grounds. But when we reduce
the possibilities to one, we cross the line of seduction. Moments,
hours, days, or months may go by before we finally abandon ourselves and cross the threshold. But when we do, when we commit
adultery, the innocence of the marriage dies. And somewhere
within lies the terrible knowledge that things will never, ever be
the same.

When we enter the hidden world of the affair, the laws of the
universe, as we know them, cease to exist. Time never again
resumes its usual cadence. On a sexual detour, we hover in the half-
light of physical reality and emotional fantasy. There, triangles
form, reflecting an inner life we have yet to explore or fully understand.

In this hidden world of the sexual detour, there is even a subtle change in climate. The weather of secrets prevails. The secret is as crucial to the existence of this hidden world of the affair as are air and water to the planet we inhabit. Here, whispers float in air that suddenly grows heavier. A silence descends to muffle the sound of reality. Stillness emanates from the secret, weaving a cocoon for the fantasy life of the affair. Affairs live and thrive in this cocoon, where wishes and dreams take form and shape as if to prepare for flight.

Functions of a Secret

The affair is a secret triangle that serves many functions. It lures those of us who are afraid to know who we really are or who we may become. It beckons to those with low self-esteem. The secret of an affair feels safer to those of us who do not feel whole. With a fragile self, we allow ourselves to behave more freely in an affair than in our real lives. The secret affair becomes a private testing ground, before integrating into real life, for a particular action or way of being.

For some, the secrecy of an affair feels like a safer arena for the expression of sexual needs. While sex with a marital partner may be technically good, the sexually charged air of a new and different sexual partner brings fantasies to life and allows us to act them out. It may be easier to reveal our desires without consequence, and attain them without cost, when we act on them secretly. Because it isn't for real. Or for keeps. Marital partners, with the help of transference, often inherit the powerful mantle of parental figures. So instead of learning how to act out sexual fantasies with our spouse, from whom we may fear disapproval, we use the illicit playmate to experiment more freely. In secrecy, we do what children normally do. We misbehave.

Denial in the Affair

The affair stays alive best in secrecy. This keeps the sexual detour safe because it creates denial. An affair is a fragile, furtive thing, designed to serve a fragile self. Secrecy provides cover for the psychic issues within ourselves that we want to keep clamped down, hidden. It is as if the darkness of a secret protects us from seeing or feeling something within ourselves.

This secret releases a peculiar energy. I remember watching Joan pack twice as much into a day as others could in a week during the secrecy of her affair. She moved at lightning speed. She juggled the daily tasks of raising a family with seemingly great ease. Housework, driving a carpool, attending soccer practice and ballet rehearsals, working at her job, and spending time with her husband and lover seemed to go without a hitch. Watching her do life in double time, I knew of course that the frenzy outside masked an even greater frenzy within.

In the absence of external chaos, I sensed that Joan would feel the internal frenzy from which she was so desperately trying to escape. On a sexual detour, she did not have to face inner anxieties or frustrations because the affair offered escape. I could see that Joan's worry over details, about overt lies, was easier to tolerate than the tension of her inner feelings. All the dangers facing Joan seemed to lie in truth, in discovery. I knew that her affair was not a cure and would never heal, only hide.

The Secret Exchange

Marriage is a two-party system. A dramatic change occurs when a third party (a lover) is introduced into a two-party system. On an emotional level, betrayal takes place when secrets are shared. Momentary affairs, purely physical sex that do not contain shared secrets, are far less damaging to marriages. For most people, the ultimate betrayal is not the physical act but the rupture of emotional trust, the sharing of secrets with another.

Often, the distinction that enables many spouses to stay put and help the marriage survive a sexual detour is the belief that blindfolded sex took place. As if no other person were present. An activity more on the order of masturbation. No emotional boundary violations. And very often, it is true that no confidence has been broken. No secrets shared.

A couple came to me with their hearts in their eyes. Frank, the husband, had had a short affair. What should they do? Did this mean something terrible about their marriage?

When Frank described his sexual indiscretions, it was fairly clear to me, as well as to his wife, that his loyalty had remained intact. His trucker's drive-through route had become a few one-night stopovers. There, he availed himself of all the comforts of home. On the blue plate special, sex was served after dinner and secrets were kept, not shared. What I told them to do was to go home and hold each other tightly, hang onto what they had. To forget about his drive-throughs and keep their lives intact. For them, blindfolded sex had indeed taken place and no one else was involved. They could deal with the sexual temptation, the lapse in judgment. For them, no secrets shared meant that no betrayal had taken place.

In another case, Ginny felt distraught not by the sexual act but by how enormously betrayed she felt. She came to see me in a panic and rage. She was crazed. She had been told everything in excruciating detail. Her husband had revealed that he had shared all their secrets. He had told his secret lover Ginny's anguish over their marriage, even her struggle with weight. Their secret rituals had been incorporated into the affair. His betrayal ran deep. Her wounds, therefore, were deeper as well. What she was reacting to was her intimate life being taken away and given to someone else.

Ed had been my patient long before his affair began. His emotional relationship with his wife had always been bare bones. A prisoner's meal. It was watery, thin gruel, barely enough to sustain him. He longed for a rich emotional meal. Despite my efforts at encouraging therapy for them both, his wife remained isolated from any help and unable to join him in the way he wished. When he began his affair, I had a hunch that it was going to bring about the definitive end to his marriage. Not because of any wild sex, but because new secrets were being shared. New life was taking shape and carrying him far beyond the boundaries of his marriage.

Ed and his lover were both architects. They were partners in a design contest. They huddled incessantly, whispering and colluding, forming the alliance he wanted so dearly and had never been able to form with his wife. His betrayal was not in sharing secrets but in forming new ones outside the marriage.

AFFAIRS UNLEASH EMOTIONAL DYNAMITE

Affairs include all types of emotional betrayals in varying degrees. The triangle, when found out, lets loose some of the most power-

ful, rage-filled emotions of mankind. Emotional dynamite has been
set and lit. Betrayal touches on our most primitive, archaic emotions. Helen, whose face launched a thousand ships, was the wife of
the king of Sparta. She was abducted by Paris, son of the king of
Troy. Homer immortalized the ensuing ten-year Trojan war in the
Iliad four hundred years later. As I said, lots of dynamite.

Paradoxically, while we unconsciously try to avoid trouble by
going on a sexual detour, we end up with more trouble. When
problems exist, we may feel left with only two alternatives, either
one of which may be dangerous:

1. Deal with problems in the marriage by confronting the
   painful issues intrapsychically as well as interpersonally
   and begin the work of resolving them; in other words,
   improve the marriage.

or

2. End the marriage.

This do-or-die mandate of couplehood is lifted by the introduction of a third party. What is acute becomes chronic. An affair prevents the dissatisfied partner from having to face either one of the
two fearful alternatives because it presents a third alternative and
another way of having needs met.

The Dynamic of the Triangle

When the third party enters a two-party relationship, the new
geometry of love becomes a triangle. An invisible third party is
brought into the sexual arena. This third party is never the primary

relationship but is the indicator of trouble in the primary relation-ship. An affair may become the primary relation once the marriage ends, and this is what we fear when a partner has an affair.

From the point of view of the psychology of a relationship, a tri-angle is a manifestation of a problem *within* the marriage. Something has gone awry in the way the two people interact. One, or both, part-ner is experiencing painful issues *within*—notice I did not say painful issues *because* of the marriage—and has chosen an alternate way of dealing with the problem. These issues are both intrapersonal and interpersonal.

Whereas intrapersonal has to do with what goes on inside our-selves, interpersonal refers to the business of what goes on between two people. From this interrelationship point of view, emotional triangles are an extension of the primary relationship and are intro-duced when a two-party system is in trouble.

A triangle introduces distance. It prevents complete intimacy with either the marriage partner or the partner in the affair. It pre-vents us from having to face internal issues. In marriage, for inti-macy to exist, resolution of intrapersonal and interpersonal issues is linked together. In a triangle, the issues of the self and the issues of the relationship are kept wedged apart.

Problems in relationships always have a leg in the individual issues of the past and a leg in the relationship issues of the present. As a practical reality, nothing can stay in this overstretched position for very long. Intimacy bridges the gap between the two worlds. When intimacy fails to exist, we introduce a third person, like a third leg, to relieve the strain on the emotional back of the marriage.

For the marriage, a triangle most often worsens and compli-cates the relationship. Again, the universal language of the triangle as a tool comes into play. The stable nature of the tripod prevents toppling, and the problem remains unsolved. The very existence of the affair temporarily relieves the tension of internal issues and the problems manifested in the marital relationship. The triangle lessens the intensity of the primary conflict felt within and reduces the interplay of the couple. Conflict is obscured by the third party, because the triangle introduces illusion instead of the coping mechanisms that can realistically solve problems. Triangles, which prevent the system from dissolving, also prevent it from improving. The eventual fault lies in the very nature of the balance, where nothing gets better, nothing gets worse. The triangle obscures personal issues and hampers efforts toward resolution. What the triangle accomplishes best is to waste time. The introduction of a third person delays the imperative to face issues and find solutions.

Eventually, when the affair is discovered, the marriage likely will end. Sixty-five percent of marriages faced with infidelity cannot weather the storm, not only because of the internal issues that interfered with intimacy in the first place but also because the anguish of betrayal carries with it a terrible cost. Far too few of us know how to breach the break in fidelity and heal the wound that betrayal inflicts.

LIFE EXPECTANCY OF A TRIANGLE

The end of an affair lies in its beginning. An affair is a desperate search for stasis, but nothing remains unchanged forever. Affairs are fated for an early death. They usually last two to four years. If the affair becomes public, it is doomed. Reality eventually takes its toll on the affair. If the affair replaces the primary relationship, it is subject to the same emotional stresses and forces as the marriage but is twice as likely to fracture.

Conversely, although an affair survives best in secrecy, the very clandestine nature of the relationship kills it. An affair prevents binding ties from forming. Eventually the affair has nowhere to go, no way to grow. There is nothing of the stuff upon which relationships thrive and survive. Sooner or later affairs die of isolation. They suffocate in the secrecy. Affairs die for the same reason marriages suffer in the first place, only sooner: lack of intimacy.

THE OEDIPAL TRIANGLE

Often the issues that start affairs have to do with Oedipal feelings. The re-creation of this family triangle is so unique, with so many versions; the variations are endless. The most common example paints a sweeping picture of a young, single woman who becomes involved in a relationship of sexual ecstasy with a forbidden, unattainable object: the married man. The eternal triangle replayed.

The term *Oedipal,* which Freud used to describe children's preference for the parent of the opposite sex, comes from the classic myth that plays out in an adult relationship the consequences of a child's wish to overcome the rival and win the parent of the opposite sex. The Oedipal triangle is an erotic one that takes place in all families. Oedipal wishes are sweet and innocent. And very sexualized. At one time or another we all want to be the favored one, the special one. The one who gets to be in Mommy's and Daddy's bed. And we want to do everything they get to do. Everything.

Oedipal fantasies are part of the gas that fuels sexual engines. It is these fantasies that reawaken with a vengeance in puberty and drive masturbation and sexuality. Oedipal feelings are usually abandoned very early because we learn that the gratification of the childhood wish to win a forbidden parent is never granted. These wishes are given up, but the sexual fantasies remain erotically arousing. These kinds of feelings are often replayed in an affair.

Chapter Six

❧☙

Sexual Detours

It is as absurd to say that a man can't love one woman all the time as it is to say that a violinist needs several violins to play the same music.

—HONORÉ DE BALZAC

❧ What is surprising is that so many of us, at one time or another, manage to find our way into the hidden world of the affair. Nearly 70 percent of married men and 60 percent of married women have had affairs. Assuming that only one partner in a marriage is involved in an affair, at a minimum, two out of every three marriages are touched by the phenomenal popularity of this seventh sin.

The selection of a partner in a sexual detour is a snap. Lovers are easy to find, far easier than finding a marriage partner. We don't search the world over. It has to do with simple location. The person we have an affair with is almost always right under our nose. It is always someone with whom we have had occasion to become familiar. The reason we don't have to look far is that we're not choosy. In choosing a marriage partner, we work hard, consciously looking for a mate. In the hidden world of the affair, we are being driven by unconscious issues and don't even know we're looking.

Affairs as a Reflection of What We Want to Be

In an affair, we seek a reflection of ourselves as we want to be seen. We look for ourselves in another's eyes. We may not have the self-esteem to feel beautiful. So we seduce a lover and look for validation in another's estimation. We even imagine that we see what we want lying there.

The feelings we have about another person in a secret triangle have more to do with ourselves than with him or her. This is because in an oblique fashion, we look for a part of ourself that we feel missing. Ultimately, the significance of the affair lies in finding out our own identity when we are on a sexual detour. We need to know how to incorporate this new self—the one we like so much—into the real world. This is more important than focusing on whom we are having an affair with. Ridding ourselves, to the extent possible, of denial helps.

Another way we seek to enhance ourselves is by endowing another with the characteristics we wish we had. The person we are with doesn't even need to have everything we're unconsciously seeking. If there is just a smidgen there, we'll flesh it out with the creative power of romantic imagination.

In an affair, we borrow from another what we feel lacking in ourselves: youth, ability, beauty, sexuality, power. This search is camouflaged by the cover story of the affair. Sometimes what we're trying to borrow is as obvious as a cup of sugar. What is the woman with an enormous sense of responsibility looking for in an affair with a carefree, totally irresponsible man? One good guess is a sense of freedom. She wants an escape from the unremitting and unforgiving burden she most likely imposes upon herself.

In affairs we see all sorts of dog-and-pony shows: the collector who has an affair with an artist; the cold, stiff politician who falls for the showgirl along with her bohemian lifestyle; the heiress who runs away with her chauffeur. Age and youth. Beauty and brains. Rich and poor. We've heard the clichés before, because they're truisms that exploit the contrast, the differences. Unerringly, we're drawn to what we think we don't own or can't have. We find elements in the partner of an affair that we try on, like costumes in a masquerade, and act out a story uniquely our own.

In fortunate instances, an affair sets free in us something vital, lasting, even though the liaison is temporary. The experience may unleash forces in our personality that remain long after the affair is over. And to the extent that a sexual detour is a catalyst for change, it can be a positive force. Unfortunately, the reverse usually happens. Too often the secret affair is a regressive way of avoiding the real work of change. Rather than becoming, we run away from a marriage and hide in an affair. When this happens we deny ourselves the fulfillment of our own potential.

The Triggers for an Affair

The psychic groundwork for an affair is laid long before marriage, but the trigger for an affair is usually a specific life stress more apt to occur at one particular time of our life than another. Stress decreases our ability to tolerate the frustration of unmet needs and thus increases our vulnerability to the quick fix, the easy escape into ecstasy. The more contact we have with the outside world, the more likely we are to take a sexual detour. This is particularly true if we do not have to account for our time.

We often have affairs when we need a change. Indeed, many have said that the cropping up of romantic love is about being in need of change. Like a catch-22, change also harbors stress. Stress occurs in times of change because there is a need to realign and readjust. Our emotional gears don't always mesh smoothly, much less fit in with someone else's. Specific stresses can lead to affairs. A demotion in a job lowers our self-esteem, and we may look for it elsewhere. A promotion shifts our sense of ourselves the other way around, and may underscore our insecurities and present our vulnerabilities in a new way.

There are various stages during marriage where natural transitions occur, and sometimes, in these stages, the stress leaves us vulnerable to sexual detours.

EARLY YEARS AND CHILDBIRTH

The early years of marriage are volatile. Pregnancy and the birth of a child usually bring partners closer together, but many are also driven farther apart. The fears and responsibilities awakened by parenthood send many scuttling for escape under the covers of an affair.

THE CHILD-REARING YEARS

Many men feel a sense of loss as the wife is taken up with child care. Similarly, the loss of a husband to career leaves many women longing for companionship, and they seek a male who offers friendship and is simply more available.

MIDLIFE

The phase of marriage that midlife partners face is one of the most stressful. Couples confront complex issues that include coming to terms with the loss of their dreams. They face an empty nest as children are launched into their own adulthood.

LATE MIDLIFE

Later midlife brings a perceived loss of sexual desirability. Breasts drooping, hips spreading, business downsizing, Dow falling. We fight against gravity, trying to lift our failing powers of seduction. Men may feel their diminishing power in the external world and assuage themselves by exercising prowess in the sexual realm. And for the fading beauty, the reaffirmation of sexual desirability by having an affair reflects what her mirror no longer does.

Acting out an Affair

Mature adult behavior can tolerate frustration, live more peaceably with unmet needs, and find fulfillment. When we have not developed a whole sense of ourselves, we tend not to be able to withstand any deprivation. We act in ways that are more unruly, unreasonable, and sometimes self-destructive. Adolescent. Technically, having an affair is "acting out." In the language of psychology, this means that what is going on inside, rather than being felt or dealt with, is being displayed in behavior. We are literally acting out what is inside our unconscious world in order to eliminate the negative tension, instead of understanding it and modifying our behavior.

When we do not have a sense of a whole integrated self and cannot tolerate our inner conflicts, we instinctually have a knee-jerk reaction designed to avoid the tension of negative feelings. We must rid ourselves of them. Our unconscious tensions are like thunderheads looming below the horizon of sight, creating an electrical discharge of behavior that often leads to a sexual affair. Psychic lightning.

Acting out is *doing something*, but it is not a consciously understood, planned *something*. A sexual detour is hardly ever a conscious goal or planned activity. The behavior does not fulfill a conscious directive like enrolling in a class or taking a bus to the museum. The doing something is an unconscious attempt to avoid feeling the anxiety of our inner self. It is designed to keep the feelings of unbearable frustration, terror, or anxiety at bay. Sexual acting out is only one small segment of this kind of behavior. Acting out behavior encompasses rage, depression, and all kinds of obsessive-compulsive addictive behavior.

Sexual acting out behavior masks feeling the frustration and anxiety that accompany our inner conflicts. Naturally, when we avoid the issues we fail to come to terms with our problems. The critical feature in adult psychic development, in growing whole, is the ability to deal with our problems in constructive ways. With a whole sense of ourselves, we can more easily tolerate frustration and anxiety and find acceptable solutions.

As a therapist dealing with the internal conflicts that are frequently demonstrated by sexual acting out, I get advance reviews of sexual detours. I'm given a brief outline of the story and then a lot about component parts. I get promo pieces of leading characters, skewed views of the opposition, a line or two about the supporting cast. I get snapshots, posters, and picture postcards advertising the land of lust and longing. I get sound bites about firm flesh slapping against the thighs versus the flabby version. I know about high-hard versus soft-natural. I get reviews that quantify and qualify. But one thing's for sure: Nothing I get approximates what is really going on in the inner world.

It is perhaps an irony that looking at a wedding cake may lend understanding to sexual detours. Like a wedding cake, there are three levels, or tiers, to every affair: The first level, the top tier, is the presenting symbol. It's decorated for allure. It's lovely. Like romantic love, it is also more symbolic than substantial. It consists mostly of frosting. This top tier is the cover story. The sexual detour. The affair.

The second level, the second tier of this cake, represents the marriage and the way the couple interacts. This is the marital relationship. How the couple communicates and builds intimacy is reflected in this level of interrelatedness.

The third level, the bottom tier of the wedding cake, is the least decorated. Not at all beguiling, with hardly any frosting, it doesn't taste as good. This biggest layer is, predictably, the most important layer. It's the foundation for the entire wedding cake. This represents the inner world and the fissures in our feelings about ourselves. What goes on here works its way up and comes out in the second layer. Therapy is about getting into this bottom third level. A good result here helps us deal with what goes on in the second layer and even affects whether or not there is a top tier.

Reasons Behind Affairs

Affairs are a complicated drama, like the characters who play in them. Often, many issues intertwine and touch on one another to form a complicated piece known as an affair. Sometimes it's a simple melody and it's easy to hear one major chord. Sometimes there are multiple issues that combine into more complex entanglements. The following chapters illustrate case histories that point out the predominant feature of what function the sexual affair plays. This function is usually hidden in the cover story of the affair and is the issue the person on the sexual detour wants to avoid. While the reasons for sexual acting out are as unique as the people involved, there are some broad categories that can illustrate how affairs provide cover stories for the conflicts going on within ourselves. The sexual detour may serve different functions for the individual and/or the marriage. Generally speaking, as they pertain to the individual, they are:

    ✐ *A search for identity.* Sometimes we look for ourselves in the lives and accomplishments of others. Their lives seem to provide something our own life lacks. Another person's power, beauty, career, or personal attributes are sought to give us a sense of our own identity.

    ✐ *An avoidance of profound life issues.* The emotions aroused by a sexual affair may function as the way we deny and distract ourselves in order to mask the terror, anxiety, and chaos of internal conflicts brought about by unresolved life situations or profound events.

    ✐ *An escape from anxiety.* Stress is reduced by masturbation or sexual activity. Sexual affairs that take on the nature of obsessive-compulsive behavior fall into the category of an addiction.

☞ *A substitute for intimacy.* Those who fear abandonment and loss or fear engulfment and control and are uncomfortable with intimacy use sexual behavior as a substitute for emotional intimacy because intimacy provokes fear, and sex is something over which they can feel they have control. Sex, because it is used as an excuse for emotional intimacy, provides distance in the relationship.

☞ *A source of self-esteem.* Sometimes we look for ourselves in another's eyes. A desirability contest is won with a new sexual partner. For both, an affair may be sought for reassurance or repair in an effort to rebuild damaged or nonexistent self-esteem. Men may assert themselves sexually to combat fears in other, more daunting realms. Women may seek to combat fears of aging with sexual desirability.

☞ *A weapon of power.* Self-esteem issues are also present here, but there is an underpinning of hostility toward the opposite sex. Sex is used to control, to defend, and to manipulate. Men seek power in the sexual realm, and otherwise powerless women can become overtly seductive. In seduction, both men and women render the opposite sex less powerful and thus by default become more powerful.

☞ *A method of sustaining the marriage.* An affair may function to sustain the status quo and avoid dealing with issues in the marriage that necessitate change. The affair allows the marriage to continue when the needs of one or both partners are compartmentalized and fulfillment is sought in other ways.

Chapter Seven

❧❦

Marsha: A Search for Identity

We carry within us the wonders we seek without us.

—SIR THOMAS BROWNE,

RELIGIO MEDICI

❧ Many affairs remind me of a fable called "The Bluebird." In the story, two innocent children look the world over, search heaven and earth, even the realm of death, for the bluebird of happiness. Eventually, they find it right in their own backyard. I like to think this is a metaphor for finding it in themselves.

Identities, like pieces of a jigsaw puzzle, are made up of enough pieces to form a recognizable picture and help us understand who we are. So it is with feeling a whole sense of ourselves. Sometimes when we have little sense of ourselves, we look to another person to provide something rather than look to ourselves to fill the void. Power, beauty, money, status, or even youth— these are all sought as a substitute for a whole sense of self. Inevitably, the disappointment we feel when we cannot find or feel ourselves in that futile search leads us to search elsewhere. Sometimes, we search forever. The following case history demonstrates such a search.

I felt the vitality of Marsha's presence before I even saw her. The deep, rich timbre of her voice carried an energy that crackled on the phone. She requested a double session, so I could get to know her a bit more quickly. Hurriedly, she went on to outline a rather complicated schedule. She was available only here, there, out of town, in town, etc. Could I possibly fit her into one of those windows in time? "Window in time." An apt choice of words, I thought, for someone in a hurry.

We spoke briefly in the shorthand of quick intelligence. The date and time were echoed back to me, accurately memorized. She assured me she wouldn't be late and she needed no directions. Not for a moment had I a doubt of either.

Marsha had an arresting physical charisma. In her mid-forties, she was an attractive woman, even beautiful, in a strongly handsome way. The navy blue of her eyes seemed to intensify as she looked directly at me and took my hand firmly. In reality I'm a small person, but I seem large. In her handshake I felt tiny, in the grip of a powerfully competent woman. I wondered if she felt that way about herself. I didn't know it yet, but the way she experienced her self-identity was as fragile as a house of cards.

Marsha settled herself into the depths of my overstuffed couch, comfortably tucking a leg under her. She glanced around, took in the surroundings, and with a quick nod of approval, smiled at me. Then, as if readying herself for action, she notched some of her hair behind her ear, leaned toward me, and launched into a lively description of her life. She had been married for twenty-odd years to a lawyer. They had met in college, and upon marrying, she had dropped out. He went on to law school, she to raise their family. Their two grown sons were now living away from home.

Marsha was psychologically aware, physically active, and intellectually accomplished but had not availed herself of what a career might have to offer. She had returned to school when her children were young and dabbled in a number of subjects. Over the years, she had held several high-level managerial jobs but felt mainly unknown for her efforts, unrecognized for her talents, and mired down in the bureaucracy of her work.

This theme of being unrecognized extended into her marriage. She felt that her husband looked through her. Past her. He was flirtatious with other women but, to her knowledge, not unfaithful. She knew only that she felt less important than him. Not exactly belittled by him in word or deed, but smaller somehow. She had felt the same way with her father, as if he never really saw her. Her father, too, had been absorbed in his own life, as if he lived it alone. She felt she didn't get credit for being a daughter, as if she mattered less to him than his fatherhood did.

She confided that her marriage seemed perfect to outsiders. Everyone thought they were a terrific couple. "Everyone" included her husband's therapist. Her therapist. Their marital therapist. Even the circle of friends included therapists. So much for therapists, I thought.

Marsha assured me that her problems were not due to lack of psychological insight. She had insight in spades and had availed herself of all the psychological help anyone could possibly want. She had been quite thoroughly analyzed. She'd followed analysis with a number of other therapists. She assured me that sex wasn't a problem. As a young woman, she had always felt sexually attractive and had been sexually active. Her husband was proud of their sexual relationship. But then, she added almost as an afterthought, sex wasn't an issue simply because sex was always good. It had been good with a number of the men with whom she'd had affairs. It was in this way, rather blithely and obliquely, that she revealed the fact of her lovers.

Her husband knew nothing of her affairs. None of these affairs had seriously disrupted the marriage. She wanted clearly to make the point that the problem was chronic. That she had always been searching for something. Someone. Notice it hadn't been for herself.

It was then, with a mixture of somber reflection and luminescent wonder, that she told me what brought her to me. Finally, after twenty-three years of marriage, she had met the right man. I could tell by the breathy sound of her voice and the somewhat reverent air on which her sigh floated that I had to play for time. Her discovery of this person had been such a long time in coming that the pressure beneath the affair was like a gas leak under concrete. It could threaten to blow sky high at any moment. Whether this explosion was right or wrong, good or bad, I could not yet know. I knew only that explosion per se was not good.

I asked her to tell me not about this right man, but about the wrong one. I asked her whom she had been living with for twenty-odd years. She bolted upright, hooting again with hard, long laughter as she stabbed a finger at the region of her heart, ready to implode:

Who? Who? Me. That's who. I've been living with myself.

Even though she had created her husband from collage material, created every inch of their life together, he didn't recognize her great accomplishment, didn't realize who she was. And as for Mr. Finally Right, Marsha exhaled, the implosion staved off for a moment, as she relaxed again:

Leonard is the only one who really sees me.

And that was my first introduction to Leonard, the man who was her partner in an affair. The right man Marsha finally found and loved.

I wanted to learn more, not necessarily about Leonard but about whom it was that Leonard saw. When I pressed her in the ensuing session for *whom* it was Leonard saw, what that person felt like, Marsha could respond only with who *he* was. Leonard had a cachet about him. He was a successful writer, with a long list of publications. He had a glamorous life and an even more glamorous past. Leonard was passionate. Sex was wonderful. They spent long, lazy afternoons making love. Leonard had time to spare. He was in the midst of writer's block. That gave him a lot of time. Leonard was described as a sensitive, deeply insightful person, who confided all his fears. Not at all like Marsha's flimsy husband who was filled with bluster. Leonard had no arrogance. Leonard made her feel needed.

Although Marsha told me she wanted to explore where she was going, I feared she already knew. She was in a hurry. Knowing she had decided, I told her in my general opinion that wherever she was going, it was too fast.

Marsha began seeing more of me, but it was almost as if it were to legitimize and accelerate her pace in the affair. Her husband still knew nothing, even though she wasn't particularly trying to hide anything. We had a tacit understanding that I was trying to put the brakes on a runaway train. She knew I was not content simply to witness her life. I wanted to meddle. I wanted her to slow down, but as the winds of change rushed past my ears, I heard chaos breaking around the corner. I resorted to one of my less subtle ploys: outright shouting.

Are you crazy?! Let's tread water awhile, Marsha.
I'm drowning and you want me to tread water?
Leonard, as dry land, is a dangerous notion. I'm dry land. Here.

In therapy, we like time. We don't want intense emotions to be acted out and discharged with abrupt behavior. We like issues to be tolerated, looked at, understood, and examined long enough perhaps to be modified. Therapy creates an emotional space where intense emotions can exist and be communicated in ways other than in the unconscious knee-jerk reaction of psychic lightning.

Play it in quarter time, I urged. I wanted Marsha to gain more of a picture of how Leonard was allowing her to feel, who it was she thought Leonard saw, in the hope that we would discover who Marsha really was. Because after twenty-three years of living with the wrong man and seeing all the right therapists, Marsha still didn't know all of who she was. She had no real sense of herself. She wasn't whole. She needed to have an identity, not borrow one.

But Marsha was too hot to slow down. Within the month she was leaving. Leonard and Marsha were going to spend three weeks together. Explanations to her husband were vague, reflecting the empty space that filled the marriage. She was going to introduce Leonard to the physical world, teach him how to hike, maybe even ski. Leonard, for his part, was going to introduce her to his three grown daughters.

I remember vividly the session upon Marsha's return, if only for its vibrancy. The leaves were blowing off the trees. It was a glorious, blustery fall day, filled with color, full of action in the sky. I should have taken it as a sign. Marsha blew in, aglow, cheeks ruddy, eyes sparkling. She had met all his girls. Leonard's women. They loved her. She loved them. Everyone loved everyone. She was dying to make them pumpkin pies, lemon tarts. Make their lives festive. Make them a family.

And your own children. What of them?
They'll love Leonard.
Are you going to tell your husband, or just let him find out?
Actually, I've already told him.

I could hear the distant sound of the family fracturing. Like fine old crystal, worn thin by time. But I could see the stars shining in Marsha's eyes, obscuring vision. Feeling the vortex, I held onto the trappings of reality.

To Marsha, for the moment, a whole new world beckoned. Marsha held a vision of what she and Leonard could attain together. Glamour. Success. Leonard offered an alternative to feeling unimportant. His was a world of status, creativity. She felt she could do with him what she was incapable of doing herself. She could fulfill herself. Be whom he saw. What that said to me was that at last she could have an identity.

Marsha's marriage dissolved before my very eyes. It was rather easily accomplished, in a matter of weeks. It is amazing, once the die is cast, how quickly events ensue. True, it was made easier by the fact that their sons had already relocated their lives. True, it was accomplished speedily by the greased exit of Marsha's husband, who soon became involved with another woman. What seemed to affect Marsha the most was selling the family home and dividing up their finances. This shook Marsha to some degree. But Leonard was successful. There was a new life in store.

The divorce brought our sessions to an end. From start to finish it had been barely five months since Marsha had first called.

They were going to stay for several months in Mexico. The enchantment appealed. Serenades beckoned. Leonard could work from
there. The new life and new identity were close at hand. In fact, she
had a project in mind for the two of them. I felt strangely
depressed, not able to taste the optimism that flavored her
announcements, feeling I had somehow failed, in that wink of an
eye, to help her. And as quickly as she had entered therapy, Marsha
left. Flew out that window in time.

From time to time, I received notes from Marsha. They had
decided to stay in Mexico for a year. The house was on a piece of
land jutting out to sea. Glorious. An announcement of Marsha and
Leonard's marriage drifted in like a piece of kelp. Then:

The house up here is too narrow. I feel like I'm in a tunnel.

Space sometimes opens up possibilities within, I thought to
myself. Maybe even gets blamed for the lack of potential we feel
inside, for what we are restricting ourselves from becoming. Then,
nearly a year later, I received a phone call:

Hey, is that window in time still open?

Marsha blew in with the same energy and vitality I remembered. She looked a bit different. She sat in the same at-ready
stance, quick to banter and laugh, but a worried look haunted her
eyes. The new place, the new start, were new all right. What that
translated into was strange. Unfamiliar. Even a past that had not
always felt good was familiar.

The realities of her new life rankled. She didn't like being a
stepmother to Leonard's daughters. She found them irritating. They

drained Leonard of financial resources. He was besotted by their need of him and refused to urge them to become financially independent. The writer's block that had left so much time for sex was taking a toll on her new identity.

The project she had envisioned working on, their debut as a writing team, still hadn't happened. I suggested that perhaps working on her ideas and not waiting for him might be an option. She might discover what she could do without him. She might discover a way of opening up that narrow house.

In time, Marsha gave up Mexico and they returned to California, where Marsha's energy and vitality were poured into real estate. Her search for a new life became an effort to find roots. They purchased a house, which she went to great lengths to restore. But it became painfully obvious that just as she had created the last life looking to her husband for an identity, she was doing it again. The new life with Leonard was beginning to resemble the one she had undone. Away from the rosy glow of the affair and in the glare of marital reality, her new life was beginning to make her feel like her old self.

The house never really became a home. In the ensuing year, the ominous signs that had been there all along became more and more apparent. Leonard's endearing fears became annoying. A chronic depression plagued him, and it became clear he needed her to lift him out of himself. Marsha felt emotionally drained by his depression and dependency on her. She was indeed needed as she had seemed to want, but this was not the new life she had imagined. She had envisioned a team. Now she felt responsible for the dogsled. She felt as if she was hauling the emotional load. She said she felt like a nurse. She wanted a divorce.

The vision that had entranced Marsha, the person she thought Leonard had really seen, was not who she really was. It was who and how *she wanted* to be seen. The affair was a cover story hiding the lack of her own identity and the fact that she was not a super-woman but a person needing to find strength and fulfillment. First the affair, then the marriage, had extended the charade. The affair allowed them both to buy into the smokescreen Marsha represented to the world. A woman in charge, in control, able to do anything and everything. Create lives. Except one of her own.

Marsha began to see and feel her own vulnerabilities and understand the dynamics of what had been the pressure under her divorce and remarriage. She began really to know herself and become whole.

As much as Marsha's insights were a beginning, as much as they helped her grow whole, they ended her marriage to Leonard. Like many relationships born of affairs, the second marriage that had been so hurriedly grasped in fantasy evaporated with reality. So as the winds of change howled fiercely around us, I held on more tightly than ever. Until on a particularly strong gust, I let go. Marsha flew out that window again, this time a bit more whole, and charted a course toward the unknown.

The bulletins still drift in. Home is Manhattan. Marsha went back to school and is finishing her doctorate. She began writing about her own insightful and unique experience of finding herself at such a late stage in life and is looking forward to seeing it published. Now at what is so graciously referred to as a woman of uncertain age, Marsha feels radiant, alive, and well. Peacefully empowered. It was a long journey home. And like the journey we all share, while still containing uncertainty, it is also filled with potential.

Chapter Eight

❧❧

Norma: An Avoidance of a Life Issue

Life is as tedious as a twice-told tale.

—SHAKESPEARE

❧ All sexual affairs are detours of one sort or another. Rather than feel what takes place within the inner world, the acting out behavior provides a cover story. This is seen most clearly when the affair serves as a distraction from a profound life issue. I want to make clear that by distraction I in no way mean to convey a flighty, pleasurable diversion or diminish the emotional power in an affair. Rather, I am trying to convey how a sexual detour can represent an escape from a profound unconscious event we are desperately seeking to deny. We avoid dealing with the enormity of inner conflict by pouring ourselves into the very seductive emotions present in an affair. The problem, of course, is that, in time, the affair ceases to mask the issues. The inner problems that are not faced or resolved resurface.

The case that best illustrates the divergent nature of affairs, the errant deflection that skews and diffracts our consciousness so that we actually stray from the matrimonial path, is shown by

Norma. In her case, the compelling emotional work of dealing with separation and loss was a profound life issue that needed to be undertaken in order for her to move comfortably forward in life. Instead, she flew into fantasy and illusions and buried her emotions in an affair.

The sexual affair, which seemed to provide the romantic dream come true, was an escape from terrors Norma had managed to disguise in many ways until the death of her mother and the separation from her daughters when they left home. The terror of separation then became too great to handle, and Norma escaped facing these feelings by fleeing into an affair. The circuitous attempt to avoid and deny did not last, for in the end a crisis with her beloved grandson served to bring her, as the poet T. S. Eliot wrote, back from where she started. The beginning.

Like perfume, the memory of Norma's story lingers. I was called in during a crisis, when her losses were mounting, to stop the flow, ebb the tide, before she was drained of what she felt to be her lifeblood. I had met Norma fleetingly, through a circle of associates, a decade earlier. I remembered her as a bright, beautiful woman. The appearance of the woman who walked in the door ten years later shocked me. Norma, on the downslope of fifty, seemed greatly aged. She carried a great weight, not just in the excess poundage she had cloaked herself in, but also in her bent head and the look in her eyes.

The acute crisis that precipitated her seeking my help was her daughter's impending divorce. Norma had been the primary mothering figure to her grandson since his birth six years earlier. The custody issues of the divorce meant that she would see less of her grandson. Norma obviously had a deep and passionate connection to him and he to her. She was distraught over the pain he felt and the threat of losing the boy. Her fear and rage about this were ripping the family apart and threatened to tear asunder any remaining ties to her daughter. The seams of Norma's life were coming apart before her eyes, as cover stories often do.

Norma was the only child of elderly immigrants. Norma described great freedom in her childhood. But what this translated into was that Norma had raised herself. She was accustomed to awakening after her parents had left for work, eating breakfast, and taking herself to school and back. By the age of six, she was on her own every day from seven in the morning until just before dark. Norma took care of her parents by taking care of herself. The subtext of loneliness and danger colored her life but was never openly acknowledged. Norma had such denial of her terror that—unfelt and unrecognized—it governed the rest of her life.

At the ripe age of eighteen, feeling twice her age, Norma married a knight complete with shining armor. In quick succession they had two daughters. She felt that her real life had finally begun. Norma marveled at her good fortune: a home, children. What mattered most to Norma was that her children have a mother who was always there. Finally, in becoming the kind of mother she had unconsciously longed for, she had one. She remembered wishing time could stand still.

Then the past intruded. All the fear, all the terror Norma should have been able to feel in her young fragile childhood, she began to feel in her safe and secure adulthood. Soon after the birth of her second daughter, she began to awake in a panic, forgetting where she had put the child, fearing that the children were lost. She picked up the children at school drenched with sweat until she caught sight of them. Relentless, and in pursuit of the past, her unconscious fears tracked her. As her children grew, so did her panic attacks and agoraphobia. Her past was being played out for her in the music of the unconscious, like a record stuck in the same old groove.

Suddenly Norma's father, then her mother, died. The shock left Norma grieving and assuming responsibility for their deaths. Often children of abused childhoods cannot give up the role of taking care of others. But they never learn how to take care of themselves. The burden she had always carried suddenly grew heavier under the full measure of her tremendous guilt.

Within months after the death of her mother, her daughters left to go off to college. Norma remained in shock. They were all gone. Bereft of her attachments, reeling in place, she tried to stand still, to grasp what was already gone. Appalled, she realized that all the ones she had taken care of, all the ones she had given her life to, were no longer there. They had left and taken her life with them. They had left her with the life she had created for them. Like an empty sack.

The issues in Norma's marriage had been shelved in the press of the child-rearing that shaped her life. Although her knight enabled her to create the world she lived in, she lived alone. Her husband lived an interior life, embedded in work. Norma's main sense of an interactive life had come from her children. Norma didn't really foresee that the place that felt so safe, the place she had inhabited as a refuge, mothering, caretaking, was a dangerous place for a shattered self to be.

As is so often the case when children are launched, even when a full, rich marital life exists, and even when a whole sense of self is alive, enormous pressure and stress are put on the system. The marital system that had been established in Norma's case was not able to provide for her unmet inner needs. As is always the case, her marriage was unable to save her from herself. The current life issue of separation and loss evoked inner terrors that mounted until she could no longer handle them and began to act out.

Norma began compulsively to overeat. She gained fifty pounds. In desperation, she sought help. She found a well-known diet guru, a nutritionist. He was charismatic. He paid attention. He listened. It was predictable looking back what would happen next. She looked at me for a moment, hesitating before telling me the story.

You know what happened next, don't you?
Yes. I can guess.

Of course I could. It happens all the time. For the next few years she kept the issues of her terror at separation and loss hidden under the cover story of the affair.

The cover story worked well enough, at first. In the early stages of her affair, Norma shed her weight like a garment. Norma saw an illusion of herself in her lover's eyes that did not resemble the terrified, bereaved, obese woman in the mirror. With him, she could be someone else. She reinvented herself not as a daughter, or wife, or mother. In a hauntingly familiar role, replete with all the fractured pieces of her broken self, Norma's path turned away from feeling her terror, and dealing with it, into an escape. It was so much easier to drown in the emotions of the affair than to feel separation and loss.

Norma filled the empty sack of her life with a new version of reality, one laced with fantasy and romantic illusion. Her terror and grief dried up because, as she told me with an ironic smile, mascara runs if you cry. The affair became the place where she did not get over her terror, guilt, or grief; she simply bypassed it. She dealt with her children leaving home and her mother's death by leaving, too. I smiled at the clever reasoning and the sly tricks the unconscious plays on us. As if we were outfoxing the drama within.

Sex, even though it may stretch like a cat in the overheated, charged air of attraction, is not the primary motivation for many sexual detours. Feeling pain, feeling powerless or alienated, our link to a comforter and ally becomes sexualized and acted upon when change within ourselves might suffice.

Now, the trigger for the terrors that had lain dormant under the avoidance mechanism of being in the affair was the threat of losing her grandson. The current terror of separation and loss resurrected her old terrors. Norma's current distress spoke volumes. Echoes of fear-filled lifelong chords were not difficult to hear. All the old feelings Norma had felt ten years ago, which had been buried under the cover story of her affair, were now surfacing. Not only were the same terrors returning, but also the weight gain. She began compulsively to overeat once again, just as she had when her daughters left and her mother died. The wounds that Norma had sustained as a child were being laid bare once again.

The affair had been about escape from the very emotions Norma was now feeling. She had avoided her inner pain in an affair that served to make her feel better, even look better. On the surface, that sounds good—cover stories always do. But it was only a temporary fix. Now she no longer had the fantasy and illusion of a fresh affair to mitigate the pain of impending loss. Norma had used the affair to mask the issues of separation and loss, but now the affair held no power to enchant, offered no place to hide. Norma's affair had lost its power to conceal real issues. Norma would have to deal with what she had always feared and avoided. She would have to face her feelings. She would have to confront her terrors.

There is no painless way to heal ourselves. It's always a mistake to try to avoid this experience of pain. We try to go over or under and take the painless route, but there is none. Often we cannot see the way, or only in hindsight. None of us can assume the mantle of parenthood without inheriting the leave-taking that must accompany it. It's not easy to let go. We so want to hold fast. Finally, Norma would have to keep her date with destiny and go through her private tunnel. My thoughts, as yet, remained unspoken:

> *Can you see how you fled for your life into motherhood?*
> *Can you see how you have sought refuge in the affair?*
> *Can you see that there is no refuge, only risk?*
> *Can you see that the only safety we have is within?*
> *Can you see what we have to do here?*
> *Can you see that I will have to help you let go?*

Norma had never faced the fact that her inner life was not being sustained in any satisfying way in her marriage or as an individual. Did she want to work on that? This sense of inadequacy was heightened by the fact that she could lose her grandson. Did she want to face that? She was beginning to face and feel that her special affair, now a well-worn shoe, was changing and slowly fading into a friendship, not a romantic dream come true. Was she going to continue with that? Or was Norma going to address the issues in her life and try to rebuild intimacy into her marriage?

As yet there are no hard-and-fast answers. Norma's work of

growing whole began and continues as she faces the loss of a grandson who is growing into a life that will include less of her mothering. Norma's affair ended, but as old friends, they still share a corner of their lives. She is working hard trying to clear the runway of her emotional debris, a valiant warrior bearing scars, hoping finally to soar. Sometimes, that's all any of us, even the best of us, can do.

Chapter Nine

❧❧

Luke and Travis: An Escape from Anxiety

> *A very popular error, having the courage of one's*
> *convictions: rather it is a matter of having the*
> *courage for an attack upon one's convictions.*
>
> —FRIEDRICH NIETZSCHE

❧ Part of sexual pleasure is the soothing it brings. The physical intimacy felt by the infant in the mother's arms as we were physically soothed by being rocked, kissed, and held is carried forward into adulthood by sexual activity. Masturbation as practiced in adolescence is a learning activity as well as a self-soother. This segues quite naturally into the interactive sexual activity of our adult relationships. Sex as a soother is integrated into the many functions sex fulfills.

Sometimes, the self-soothing function of sex predominates to the degree that sex becomes the major way we deal with the stress and anxiety of inner conflicts. It is used like a drug and represents addictive behavior. Often, despite the presence of a primary relationship, multiple partners are continually sought. When sexual activity becomes something that is needed in order to reduce anxiety and is an obsessive-compulsive experience, it functions much the same way as does any substance abuse. Relationships, which are anxiety-producing, are avoided. Sex partners are perceived as necessary to satisfy sexual needs rather than as emotional partners in a more three-dimensional relationship that satisfies other needs as well. Variety becomes a stimulating sex aid needed to help stoke the sexual fire to cover anxiety.

The men illustrated in the two case histories here, while dealing with different circumstances, read much like the same person, because both compulsively use sex to deal with the tension, anxiety, and conflict states of their inner worlds. Their inability to be faithful, due to any number of excuses, is the cover story. The inner truth is that they use sex in the same way drugs, food, or alcohol are sometimes abused. These men are sex addicts who rely on sex to mask their inner state of anxiety, confusion, chaos, and despair. The problems have never been faced, or solved, because they have not been allowed to surface through the constant, soothing, druglike balm of sex.

When numerous sexual affairs continue unabated in conjunction with another seemingly primary relationship, sex as a form of addictive behavior needs to be faced. The resolution of sex addiction requires the same treatment program as that of drugs or alcohol. Twelve-step programs have been highly successful. Therapy and support groups are helpful, indeed even necessary, but the primary focus is on abstinence and the hard work of continuing that abstinence. Oftentimes therapy brings about the willingness to initiate a program of abstinence because, as with all change, people must be ready to admit to their behavior and actively want to address it.

✒ *Luke*

Luke blew into treatment like a storm. A bristling hostility surrounded his body. He was in his midforties, his hair graying, but something about his manner made him appear decades younger. He reminded me of a fidgety adolescent. Perhaps it was the wad of gum he constantly chewed or the fact he couldn't sit completely still. One foot silently tapped the air, keeping time to a beat of his own. He kept glancing at his watch, as if trying to get through the hour when, at last, he would be set free.

Luke felt he was under a tremendous amount of stress despite a relatively easy, secure job and no real family obligations. Still, he was easily overwhelmed and very brittle. He was in the midst of a fleeting affair, which was flavored with visits to prostitutes, and another impending divorce. Technically his second, but really his third. Each of the marriages had lasted barely a year. The recurring theme that had prompted him to seek my help revolved around his soon-to-be-ex-wife, Gloria. Luke wanted my advice about how to handle her. He wanted to give therapy a quick look-see. Could therapy offer him something that would help him keep "his ex" (as he referred to his current wife) off his back? The help he hoped I could give him was designed toward emotional freedom to pursue what made him feel good: sex. He wanted out of the jungle of relationships. He even wanted to get out of therapy before it really began.

Relationships of any sort were stressful to Luke. He had no close friends or associates. In his view, sex was enough of an emotional existence. I hesitate to use the word *relationship* in describing his sex life because his sexual activity, begun in his early twenties, consisted mainly of sexual encounters with different women and masturbation. Sexual contacts continued throughout his brief mar-riages. Variety was an aphrodisiac. Luke couldn't get enough of sex, and for weeks on end it seemed as if he couldn't get enough of describing it to me, as if that, too, were a sexual performance. What he described was sex; what I heard was a plea for approval, and a lot of obsessive-compulsive, anxiety-reducing behavior. He was ad-dicted to sex, unable to become emotionally attached, and depend-ent upon the kindness of strangers: prostitutes.

The underlying theme of resentment toward his family came forth loud and clear. Luke was seething. His history described a father who was withdrawn, generally trying to steer clear of his wife's wrath. Luke's mother, a lawyer, was the machine behind the medical clinics that carried his father's name. She was a smothering, judgmental, emasculating woman who was never interested in Luke as a person and wanted only a flattering reflection of her son.

Luke's mother had high aspirations for him, and she kept him on a tight leash, but he never lived up to her expectations. Luke felt he was a serious disappointment to her. He failed to enter either law or medicine and so had been given a job managing one of the less important medical clinics. He felt owned by his dependency on the family business, and his independence had been stifled. He believed that his mother hemmed him in, manipulated him, and he suffered from a constant state of tension over his inability to per-form well enough for her approval. Sex calmed him down and made him feel good about himself. He had learned early on, in an adolescent frenzy of sexual activity where he masturbated several times a day, that sex made him feel good.

Masturbation calmed the emotional frenzy within. After adoles-cence, Luke's self-soothing segued into sexual contacts that func-tioned as the masturbation had. If a girl was particularly pleasing,

Luke would continue to see her for weeks. He never grew emotionally involved because he wasn't able to be close. As a young man, Luke's sexual contacts were easily obtainable, but they became more complicated when casual sex fell out of favor. Health concerns became an issue for women, and he found ready and willing females in short supply. In an early drunken spree, he woke up to find himself married and quickly had the marriage annulled.

Luke's mothering experience left him with severe difficulty in attachment. He avoided the danger that women represented by obtaining sexual gratification in fleeting affairs instead of in an ongoing relationship. The women in casual sexual affairs were never in a powerful enough position to harm him. Caught between the need for sex as a constant source of anxiety reduction and the need to remain emotionally detached, Luke didn't have much choice in sexual partners. He became dependent upon prostitutes. They were a drug to which he was addicted. Luke was held together by this kind of sexual glue.

Seven years after the annulment, Luke found himself in another marriage and again immediately regretted his decision. That marriage ended quickly in a divorce, and he returned to his pattern of temporary sexual relationships, heavily sprinkled with visits from prostitutes. His present wife, Gloria, was a sexual partner of a different sort. Their sexual liaison lasted for many years, along with his continued visits to prostitutes. Somehow, Gloria gave him a feeling of safety, and he drifted once again into marriage. It may have been, in fact, a spark of good judgment because Gloria seemed sincerely to want to provide a good emotional home for him. The marriage, however, now threatened to put a crimp in his sexual style.

Luke needed help recognizing that he had a profound choice to make. He could continue living his two-dimensional existence in which he used sexual behavior to allay his anxiety, or he could recognize what was taking place on the inside and perhaps give this marriage a chance. Acknowledging that he was a sex addict was crucial. I had the feeling that Gloria would willingly help him in the struggle he would eventually have to undertake in his life if he were to become whole. However, asking Luke to relinquish his sexual freedom was the same as asking an alcoholic to refrain from drinking or a drug abuser to give up drugs. He would have to be powerfully motivated.

What were Luke's choices? He was addicted to sex, but he couldn't continue living with prostitutes forever, could he? Perhaps he would be willing to give his marriage a chance. Maybe we could take the edge off those brittle feelings. Gloria was, as I suspected, sincerely interested in working out her marriage, but could she live with the possibility of Luke's sexual detours?

I also had a choice to make here. Antidepressants seemed a logical addition to therapy. Antidepressants are anti-irritants, helpful in mood disorders and turning down the burner on anger as well as anxiety. With the use of medication, perhaps Luke would remain in treatment and in his marriage—at least until therapy had a chance to have an effect upon him. But I didn't want to broach the subject yet. I encouraged Luke to give treatment a chance. I warned him that it would require a lot of work and I would probably be experienced as another deficient woman in his life.

Would you prefer a man to treat you?
Got someone in mind?
No, but you seem reluctant.
I am, but not because you're a female.
Then let's give it a go.
You've got enough enthusiasm for the two of us.
Yes, I do.

He slowly learned to trust me, and we ultimately began a course of medication that seemed to work in controlling Luke's short fuse. Buoyed by this success and to help him deal with his deep sense of isolation, I gave him a book about a twelve-step program. During the next few weeks, when he failed to respond, I gave him others. It was then that I discovered he had dyslexia and couldn't really read. I hadn't blundered into enough medical miracles and had spilled milk. Mopping up, I apologized for not getting a more accurate picture in a less insensitive way. I apologized and apologized. I could see I had wounded what little pride he had and raised his anxiety about therapy with me in much the same way it was already present in his life. Could Luke trust that I wouldn't wound him again? Here I was, in the same bucket as his mother. Another woman trying to control, change. Couldn't I have just accepted him as he was? Couldn't I at least have known what he needed? Couldn't I, at least, have helped? I remember the session all too well. His jaw clenched, his foot jiggling.

I'm leaving for Cabo.
Are you staying long?
The women are to die for.
Can we make a time for another session?
I'll make an appointment as soon as I get back.

More than a month later, Luke finally called. When he returned, he told me that I hadn't paid attention to him or been considerate of his feelings. He was right, of course. He had made a major developmental leap into agreeing to try therapy on my ground rules. He was vulnerable, and I had failed to take all possibilities into account in order to make the therapy feel safe. The fact that he could tell me these feelings meant more than his continued sexual acting out. His ability to return demonstrated that we were actually building a connection that might one day give him the capacity for a satisfying relationship, even if he couldn't stop his addictive sexual behavior immediately.

We began again, and this time Gloria came to some sessions with him. She was willing to have a trial separation, as she really didn't want to divorce him. Luke, too, was now willing to postpone the divorce. He couldn't promise anything. Although his sexual contacts were diminishing, he still acted out. I couldn't promise anything, either, except that we were making progress. I didn't want Gloria to fool herself. Would they be able to continue on, perhaps even live together, not knowing what the outcome might be? No one knew.

In our sessions, Luke began to see that he had never been considerate of Gloria's feelings, since she had never existed as a person to him. Luke had never taken anyone's needs but his own into account. Now he felt more attachment, not a lot or enough, but more. At least he wouldn't flaunt his escapades and would work on being more emotionally present in a relationship with her and protect her from his behavior. Perhaps someday he would commit to a program of abstinence. For now, he would continue to try to grow whole. And in my book, *try* is a nonfailure word.

ॐ Travis

Travis wore a halo of a different sort. He, too, was a sex addict but more on the angelic order. Despite the wings, however, Travis was a blight on fidelity. He was a well-known country western star who sang his way into my office. He had thousands of fans, and clearly he was determined that I would be one of them. He was charismatic, but it masked a deep sense of anxiety about his adequacy as a person and, more, as a performing artist. He toured regularly, and while he didn't use drugs, sex had become the drug he relied on to combat anxiety about his self-worth. Availing himself of sexual favors made him feel special, unique, and wonderful, and allowed him to believe in himself enough to perform. Each sexual affair was a bulwark against the constant anxiety and crippling stage fright he felt on his concert tours.

Travis had an abundance of physical charm. He was a grown man with the appeal of a little boy. The combination was like catnip to the ladies. When he was on tour, he was sexually swamped by a great many adoring females. Women found him irresistible; they lavished him with attention and affection, and he graciously returned the compliments. He always found time to take a lady to lunch. He was always fair. Going in he would tell them it wasn't going anywhere. Going in he would tell them he was a family man. Going in he would kiss them good-bye.

Travis came by his way with the ladies quite honestly. He had been well tutored. He had descended from a long line of lotharios, all famous in their day, all of whom suffered from the same overabundance of charm. His grandfather, father, and uncles all had the same affliction of being besieged by women. Indeed, it was with more than a touch of pride that his grandmother regaled Travis with the plight of the devilishly handsome men of the family. Those poor wretches. Women swarmed all over them, like bees on honey. His mother, grandmother, sisters, and a plentitude of aunts clucked the same chorus. It was a legacy. Who could fault Travis for believing in his destiny? It was a myth he carried with him all the way into my office. It provided a cover story for his sexual addiction and a method of dealing with his inner anxieties.

What prompted Travis to beat a path to my door was his wife Loretta's change of heart about the family myth and his career. Financial success meant that it was no longer necessary for him to be on the road to such an extent, and she wanted him to stop touring and stay at home to be more a part of the family. His career required performing in concert, and for Travis, going from one concert to another had been like a political tour in an election year where he hoped to be voted most wonderful and most loved. If a woman indulged him, he felt sunny. If she refused, he sulked and brooded like a child, taking the lost sexualized contact as lack of approval, an indictment that he was worthless, and his stage fright would soar.

Despite his financial stability and the lessened need to tour, Travis was now in a panic. He felt he was between a rock and a hard place. He worried that without going on the road—and all that it meant—he would never be able to write another song, or perform, and that he would lose his identity. He needed his home to be safe in order for his identity to exist. His loneliness and fears were eloquently expressed in his music, and his anxieties about performance were assuaged by the sexual adulation and indulgence that made him feel irresistible. He didn't want to give up *anything*. What do you do when women flock? When a sexual embrace with a new woman lends wings? How do you retain that feeling? Better yet, how do you willingly give that up? How do you stop wanting that?

As a child, he was protected by the safety that his mother and his grandmother offered. In adulthood, his wife provided a haven. During the nearly fifteen years of their marriage, Loretta had turned a blind eye and deaf ear. She had essentially sung the same song as his female relatives, but now her feelings had changed. In despair, Travis brought her to a session, thinking I might convince her to change her tune.

Loretta was not going to change anything. She made it clear that this was strictly something Travis had to resolve alone. She wanted Travis home. She wanted some of the intimacy she had put aside and had partially fulfilled through her children. She no longer wanted to accept the blame for his wandering eye and didn't want to make excuses for him anymore. She wanted a partner in bed to keep her toes warm and body alive and a father home with her children. After all, she was forty-five and had put it off long enough by distracting herself. In my presence, she repeated her ultimatum. If he wanted her, if he wanted to keep his family intact, he had to do something about himself. Get help, get it fast, get cured, or get out.

Travis was genuinely perplexed and clearly at a loss. He was shocked by the turn of events. How could she blame him? Didn't she know it wasn't his fault? He was able to go out and perform nightly, but at great cost. He needed a haven. But his involvement with "the road" felt like his source of energy. His life force. What made him feel good about himself and allowed him to be successful was inextricably entwined in the way he had constructed his life. Communication between Loretta and Travis had failed, and he needed help to understand that while they had colluded in creating a person who was unaccountable for his sexual behavior, it was eventually going to destroy their marriage. Loretta could no longer be part of the unconscious contract they had made, and change was in order.

After it became clear that Loretta was not going to be swayed from her position, the need to maintain the safety of his home base was motive enough for Travis to commit to the idea of therapy. He announced that he would do *anything*—he was willing to be in therapy *forever* if that was what it would take in order for him to keep the marriage intact. Each time he came in, he made a little play of trying out several chairs, earnestly explaining that he wanted to make himself comfortable since he would be staying so long. He promised he would be my best patient *ever*. The naive endeavor, to plant himself in my office and grow like a tree, was endearing, but his anxiety was obvious. I could see how his playfulness masked the deep anxiety about whether he would be able to "perform" in therapy.

He continued sessions eagerly, but his self-image could not stand alone, not for a moment. He needed constant reassurance from me that whatever he said was okay. He was not a lost cause. Yes, I could help. And yes, things could resolve. He felt great guilt. His remorse about his sexual misadventures came in great waves but dissipated in proportion to his wife's forgiveness. He was grateful when she forgave him and eager for any sign of approval.

Travis had no idea that he was addicted to sex. He prided himself on the fact that he didn't use drugs, but he had no concept of his use of sex as a drug, or for that matter how he operated internally. Travis had to work on the parts of himself that were fractured, for he could not feel any ongoing sense of being internally safe or internally creative. All of these aspects of himself seemed to depend on the outside world. The anxiety this generated was abated by the sexual activity. The image of weak, sexually active knights that was passed on to him from generations hid a great deal of shame. Travis did not feel like an irresistible or worthy man. Shame was something Travis would have to let go of.

Just as Luke, our other sex addict, had to employ all of his being in order to recover through a twelve-step program, so too would Travis have to mobilize all that he could in order to change his behavior. To change, one must take action, often an action that one has never experienced before. It is painful when you don't know where you're going and you feel as though your world will end if you change anything. The idea that I believed in a different way for him to feel good about himself, and not suffer from such crippling anxiety at each performance, was a beacon of light that gave him hope.

In my job to shine some light into the darkness, and in my own customary unsubtle manner, one day I simply announced he was a sex addict. Travis looked as if something had hit him in the head, which of course is exactly what had happened. I then more gently went on to explain that in order to be creative without such crippling anxiety, and to keep his marriage intact, he had to admit to certain truths about himself: He used sex to allay anxiety, like an addiction.

He thought about that for a long moment, rubbing his chin, then agreed. Like a compliant child, he dutifully repeated the phrase, then asked me what came next.

Then you change.
Change?
Like a writer learning to write without a cigarette.
That's all?
That's all.
How long does that take?
You do it one day at a time.

We would deal with how hard forever was later. Travis's spirits were buoyed by what he thought was this easy turn of events. He began to feel more optimistic, a bit beguiled by the prospect of changing, relieved that his wife had been delighted, although I knew she was delighted because I was playing hardball. He seemed reassured that he was on the right track, that he had a way to keep his life from falling apart. In the ensuing sessions, Travis wanted me to repeat the program and tell him again and again what he was going to have to do. Soon he caught on that it wasn't as simple as it sounded. He was going to have to give up the sexual behavior. He was going to have to give up what made him feel irresistible and soothed his anxiety about his talent. How would he feel then? It wasn't going to be so easy after all.

But I may never stop flirting.
Maybe never.
Then what?
Give up having sex with the lady you're flirting with is what.
Just like that?
Just like that.
So I just stop cold turkey?
You just stop. Cold turkey.
Like I'm an alcoholic?
Like an alcoholic.

He wasn't going to stop feeling the anxiety, but in time he would learn to do without the actual sexual activity. The experience of new behavior combined with therapy would help. He didn't even have to stop *liking* the girls. Just the *doing* part. They could still adore him. But he would have to take adulation on faith and the psychology in small doses. He was a talented performer and would eventually be able to recognize that source within himself.

Travis's initial good cheer at the prospect of change became laced with anxiety when it began to sink in that change would be long and hard. With his sincere desire to maintain an intact home life, and my beacon in front of him, he was fortified enough to begin.

> *So, when do I start?*
> *Right here. Right now.*
> *First, can I take you to lunch?*
> *Not if you want to feel irresistible.*

He grinned, easing himself into the banter, already back at flirting with me, feeling good about himself. There was hope. And with it, we would proceed. One day at a time.

Chapter Ten

❧

Shawn: A Substitute for Intimacy

If I, by miracle, can be this live-long minute true
to thee, 'tis all that heaven allows.

—JOHN WILMOT,

EARL OF ROCHESTER

❧ Many times the nurturing experiences of our early lives leave us with a fear of intimacy. We grow into adulthood not really wanting to be too close to our own or anyone else's emotional world. We avoid intimacy, perhaps because we fear abandonment or fear being controlled. We avoid intimacy both consciously and unconsciously, as if we were in danger of losing ourselves. It doesn't matter that this is not possible—it feels real.

Sexual detours in marriage maintain the emotional distance that is usually present with a fear of intimacy. Intimacy provokes fear because it is something over which we feel we have no control, and sex is something we can control. Because sex is such a physically intimate experience, it can easily be confused with intimacy. Sex is often substituted for real intimacy and sought after in order to fulfill this lack of intimacy. When a relationship lacks intimacy, usually both partners uphold the emotional distance, then blame it on each other.

Some hide from intimacy with a true self for so much of their lives that they don't know what emotional intimacy feels like. Sometimes physical intimacy is their closest attempt at approaching emotional intimacy. The only thing that feels familiar is something hidden. The following case history demonstrates how sexual detours and a fear of intimacy can collude with each other and threaten to destroy a marriage. When sexual needs are used as a substitute for intimacy, as a bulwark against intimacy, we may end up seeking an illicit relationship.

It was a long time before I knew the color of Shawn's eyes. They were downcast much of the time, and he had a great deal of trouble looking directly at me. Shawn was in his late thirties, but he seemed far younger and was achingly immature. He was confused and desperately in need of a friend. He was separated from his wife, Anne. Even though he was deeply involved in an affair, he had mixed feelings about divorcing his wife and breaking up the family, which included one young son. Although he denied that the lover had anything to do with the separation, it was clearly a case of the lover or the wife. Shawn didn't seem strong enough to have the option of living alone. He had no interest in being what he called a "bachelor," a word I hadn't heard in twenty years. He had nothing to pinpoint except his own miserable muddle.

The conflict Shawn seemed to be in was one I had often seen before. There was nothing wrong with his wife. And nothing especially better about the lover. At least not enough to justify having an affair that would break up a family in which a young child was involved. Shawn was so conflicted about the issues that he couldn't even quite frame the conflict he was in. He couldn't bring himself to ask his wife for a divorce even while moving out of the house and into the arms of his lover. Yet he could not end the affair and work on the marriage. What did he want with me, I wondered, knowing the answer even as I thought it. He wanted a relief from the emotional pain.

Shawn couldn't frame a concrete statement to me. The same emotional paralysis that inhibited him from finding a solution to his marital conflict was exhibited in his therapy. He couldn't directly ask my opinion, such as should he stay in his marriage or leave for a new life with the lover, nor could he state what his goal was in seeking therapy. He felt quite a bit of self-pity and spoke more about his feelings of confusion than anything else. He seemed to feel that he loved his wife Anne. She was a good person . . . but. But what? He didn't know. She worked hard, loved him and their small son, and was distraught and destroyed at the thought of losing him. She was panicked at the thought of another woman spending time with her child and jealous over the time Shawn spent with his lover. She wanted her family.

Shawn had met Anne in graduate school. Both of them came from small midwestern towns to attend a prestigious graduate school in the city. They met through a common friend who thought they were as alike as two peas in a pod. Shawn was studying to be an engineer and Anne was pursing a teaching credential. They hung out together, weathering the stress of school. Shawn remembered enjoying the common bonds of their similar backgrounds and the happy early years as he and Anne discovered their new city together. Anne, a soft-spoken but strong-minded individual, had a quiet strength about her. Shawn, undemonstrative and uncommunicative, nevertheless felt a bond to Anne. They had a lot in common and moved in together. A year later, when they graduated, they married.

Shawn began to feel edgy about a year into the marriage. They had moved back to the Midwest, and Anne was pregnant. He had been offered a lucrative job that involved quite a bit of responsibility. Shawn found a million reasons not to accept the position and began to work instead in the nonprofit sector as a fund-raiser. Anne, in the late stages of pregnancy, tried to be cautiously supportive. Shawn's parents were horrified. They were incredulous that he could throw away a career. He remembers feeling very angry at their reaction. He denied having any anxiety about performing in the high-powered job that demanded more of him than he felt he could give and found some vague rationale for working part-time. Looking back, he could see how his feelings of inadequacy might have something to do with the current marital situation. After the baby was born, life took on a different emotional tone. For one, Anne was involved with the baby. And two, Shawn had met another woman.

Shawn met his lover at a coffee shop. It was an idle moment, a simple conversation, nothing more. He was attracted to her youth and vibrancy. Her exuberant interest in the campaign he was involved in led to one thing. Then to another. And another. Before he knew it, he was involved in a passionate sexual affair. The sex drew him out of the social and emotional isolation he felt, and, strangely, the secret life he began to lead somehow comforted him. He felt enormous guilt, but the guilt increased his pleasure in the sex. He felt free in a way he had never experienced with Anne. He also felt strong and capable with the other woman while meek and submissive with Anne—even though his wife was not controlling or demanding.

In his treatment sessions, Shawn's physical demeanor spoke volumes. I could see by the hesitation in his voice and the message sent by his sagging shoulders that he felt enormous conflict. Shawn's gaze was fixed out the window as he hunched over and hugged himself, speaking as if under siege. He made excuse after excuse for what he was doing and rationalized his choices and actions with spurts of hostility that rained blame on everyone in his life. He was gracious in his description of his wife's good character and what he professed to think about her. I suspected he was deeply disappointed with himself and unable to face that fact or cope with how he was handling his marriage. I wondered if he was able to be straightforward and honest with himself. I suspected he wasn't with his wife, and he certainly wasn't able to be open with me.

Shawn lamented Anne's inability to be angry at him. He wanted her to be mean and surly. It would be more understandable to leave her if she gave him something to hate. He wanted to escape the responsibility for making what everyone in his family felt was a heinous choice. He needed to blame the state of affairs on Anne. But that was hard to do. Not only did his family love her, but Anne's sorrow and distress made it difficult for him to be angry at her. Arguing certainly would have made leaving the family easier and would at least have given him a position to defend. This way, all he had were the consequences of his own actions. His confusion and ambivalence wrapped around him like a heavy wet blanket.

Shawn's history revealed that he was an indulged and adored only son. He had been a model child, a nonrebellious teenager, and up until his marriage, heir to his parents' hopes and dreams. Shawn was bright. He was a chemist with an advanced degree in chemical engineering, but had chosen to work on fund-raising campaigns for a nonprofit agency. While potential earnings in his field of training were much higher, he sacrificed the income for interaction with people and the ease and comfort his nonpressured job provided. While his parents had been delighted when he married Anne, their consternation at his choice of a career tipped the scales in the other direction. They were not shy about expressing their dismay.

Both of Shawn's parents had been high achievers and had been pleased when Shawn chose to follow in their footsteps by getting an advanced degree. Now, however, Shawn was bitter about their less than joyful reaction when he announced he was choosing work outside of engineering. Listening to him, I had a hunch that they had dragged him up the path of postgraduate education and that he hadn't followed their footsteps willingly at all. I wondered if, for most of his life, Shawn had done a magnificent job at deceiving his parents by never revealing who he really was. If the affair was any indication at all, a good part of him had certainly been buried. Until the affair, that is.

When Shawn chose not to use his degree and then abandoned his wife to take up with another woman, it dropped a bomb into the family dynamics. Shawn's parents' shock and dismay began a merry-go-round of resentment and anger. They were deeply disappointed and wanted him to give his marriage a chance to work out. For his part, Shawn was suffering with his own brew of remorse, bitterness, and hostility. Within a space of a few months, Shawn and his parents weren't speaking to each other. In therapy, Shawn chipped away at his parents' value system, as if needing to excuse his own behavior. I knew that he had disappointed not only his parents but himself as well. Shawn's anger toward his parents was obviously something that he had suppressed for a good deal of time, but it was easier to feel than examining his own sense of inadequacy.

The separation from his wife and son was difficult to bear, but it seemed equally difficult for Shawn to adjust to falling from grace in his parents' eyes. When I asked Shawn if it was hard being a model only child, he shrugged it off as if it wasn't an important element in his present-day conflict about his marriage. He found it difficult to connect his earlier life with his parents to his present life with his wife. I didn't find that difficult at all. In fact, it was all I could do. But then, I was the therapist. Shawn couldn't feel sorrow at giving up the image his parents had of him. He felt anger instead. It was as if he had built an illusion of a person, and the fragmented person who faced him in the mirror now was simply someone whose existence he could not acknowledge.

The woman with whom Shawn was conducting his affair was young and naive, with a great deal less formal education than either Shawn or Anne. She had not completed high school and worked the night shift at a fabricating plant. She was bright, intuitive, and ready to commit herself to Shawn. She wanted a family and displayed enthusiastic tenderness at the idea of being a stepmother to Shawn's son. The trouble, aside from the fact that Shawn didn't want what she wanted, was that what she represented to Shawn had nothing to do with her. She was an escape route for him *away from* something, not necessarily *toward* her. My job was to help Shawn discover what that something was that he was running away from. I had a hunch it was the burden of being a model son. It had left him without a sense of himself and fearful of intimacy.

Shawn's history confirmed the fact that he never truly was able to reveal himself to his parents or to himself. His parents were just too powerful for one small model son to take on. His father was brilliant. A hard act to follow. He wasn't cruel, but he was undemonstrative and often caustic. Shawn's mother glorified

Shawn. Whatever he did she applauded. The result was that Shawn never knew what talents he had in reality. All he had to do was exist as a screen for her idealized image of him. She never saw him for who he really was. *It was as if he didn't exist.* Both his parents had good intentions. Good intentions, however, don't always count. To small children of powerful parents, especially ones with their own agenda, developing a sense of self is difficult. The desire to please overwhelms the fragile self of small children, and in the face of rejection or fear of their true selves, they develop a false sense of who they are. Shawn never knew who he really was.

As for Shawn's problems in his marriage, were they ones that could be fixed? Where were his actions going to take him? Was his affair designed to substitute one family for another? Was that what he really wanted? What exactly would be gained, I wanted to know, by substituting the lover for his wife? The only thing Shawn could stammer out for certain was that his sex life was better with his lover than it currently was with his wife. Not a surprising statement. Certainly sex was a good cover story. As good for Shawn as the countless others on sexual detours before him. We would have to find out what fueled the better sexual relationship on his sexual detour and what was blocking a better sex relationship with his wife. I doubted that sex was the culprit, even if more sexual attraction and better sex were present in the relationship he had with his lover. By all accounts, I knew we were not yet at the crux of his affair.

Not so curiously, Shawn did not want to get into the nitty-gritty of his sexual attraction to his lover versus his attraction to his wife, any more than he wanted to discuss his growing years and the burden that being a model son had placed upon him. I knew it was easier for him to allow the conflict in his life to remain status quo.

He wanted my help in dealing with how that felt to him, but he did not necessarily want to prod his inner life, for fear of drawing blood. He was hoping I could remove his guilt and the pain of his separation from his family without attending to the cause of the problem. I felt like a surgeon who had been asked to forgo surgery and provide painkillers instead. There are no painkillers for emotional wounds.

Shawn's affair meanwhile was heading for a life of its own, one he was not quite prepared to accept. He became increasingly uneasy as his lover began to want more of a relationship. She wanted to be introduced to his parents. She wanted to mend rifts and heal wounds. She wanted to build bridges and plan a future. She wanted what someone who is able to achieve closeness desires: intimacy. She wanted a *relationship*. This put Shawn in the uncomfortable position of recognizing that he did not especially want a *relationship*. Certainly not another one. What had made him feel strong and powerful was now feeling like a burden. One from which he wanted to flee. As soon as his escape route began to propel him toward the intimacy which he had so desperately sought to escape, he wanted to run the other way.

The sexual relationship in Shawn's affair was good, but it didn't take a rocket scientist to point out that it was hardly a fair comparison to make with the sex in his marriage. While his early relationship with Anne had been sexually rewarding, having a small child at home had wreaked havoc. Unless safeguards are introduced into a sexual relationship, it is vulnerable. Couples raising small children need to protect and nurture their sex life as if it were a fragile seedling in danger of being destroyed by a typhoon. Sex needs to be transplanted to vacations, romantic interludes; in other words, sex needs to be enhanced, sheltered, and nourished by special attention designed to nurture sexual needs. Shawn and Anne never talked about their sex life, let alone did anything about it.

Shawn admitted that his affair had given him a way out, but he wasn't sure out of *what*. I noted that at least we were getting somewhere. Shawn was now aware that he needed a way out instead of just better sex. As a way of finding out what he wanted out of, I suggested that we spend some time talking about all the things his parents never knew about him. Simple things that were secrets he kept about himself. Despite his puzzlement at where these kinds of discussions would lead, we began with the late-night pizza hunts of his teenage years.

Shawn divulged that as a teenager, sometimes long after his parents were asleep, he had the habit of driving the streets looking for a pizza parlor. He could have had pizza delivered when they were awake, but that would have meant explaining why he liked the pizza, what was wrong with the gourmet dinner they had prepared for him, and why he hadn't told them that earlier, before they went to the time and trouble of preparing such a great meal for him. In his mind's eye, they were such a formidable pair that it was too much trouble. Having pizza his way was far easier without their knowledge. The emotional price was less. He wasn't even sure if he liked the pizza as much as the fact that the hunt was solitary. It was *his*. His self went in search of pizza; the model son ate the gourmet dinner his parents lavished on him every night.

I knew without asking that his engineering degree was not his idea. As far back as Shawn could remember, his parents had inundated him with educational toys. Science, chemistry, engineering. He couldn't remember playing with anything that wasn't part of some kit designed for older, brighter boys. He continually had to improve himself. He had always felt as if left untutored he wouldn't be good enough. His child's play was working at a game to please his parents. He went to engineering school because his parents felt that it was the best choice for him. He didn't know where else he would have gone or what direction he would have taken if they had less of an opinion.

At first Shawn didn't see that the direction we were following in examining his early life with his parents had anything to do with his having an affair. I had a different agenda because what I saw was a different scenario. I saw a boy working so hard at being a model son that he didn't know who he was. I saw someone who had never been able to say to himself, let alone to his parents, *this is who I am and this is what I want*, for fear of his parents' disapproval. I saw someone who was desperately trying to find himself and feel himself with his affair. I saw someone who was able to experience himself only in a physical sense because he was so emotionally hidden as a human being. I saw a man who couldn't allow himself to be emotionally intimate and who instead was clinging to the intensity of a sexual experience as a life raft defining who he was.

The trouble with the sex in many affairs is that it has to remain illicit in order to stay intense. When the covert nature is taken away and the ordinariness of life is allowed to seep into the equation, the sex changes. When a real relationship begins, the sexual aspect eventually becomes more like an ordinary sexual relationship: that is to say, it has potential for being very good, or not, depending upon how we understand ourselves and what we allow to impact the sexual arena. Shawn's married sex was battered by the emotional force of his escape from intimacy. He and Anne never had a chance to try and improve their relationship or their sex life.

When Shawn went into a sexual relationship outside the boundaries of marriage, he could feel free because he was escaping from the inhibitions intimacy posed. His married relationship to Anne brought too many of his conflicts with his parents to the surface. Issues of transference colored his feelings, and intimacy was something he feared. His illicit relationship, like his pizza hunts, felt like it belonged to him because it wasn't really a shared experience. His lover, who was becoming hungry for a real relationship, intuitively knew that sex was being used as a substitute for intimacy.

Shawn's affair was a cry for help. He needed desperately to have a better sense of himself and get in touch with his inner needs. The false self Shawn had developed for his parents was destroying his marriage. When we carry around a false self invented for our parents' approval, instead of feeling a good sense of ourselves, our emotional and sexual lives suffer. Shawn wanted to escape, but he was running away from the wrong thing. He needed to take a stand and face himself. Fortunately, Shawn felt pain. Pain would motivate him to work. He was in my office. So there was hope.

What I ultimately suggested to Shawn was that he give his marriage a try. A real try. That did not mean moving back in with Anne, at least not yet. It meant taking some emotional space to discover who he really was, where he wanted his life to go, and why. And he needed to do it alone, without a partner in an affair. Along the path of the journey into his inner world, if he wanted to, he could try and see if he could form an intimate relationship with Anne. He ended his affair, willing to take a chance to be alone for the first time in his life and find out who he really was. Eventually Shawn wanted to see if he and Anne could be truly intimate, and they both came to see me.

When Anne and Shawn met in my office for the first time, there was nervous laughter. Both were uncomfortable with the thought of doing something *together*. They had lived fairly parallel lives, and neither of them had ever looked the other in the eye and tried to have an intimate conversation focused on the other. They were both willing to work toward making their relationship last but didn't know how.

> *I think you're both afraid of intimacy.*
> *Both of us?*
> *Both of you.*
> *Intimacy?*
> *Intimacy.*
> *Do you say that to all the couples?*
> *Eventually.*

Having missed out on many of the skills that are required to make a real relationship work, they didn't know what to do. I had doubts as to whether they would be able to do what was required. Each of them, in his or her own way, was afraid of establishing a truly intimate connection. I hoped their dedication to making it work with each other was the cement that would carry them through. First, though, they needed to learn how to relate to each other in an entirely new way. This meant they would have to recognize their own fears and vulnerabilities and then be able to reveal them to a partner who was prepared to be empathic.

> *What do we have to do?*
> *For openers, talk to each other.*
> *We talk a lot.*
> *By talk, I mean listen.*
> *Listen?*
> *Listen.*

By the way they looked at each other I knew that they had a lot to learn about not only themselves and each other but also the business of making relationships work. I didn't know if the word *intimacy* was part of their vocabulary or if the concept of communication as it applies to intimacy was something they understood. If it wasn't, it was going to be.

Over the course of the next year, as Shawn and I dealt with the individual issues of helping find out who Shawn really was, I coached Shawn and Anne in a method of communication that would allow them to travel a more intimate path. It took a lot of educating to get Shawn to understand that talking to Anne about his fears and fantasies, not acting them out, was the only way they could build the kind of intimate ties that last. Shawn felt that the sexual relationship he had formed with his lover gave him some valuable clues about the kind of physical relationship he hoped to build into the marriage. He also knew that sex, separate from emotional intimacy, was simply not going to hold. He ended his affair easily and with no remorse.

The following year was by no means easy for Shawn or Anne. Neither one of them had any experience working on themselves or on a relationship. For both, being in an empathic, nurturing position, which is what intimacy requires, felt dangerous. Both had issues of abandonment and control. Shawn feared being overwhelmed by the needs of the marriage in the same way that his parents had swamped his sense of self. His fragile emerging sense of who he was and what he wanted demanded a great deal of understanding from Anne.

Shawn addressed what his life's work was going to be in a unique manner. He had a child to support and couldn't spend his adult years in an adolescent rebellion against his career training.

A compromise was to earn money as an engineering consultant, which would garner Shawn an adequate lifestyle, yet allow him to function in a voluntary capacity for many nonprofit causes. He worked out a system of economic power and social responsibility that was rewarding and practical.

His relationship with his parents improved as he was able to feel stronger and more functional in his life. He developed a tolerance for who they were. As Shawn grew in experience as a parent, he was able to stop being an angry adolescent with his own parents. Shawn began to accept them for who they really were. They were no longer parents of the little boy who had been so overpowered by them. They were an aging couple. Vulnerable. Well intentioned.

Shawn's sense of self faced obstacles, but ones that he learned to overcome, and eventually he and Anne decided to repeat their wedding vows. Although Shawn had no real intention of being unfaithful, moving back in with Anne felt as if he were stepping off a cliff. He was frightened that he would disappear. He feared he would dwindle down to nothing once again, as he had with his parents as a child. Like many who fear intimacy, Shawn spoke of losing himself as if it were a real possibility. We can no more lose ourselves than lose our skin, but we can become overwhelmed by the emotional danger such feelings engender. Shawn would have to take a leap of faith that his feelings were not facts.

Staying committed and remaining sexually exclusive became goals that Shawn and Anne were determined to achieve. Shawn learned to distinguish fact from fantasy and not allow his fantasies and fears about intimacy to sabotage his connection to Anne. As Shawn began to establish intimate communication, their sex life improved. He and Anne immeasurably improved their marriage by learning to confide and contain their sexual fantasies in and with each other. Intimacy, something Shawn had not thought possible, became a force alive and well in his life.

Chapter Eleven

❧❧

Neil: In Search of Self-Esteem

So much is a man worth as he esteems himself.

—FRANÇOIS RABELAIS

❧ No matter how sturdy our sense of self-esteem, we feel good about ourselves by the reflection of approval and validation from others, most importantly the intimate partners in our lives. Getting back a good picture of ourselves is an important function of a healthy relationship. No one wants to see an image that shrivels the soul. None of us wants the person we love to reflect back his or her disappointments in our shortcomings rather than acceptance of our flaws. We all have them. We are all imperfect creatures in one way or another. Good relationships require the ability to accept each other for who we are and not as we want each other to be. Self-esteem is a substance that needs to be replenished.

Self-esteem issues stem from our early nurturing experiences. We all have suffered some degree of mishandling that has left dents and bruises on the formation of our self-image. Even with an as-good-as-it-gets early childhood, it is an ongoing struggle for many of us to maintain a good sense of self-esteem in the challenging world of adulthood. Career pressures and the demands of parenthood can deplete self-esteem reserves. Often, the ravages of low self-esteem have a corrosive effect on our relationships.

In an ideal world, not only will we develop a good self image, but we will choose a marital partner who enhances this sense of ourselves. But we don't live in an ideal world, so often this is not the case. Low self-esteem plagues us in hundreds of different ways, and a sexual detour can beckon with a mistaken reprieve.

Sometimes self-esteem is depleted by the way our partner deals with us. Many of us don't recognize how we transfer all our disappointments and conflicts onto our marital partner and erode his or her self-esteem. When self-esteem plummets, it makes us vulnerable to a sexual detour.

Sometimes unexpected life situations, such as sickness, job reversal, or even financial success, can send the self-esteem elevator plunging down to the basement. As we try to deal with the challenge presented, we may find ourselves diving under the covers of an affair. In yet other cases, no matter how well we interact in a relationship, or what accomplishments we seem to have, our self-esteem is so low that nothing seems to push the up button on that elevator. Nothing except the fantasy and illusion that surround an affair.

In an attempt to elevate self-esteem, some of us look for a temporary illusion of ourselves in a lover's eyes. A large component of what we see is usually our own delusion. What we see reflected back to us in an affair is what we would like to feel we are. Secret lives of an affair become fantasies come to life. There are variations on the theme, but they all pivot off of desirability. Sex, per se, is not as important as the fact that we are found enchanting. Desirable. What we find in the eyes of a lover boosts our low self-esteem.

Whatever the boost, the illusion of a temporary reality cannot sustain self-esteem for long.

Eventually we have to develop a self-esteem strong enough to balance the elevator so that we don't bounce around to a lot of floors. That confidence comes from knowing who we are and accepting ourselves, not in denial of our problems. When our internal self-esteem is balanced, it's easier to avoid the pitfall of an affair. We don't need to rely on illusion to prop up fear of aging, diminishing sexual prowess, competency in the workplace, or a host of other issues when we have a strong and accepting sense of ourselves.

There are many ways the search for self-esteem leads to sexual detours. This case history demonstrates one type of self-esteem issue and how that resulted in the kind of sexual detour that changed the course of this man's life.

Neil came to see me hesitantly, feeling immensely guilty and sad. His guilt stemmed from the fact that he was having an affair. He didn't want to be involved in an affair, but he felt desperate about his life with his wife and he didn't know what to do. He had not told his wife that he was coming to see a therapist and felt it was almost as great a betrayal as his sexual detour. His wife of fifteen years, Amanda, was a beautiful, exciting woman, but she was a mountain he couldn't climb. He didn't see any way around what he felt was a heartbreaking dilemma for him.

Neil met his wife in college. It was his last semester and her first. They began an exclusive relationship almost immediately, and it continued while he attended dental school. Upon her graduation, they married. From the beginning, Neil was attracted to Amanda for what seemed like many good reasons. Her snow-white beauty and appealing vulnerability hid a rapier-sharp wit and agile mind. This seemed to him her crowning glory. They had the same background and the same goals. Or so he thought. And she needed him desperately. He liked the feeling it gave him. He felt strong and powerful. He was smitten and committed.

Within a few short years they had a son. Amanda, although fiercely devoted to her son, did not want another child. Finances were a problem from the very beginning. Neil's solo practice began slowly. Although their finances were strained, they were supported by strong gifts from his family. One year it was a car, another it was a down payment for a house. He stretched the money so that their life appeared to be one of greater solvency than it actually was.

Neil liked being a provider and had mixed feelings when his child began school and his wife went to work. She worked in the entertainment industry and rose quickly to executive levels. She commanded as much in salary as Neil's practice generated. While this took the strain off their finances, Neil missed feeling that he was caring for his family and protecting them against the world. There weren't enough hours in the day for Amanda, whereas Neil's manner of operation in all things was slow and thorough. He had a lackadaisical stride through life that countered her frenetic one. He felt it was a good balance until the balance began to shift in a way that eroded his self-esteem.

In looking back over the long history of his marriage, he was able to see that the first sign of trouble came early in the marriage with the birth of their son. The child was the spitting image of his wife. Neil often felt as if he were an unnecessary appendage, a spectator in his own family. Amanda believed that she and her son were two of a kind, a sacred unit, almost a secret sect. She demonstrated this special affiliation by zealously guarding her time with her child, often excluding Neil. For the first year or two there was hardly even time for sex, as Amanda was encompassed by the needs of her child. Neil felt completely left out.

This feeling intensified as the child grew. Neil could gain no ground with his son. Amanda brooked no interference in her care of the boy and would not tolerate any other opinion. Neil admitted that it was easier to give in than to argue. Early on Neil decided that anything Amanda wanted or acted upon with regard to their son was not something he would take issue with. Her judgment was impeccable. That was part of the problem. She was right so much of the time. The fact that Neil's opinion was not just simply overlooked, but rejected, seemed petty. Amanda's decisions were all in the interests of the child, and after a while Neil left it all to her.

Neil and Amanda's sex life improved only a small bit after the babyhood years. Amanda guarded the gate to their sex life. Neil felt sexually incompetent and controlled. The feeling of being dominated by Amanda extended into every avenue of their lives together. Their lifestyle expanded to include a larger circle of friends, and they entertained more often, but it was all generated and carried out solely by Amanda. She had a knack for knowing how to throw a party and which restaurant to go to. She organized and directed everything they did. Neil went along, allowing her to pave the way, but he felt less and less important. Amanda was the sparkle, and although Neil seemed content to shine in her reflected light, he grew increasingly despondent.

The trouble, of course, with being in reflected light is that there is no inner glow, no source of internal energy. He needed a jump start from his wife to feel good about himself. Neil started out with low self-esteem. He had less drive and energy than his wife and had allowed himself to fall into patterns of behavior with her that generated even more feelings of inadequacy. The self-esteem he did have, instead of being nurtured, was eroded by the nature of their interaction. And the trouble, of course, was that he agreed with her assessment of him, which seemed to sink lower and lower the higher her career rose.

As his son grew toward adolescence, their marriage became more and more dominated by criticism. In escape, Neil became more solitary in his social life. He cultivated a few close buddies and went out with them. They went fishing, took in a few beers, went to ball games.

The effect felt good. He began to feel less and less ashamed of what he wanted out of life. Neil liked having a cocktail or two before dinner and stopped feeling so bad about not working longer hours. He liked having free weekends to indulge his hobby of cooking. He loved going fishing. He enjoyed experiencing life at a leisurely pace. He did not like the frenetic pace and the backbiting and politics of Amanda's career, or her preoccupation with it. Neil had no real way of verbalizing the complexity of his emotions or communicating the growing dissatisfaction he felt in his marriage. One thing was clear to me: The better he felt about himself, the more he recognized that his marriage wasn't good for him.

Neil felt that Amanda was angry at or disappointed in him for not being more talkative at parties, for not being more social, more outgoing, more aggressive or assertive. She wanted him to forge ahead and make new friends, establish new contacts, in short, carry the burden of the ambition she felt. Neil didn't want more friends, at least not ones she chose. Neil didn't have the wish to exhibit more energy in the social part of her world. Amanda's assertiveness and ability to handle any social situation were more than enough for one couple. He enjoyed having a few longtime close friends. Period.

What happened next occurs frequently enough. Neil's secretary, Stacy, did not have the same high metabolism for life as did Amanda. Stacy lived at a slower pace and had a much calmer approach to everything. She did not have a short fuse and hot temper. Her tastes were simpler. She was content with a far less lavish lifestyle. She matched Neil in internal temperature. Most of all, she seemed sincerely to like Neil. She admired his skill, his tact, the gentle way he handled people. She looked up to him, respected his advice. She liked being around him. Even more important, Neil liked the person he felt himself to be when he was with her. She didn't make him feel like a superhero; it was simply okay to be who he was. He was tired of feeling that who and what he was did not measure up to his wife's standards. He liked how he felt around Stacy. He liked it more and more and more. They began an affair.

> *How do you feel when you're with Stacy?*
> *Emotionally relaxed.*
> *That you are accepted for who you are?*
> *Exactly. Amanda can be king of the castle. I just want to be me.*

Neil wanted to treat his marriage with respect and tenaciously hold onto it despite the fact that he was having an affair with his secretary. He still felt smitten with his wife, but he couldn't live with the kind of person she was. He did not want to continue having an affair, but he desperately felt he needed an escape from the way his wife related to him. The conflict was chronic and unrelenting. He needed what Stacy gave him and didn't want to give up the only place where he felt emotionally repaired. He feared he would have to leave his wife. He did not think Amanda would be able to change the way she felt or the way she related to him, even if he were able to reveal how desperately pessimistic he felt about their future together.

After hearing Neil describe his life, it was easy to see the appeal of an affair. No wonder the balm of Neil's affair felt so good. It was emotional freedom. Neil felt as if he lived in a detention home for juveniles. Amanda had him in a constant state of rehabilitation. Change the shirt, the shoes, the tie, the hair, the beard, the tone, the timing. He couldn't just be himself. Until he met someone who liked him just the way he was. The feeling he had about himself with Stacy was a good one. He liked himself more than he did when he was with Amanda.

The way we feel about ourselves is important. We rarely leave a place where we like the way we *are*. To be fair, Neil's affair cannot be blamed on his wife's criticism. The cover story was his wife's criticism and the restorative nature of the affair, but Neil's own lack of self-esteem and inability to assert himself had contributed to creating the war zone from which he now felt he had to be evacuated. Eventually that was the issue Neil would need to address.

Neil needed help from individual psychotherapy to repair and rebuild his self-esteem. He needed to understand and assert the needs that would allow his feelings about himself to rise. Clearly Neil's marriage also needed the help of marital therapy. When a couple is in marital therapy, the marriage becomes the patient. A therapist functions as a translator and referee for a couple in conflict. In the context of couples therapy, Neil would more easily be able to express his feelings, and Amanda could be taught how to relate to Neil in a manner that nurtured his self-esteem instead of destroying it. This was the only way we could see if there was a way the marriage might improve.

First, however, there was the business of the affair. Being an individual therapist makes it easy to maintain confidentiality. Being a couples therapist makes it a bit more problematic. Ethical questions arise when the therapist is privy to some information one spouse doesn't have. Some therapists refuse to treat a couple while an affair is in progress. Others feel this is unrealistic. I find it more ethically comfortable and therapeutically valuable if the partner having the affair is willing to have the issue brought out into the open, because this gives the marriage the best chance to survive. If there is a sincere effort to repair the marriage, I will not let the existence of the affair stand in the way of my help. We do not live in an ideal world and can do only what we can do. Sometimes giving up an affair is asking too much.

I advised Neil not to give in to his hopelessness or his fears about his marriage. Individual therapy would help him, and marital therapy also might hold out hope for his marriage. I suggested that it was time to stop behaving as if he were afraid, even in the presence of his anxiety, and that it was time to take charge of his life. I asked him if he was willing to tell Amanda about the affair, or if he was willing to give up Stacy. He wanted to continue with the individual therapy first, because he needed to get stronger in order to reveal his affair. He knew that Amanda's reaction would be explosive, to say the least.

The situation came to a head sooner than Neil anticipated.

Neil was right about Amanda's reaction. Before he had gathered the strength he needed to confess, Amanda found out about his affair in an extremely hurtful and unfortunate way. It was not unusual for Neil to go out to a bar once in a while. Some nights Neil went out to watch a game with the guys, other nights he took in a movie alone. Amanda saw his car parked in front of the bar. She went in to say hello, and what she saw blew the situation sky high. Neil was there nuzzling Stacy, the secretary. Amanda exploded.

When Neil came for his session after the confrontational meeting with Amanda, he needed sedatives to calm his distress. He looked beaten up, paced incessantly, and was extremely anxious. I feared he would topple over into an agitated depression. There was so much blame and guilt riding on him that he could barely keep his head up. He wanted to hold onto his marriage, if it was possible. He would stop seeing Stacy. He was willing to work on himself. If only Amanda would be willing to come in. He wasn't sure she would. He begged me to call her.

Initially, Amanda refused to come in. She wanted proof that Stacy was out of Neil's life before she did *anything*. Neil was relieved in one sense when she gave him an ultimatum because it meant that perhaps there was a way to keep the marriage from disintegrating. His relief, however, was thin layered, because underneath lay the chronic anxiety about how his marriage felt to him.

As the weeks went by, Amanda did not return my call, but her approach to Neil softened and she showed renewed sexual interest in him. He was cautious about the flavor of their seeming reconciliation and felt little satisfaction in the heightened interest because he felt it was what Amanda wanted from him as evidence that indeed she had won him away from Stacy. It was in this climate of reconciliation between Neil and Amanda, in an attempt to repair the marriage after the explosion brought about by discovery of his affair, that Amanda called requesting to see me.

Chapter Twelve

❧✿❧

Amanda: A Source of Power

Desire attained is not desire, but as the
cinders of the fire.

—SIR WALTER RALEIGH

❧ Sex has long been used as a means of asserting power. Many men and women for whom sexual detours provide this kind of borrowed strength are sexual athletes, proud of their seductive power and sexual desirability. Sex adopts the nature of conquest and is a bulwark against the feeling of powerlessness. It is used to control, defend, and manipulate. These kinds of sexual affairs have a strong component of aggressiveness. Anger and hostility transform into arousal. We may use sexuality as a lure in achieving a desired effect from another, but this often camouflages an underpinning of hostility.

Many who use sex as a means of power remember constant criticism from aggressive and controlling adults. Many were abused as children in one way or another. As the family black sheep, they usually forged their own identity through rebellion and sexual activity in an eternal adolescence full of stormy, hostile sexual behavior. Those who use sex as a means of power, or look to sexual affairs as a source of power, feel competent, powerful, and alive only in the sexual arena. The sexual realm offers a way to experience emotions they cannot experience in any other way. Strength and independence are felt through their seduction and sexual control in which their partner is rendered vulnerable.

Sexual athletes, for whom affairs are a way of life, are less than heroic at home. Often, there is an unconscious fear of attachment and a foundation of aggression. Such men and women perceive the opposite sex as dangerous and fear being controlled by them. The hostility that underlies the sexual behavior may be present to the degree that they humiliate, overpower, and overwhelm—even punish—with sexuality. Sex is often aggressive and manipulative.

Powerless women can become powerfully seductive. By seducing a man, a woman renders him less powerful and thus, by default, becomes more powerful. An innate dislike and fear of the opposite sex is present in most conquest mentalities. Fear and hostility run through the lives of men and women who use sexuality as a weapon. Women fear being taken over, invaded. Men fear being trapped. The need to be separate and protect the self predominates. I'm in charge. You can't have all of me. Affairs are coldhearted and divorces acrimonious. Derision, anger, blame, and suspicion color the relationships no matter how hearty the sexual connection. Indeed, it is the aggressive component of sexuality that characterizes these kinds of liaisons, as sex becomes a way of controlling and subduing the enemy.

It was into this category that, surprisingly, Neil's wife fit. Amanda wasn't exactly what I had expected. Through Neil's eyes, the portrait I had painted of her was softer. She was every bit as dynamic and beautiful as Neil had described. She glittered, diamond hard. She carried a burden of hostility toward her father specifically and men in general. She acted out her hidden inner feelings of helplessness by combating those feelings with seductive manipulation. I hadn't gotten a sense of this from Neil, but then he didn't know that for most of their married life, Amanda had been involved in one or another affair.

Neil had agreed that Amanda could see me alone before we proceeded with couples therapy. She had insisted on the right to solitary sessions, and Neil readily acquiesced. What often happens with couples is that each, in effect, tries to enlist the therapist as an ally. I suspected that this was part of the agenda, but that didn't matter. Neil's life was an open book and, more important, I wasn't for sale. If Neil and Amanda wanted help with their marriage, I was going to put the responsibility squarely on both of their shoulders.

When I first met with Amanda, I immediately saw the quandary Neil was in. She was beautiful, charming, exciting, and entirely captivating. She was charismatic and seductive. Those weren't the only ingredients, however; she was without a doubt the most unselfconsciously opinionated and controlling person I had ever met. No matter what I said, Amanda had a different opinion. Amanda was very articulate. Her keen intelligence was laced with sharp wit, and she was as quick as any person I had ever met. Although it was easy to like her, I could see why it would be exhausting to deal with her.

During the first few sessions, Amanda revealed her life. She was the only daughter of a wealthy midwestern family. She had met Neil her freshman year in college, the same year that her mother had died. When her mother fell ill during her last year of high school, Amanda felt her world crumble. She was the apple of her mother's eye and felt like a pebble in her father's shoe. As a child she felt pampered and protected by her mother's presence and frightened of her father. He was strict and remote with no affectionate side shown to her. She was picked up every day at school, taken home for a hot lunch, and then returned to school in clean clothes. With the illness of her mother, the thought of leaving home and going away to school terrified her. The thought of her mother dying terrified her even more.

When Amanda met Neil, he not only was a safe harbor but also appeared urbane and knowledgeable. He seemed far older than the boys she had known during high school. He was clearly bowled over by her, and she quickly attached him to her with sexual exclusivity. She felt protected by his presence, and he literally made her first year away from home bearable. With her mother's growing illness, Amanda went home every weekend. Neil accompanied her and functioned as a stalwart presence during what quickly escalated into the worst nightmare of her life. Her mother died on her eighteenth birthday.

Amanda remembers the next three years as a blur. She continued dating Neil exclusively. When he went away to dental school he commuted a great deal in order to see her. Her father soon dispensed with mourning and remarried, in the year after her mother's death, a woman Amanda felt abhorred her. Her stepmother moved into the house and quickly took possession of her mother's life. Amanda watched her father turn over all her mother's possessions to another woman. She remembers to this day the jarring nausea she felt at her father's wedding. The imprint of her grip on Neil's hand lasted for hours.

Amanda married Neil as quickly as she could and cried every day of their honeymoon. She didn't know why. She suspected it was because she was grieving for the life she lost when her mother died and for the fact that it couldn't be replaced by marrying Neil. Not that she didn't try, she added wryly. Finding herself with a baby in a strange city, knowing not a soul, she energetically poured herself into being a mother. By the time her son reached school age she had already exhausted everything there was to do or know about raising one small boy. She recognized that she would have to turn her energy elsewhere.

Amanda found the entertainment industry interesting and exciting; moreover, she found a mentor who would give her a start in the business. Her first employer was an older, powerful man. He no doubt spotted her sharp, quick-witted intelligence in an instant. He wanted her opinion about everything and everyone, something she had at the tip of her silver tongue. He liked her style. He loved her looks. Amanda went to work as his assistant and took to her job like a fish to water.

Amanda's mentor/employer had wealth, prestige, and power. Inevitably, he made sexual advances toward her. Amanda was not distressed at all. The sexual interaction made her feel safe and, more important, powerful. Her mentor was now rendered less powerful than her, because he desired her. It was a win-win situation. She had no emotion at stake. He clearly favored her, something she never felt with her father, a man she had always thought of as very powerful. In contrast, now that she had a more powerful father figure in the man she worked for, her father seemed inadequate and hopelessly pedestrian. As for Neil, he seemed more of a schoolboy every day. Amanda's boss opened the door to a whole new world, and he did so graciously and extravagantly.

One of Amanda's business strengths was making quick decisions and making the right ones. She had a natural ability to criticize and reject most material as well as an unerring ear and eye. Amanda literally made a career out of saying no. Her affair with her boss continued for years. She enjoyed being young, beautiful, and sexually desirable in an industry that revered those commodities. The added attraction of power that her sexual connection to her boss gave her bestowed license and freedom. She could go far in this business; there would be no stopping her.

Nothing did stop Amanda. She soaked up all the trappings of the entertainment industry as easily as a sponge does water. Perhaps the approval she was denied by her father gave rise to a powerful ambition, or perhaps the genesis was her distress at her mother's illness. Energy and ambition crackled about her. She wanted financial independence and all the material possessions that went with it. She dined daily with some of the most powerful and wealthy players in the business, spent hours on the phone networking and strategizing. Blessed with an uncanny memory, she had the details of scripts and the names of agents, actors, and anyone else who could possibly be needed at her fingertips and on the tip of her tongue. She rose like a comet.

Amanda ran her social life with the same drive and determination as she did her career. The social life filled a great deal of the personal life. The extravagance of the industry she worked in segued quite naturally into her life and only served to point up the inadequacy of Neil's slow-paced dental practice. She entertained and was entertained. At dinner parties the most powerful man was usually the target of her scintillating conversation and considerable charm. The man almost invariably called her the next day. Sometimes this resulted in a brief affair, sometimes in a friend forever. Either way, Amanda felt successful and powerful. The important thing was to seduce, to overcome the power with power of her own. And in this manner, Amanda collected friends and stored energy.

As with most things in her married life, Amanda was the force behind whatever got done. Plainly speaking, she was efficient. She managed all their money and paid all the bills. Before she had taken over the task, delinquent notices arrived regularly. She knew early on that Neil didn't have any ambition. Certainly not like she had for herself or for her son. Early in her career she took over Neil's income and managed their finances with all the aplomb of a financier. Neil remained in the background, in what felt to her a dragging influence on the pace and accomplishments of their lives. Neil's own steady ground, holding ordinary conversations in the corners of the parties while Amanda worked the power players, meant little to her.

Amanda grew out of one job and into another. She kept her mentor as a friend and, while occasionally sleeping with him, found a new lover. As she moved up in the industry, she met another powerful and wealthy man, this one closer to her own age. Amanda's lover, somewhat of a celebrity, hinted at marriage. She toyed with the fantasy of marriage to her lover but really felt quite comfortable in her role as "the other woman." Her connection to her husband felt quite important to her. Despite her disappointment at what she felt were realistic shortcomings, there was one overriding fact she couldn't overlook. It was of paramount importance to her. Neil was the only person she knew who had known her mother.

Amanda's second affair continued through the span of her career. He was an old guard of the Hollywood establishment, and the connection made her feel safe. He gave her advice, lavish gifts, a sense of security, and a powerful shot of self-esteem. She enjoyed being connected to someone who was a match for her. She felt she needed a superstar; at least that was her cover story. I had suspected that Amanda wanted someone to carry out her fantasies and wishes in life because she felt so powerless to do so herself, despite that reality was proving the opposite. This suspicion was confirmed when Amanda told me about a trip she had taken.

Amanda came in alone for a session when she returned from a trip to Italy. She was invigorated. She started to tell me about the trip, then suddenly got off the track and told me about her plans to go on a retreat with a self-help group whose efforts centered on enlightenment via discovering the "shadow-self." The participants were asked to bring a costume depicting what they imagined their "shadow-self" to be. At the end of the weeklong seminar, they would reveal the accuracy of their insight, or lack thereof, by donning their costumes.

What Amanda had prepared was a GI Jane ensemble. She had raided a war surplus store and couldn't wait to dress up in the full regalia. She was eager as she spoke, filled with glee, confident she hadn't overlooked one detail. Then just as suddenly as she had begun, she stopped and got back on the track of telling me the story of her trip to Italy. In the retelling, she faltered for a moment on the name of the place she had visited: Umbria. A moment went by as she stopped, transfixed by emotional vision. Then she burst into tears.

Amanda had literally stumbled over a word, across a threshold, through the door into her unconscious. The word that had tripped her and tipped her was Umbria. Shade. Shadow. She connected the word to the concept she had been explaining to me when she got off track, that of the shadow-self. She realized that the friend with whom she had spent those weeks in Umbria was a reflection of her shadow-self. GI Jane as a costume for her shadow-self was not even close. The friend was a victim of multiple sclerosis. Totally dependent. Helpless.

What overwhelmed Amanda was the knowledge that inside herself lived a helpless infant. Terrified. Lost and alone. Filled with fear, yearning to be taken care of, and seeking it through the use of her sexual desirability. The feelings filled her with fear. Fiercely driven and defended against vulnerability, she had built a bulwark against feeling those aspects of herself. Sexuality was her power base. She built herself not from the inside out, but rather precariously from the outside. She armed herself with sexual desirability as one would with a weapon. It had first gotten her Neil, whom she needed, and then she used sexuality to gain the power she needed in her career.

Although this tripping into the unconscious was a moment of emotional awareness and tearful insight, Amanda could not sustain this feeling about herself. I suggested that ongoing individual therapy would help support her as she worked through the feelings, but she would have none of it. She did not want to revisit the issue of feeling helpless except to admit that this was a part of herself she chose to ignore. She emotionally clung to what worked for her, and that was using sex as a way to empower herself and to manipulate her world. The cover story, that she was attracted to powerful men because they were more of a match for her than her husband Neil, was a fantasy that she would continue to employ. We both knew that she wouldn't give up having affairs with powerful men.

The current affair and pattern of trysts continued unbeknownst to Neil. Amanda felt completely in control of her marriage and saw no reason to change her behavior in any way, shape, or form, even when she began to suspect that Neil was having an affair. The last few years Neil had become surly whenever she suggested anything. He seemed to have a thinner skin. He resented any direction from her even though he was dependent upon her for their lifestyle and activities, social and personal. He had taken to going out more evenings when she was away. And the style of their lovemaking had changed. She felt less in control. Amanda felt as if she needed to assuage him by allowing more sexual contact.

It was in this climate that Amanda discovered Neil's affair. She was in a rage. She was angry that she had discovered Neil with another woman and completely discounted her own involvement with other men. She could not forgive the fact that he had lied and was involved with someone else. She was angry at the woman and at Neil. Amanda did not, however, see anything disconcerting or destructive in the way she interacted with Neil. The notion that he was seeking another woman in desperation was tossed out like garbage. What she did feel was that she was entitled to have Neil accept her for who she was even though she had trouble returning the favor. What she seemed most aggressively to want was to reestablish territorial control. She wanted Neil to give up what I knew was the only thing allowing him to stay married to her, his affair.

Epilogue: Amanda and Neil

A condition of Amanda agreeing to marital therapy was confidentiality. She did not want what she revealed to me privately to be brought up in the sessions with Neil. The easiest route, of course, was simply to see someone else, but she had not wanted to see a different therapist. Once again, I gnawed at the bone of revealing confidentialities. How to handle one partner having an affair unbeknownst to the other and still bring an honest effort into the couples sessions? The way I ended up doing this with Neil and Amanda was that in their sessions together, I encouraged Neil to listen to his inner feelings and not allow himself to feel manipulated. I suggested that he examine every decision he made from every angle before he acted on anything. Thus I felt I protected him from what he didn't know.

In their sessions together, the Amanda I had seen alone seemed to disappear and in her place was the woman Neil had met fifteen years earlier. She was tormented and tearful. She hoped they could bring the marriage back to where it was before Neil's affair. Even though Neil reiterated the problems, it was difficult for her to recognize that her marriage to Neil was in trouble. She did not want any particular insight into what was making the marriage such an uncomfortable place for Neil. She was even less interested in her contribution to that state of affairs. She wanted to continue the marriage, but she was perfectly content to continue to be discontentedly in control. We went on like this for several months, Neil's excursion into an affair as a search for self-esteem and Amanda's affairs as a source of power bumping into each other like giant boulders blocking the way to an intimate relationship.

The continuation of the marriage became impossible for Neil. It was almost, as Neil had feared, a foregone conclusion. The ways that each of them had of fulfilling needs was incompatible. He needed something from Amanda that she could not give. Amanda would have had to be able to really address her need for

her own sexual detours and become intimate with her own vulnerabilities in order to attend to Neil's need for an empathic
mate. Neil's need for repair to his sense of himself could not be
accomplished alone. It was a long, hard road, and he felt his marriage hindered any attempt to restore his self-esteem. He would
have continued to stay away from Stacy had Amanda given him a
smidgen of encouragement by attempting to change her behavior
toward him. However, as soon as Amanda felt that Neil was
safely in her corner, she became the same domineering and critical person from whom he had so desperately sought escape. It
was understandable and predictable that Neil would renew his
affair with Stacy in his search for self-esteem.

Eventually Neil and Amanda separated. Amanda stopped therapy. Neil continued therapy and his affair. Amanda had an angry
separation from Neil. I suspect she may have wanted to end the marriage and couldn't really bring herself to give up what Neil represented to her or take any responsibility for the end of her marriage.
She contributed to the end of the marriage not only by her manner of
interaction over the past fifteen years but also by not adapting with
changed behavior. She made it impossible for Neil to stay. It was easier for Amanda to remain angry, frenetic, and critical than to embark
on an inward journey toward change. Neil and Stacy, however, went
on to live a life where they stopped often to smell the roses.

Chapter Thirteen

❧❦

Lois and Tom:
A Way of Sustaining the Status Quo

There is nothing permanent except change.

—HERACLITUS

❧ Affairs generally divide the unity of marriage and ultimately hasten its end. However, there are always exceptions to the rule, and sometimes an affair helps keep the marriage intact. This is usually seen in long-term marriages where an affair, rather than becoming an escape route, takes a parallel road to the marriage. Sometimes the affair fills in enough of the missing blanks to enable the marriage to continue without conflict—thus keeping the status quo—but does not endanger the marriage. This kind of affair in effect helps keep the marriage going. This works well enough so that, in some instances, the arrangement can sustain the marriage for a very long time, and living a double life becomes an ongoing reality.

In other cultures, dual relationships take on a less dramatic cachet and seem more ordinary than in our culture. In European and Eastern cultures, long-term love affairs that coexist with marriage seem to be more easily accepted and in some cases ignored with a shrug. Some even become an integrated part of family life. Extended relationships with mind-boggling complications require more emotional tolerance than most of us in our culture can muster. I remember one elegant gentleman who lived quite a complicated life, a confederation of relationships replete with all the problems therein. It was, however, contained within the context of *shared lives*. This man was aghast at the concept of divorce and casting out of his life a woman with whom he had begun a family. There was only room to add, not subtract, no matter what the state of his sexual affairs. It requires, of course, a similarly minded spouse.

What happens in our culture is that lifelong affairs are always shocking. In the all-or-nothing-at-all tradition of American romance, there is no room in our hearts for anything less than divorce. But life is not a Broadway musical or a romantic movie, and is much more complicated, as my patients have helped me understand. These kinds of complexities can be seen in a long-term affair that runs alongside a marriage that, for all intents and purposes, is committed and ongoing. Affairs of this nature can occur between two people who are married to others, or where only one of the partners in the affair is married. What matters most is that all parties in the sexual affair are content with the arrangement, because stability is the name of the game.

When some important needs that are not being met in the marriage are fulfilled in the affair, the brunt of the frustrated needs is taken off the back of the marriage and, in effect, this keeps the back of the marriage from breaking. The load of emotional stress is simply less for the marriage to bear because the lover shares the load formerly placed upon the spouse. This is not to imply that these kinds of long-term affairs are a method of solving troubled marriages or dealing with our personal issues. On the contrary, affairs in this context sustain the trouble. Instead of one or both partners taking the medicine that might lead to a cure, the partners live with a permanent disability and the long-term affair is the crutch that supports the handicap.

Ordinarily, the parallel lives of a marriage and an affair are at such crosscurrents that either the marriage or the affair ends. This is acutely and especially true early in marriage, and in marriages where the rearing of young children is taking place. With long-term marriages, especially ones with older children or where extenuating circumstances exist, lifestyles more easily accommodate an altered state. However, in any and all cases, in order for the affair to work as a force in stabilizing the marriage, all the factors in the lives of all the players must stay in sync.

Balance is a key element in maintaining the duality of a long-term marriage and affair. The personal lives of the lovers and those of the people in their respective lives must stay in place and proceed as if joined at the hip. Indeed, stability is so important in these cases that the partners in the affair find themselves making choices so that everything stays exactly the same and nothing changes. Often, the spouse conspires by ignoring what is going on and in that way helps keep the marriage intact. There is little wiggle room for change or life-throwing curves. A precarious balance exists. If one element is changed, no matter how small, it can disrupt the balance and upset the triangle so that everything topples.

One way to achieve balance when leading two separate lives is to split needs into two camps. That means sexual activity almost always becomes confined to the affair. Compartmentalization of needs into two relationships is sometimes a physical necessity and sometimes an emotional one. Usually, when an affair sustains the status quo, sex is one of the vital functions that has already ceased in the marriage, and the affair takes over the sexual role. When sex is not part of the equation with a marital partner, for any number of physical or emotional reasons, it makes life easier for the affair. Emotionally and physically there are fewer complications. Isolating the sexual component of a relationship within the affair, and keeping other emotional components within the marriage, often simply accomplishes a practical purpose of balancing the scales.

Maintaining a marriage while sustaining an affair is a juggling act. Life must be simplified to the number of balls that one can constantly keep in the air. One hitch and they all fall. In this type of arrangement, the affair and marriage turn into that three-legged stool I talked about earlier, which keeps the marriage stable. The trick is to keep something from knocking down one of the legs, or to mix the metaphor, dropping one of the balls.

Whether or not partners in an affair are married to other people, the precarious balance of the triangle makes this arrangement fragile. Because the normal societal and emotional structures are not in place to help stabilize the union, this house of cards can easily fall apart. The simple act of one person having to change jobs can become a jarring complication. When the affair and the marriage proceed, unchanged and at a pace, it is usually because there are remarkably compatible conditions in place, both emotionally and, even more important, in reality. Such an arrangement needs a predictable weather report for fair skies each and every day.

Lois came into my office crying her eyes out because the house of cards that had nurtured and nourished her emotional life for more than fifteen years had collapsed. Her lover's life was changing and so, therefore, was her own. She was overwhelmed by the task of facing her marriage of thirty-seven years without the companionship of her lover to prop her up and saddened by the fact that their affair was over. She did not want to leave her family and build a new life with her lover. What she really wanted was what she had. A double life.

Lois, the middle child of a large family of seven, had married her husband, Leo, only a year after she was out on her own. Her family, unable to afford to send her to college, had furnished her with business school training, and she was already industriously employed when she met Leo. Leo, who was seven years older than Lois, was an established insurance broker. Lois had only a small string of boyfriends behind her, including one ex-fiancé, and was impressed by Leo's maturity and stability. She had no interest in dating. Three months after she met Leo they were engaged, and in another three they were married.

Lois recalled having abundant confidence in her marriage even though she and Leo were different "types." She considered herself fortunate to have found someone as stable as Leo. The man she had almost married was actually a boy, not a man, and he had wings on his heels. Bruised, but not broken, by her first brush with romance, she felt healed by the relationship she formed with Leo, even though she knew there was a primary difference in the angle with which they viewed marriage and in the nature of their personalities.

From the beginning, Lois and Leo had a bit of a different take on life. Lois recognized that she had found an unusual man in Leo, if only in the sense that he was somewhat of a throwback. He had firm beliefs about his role as a husband and father, and he wanted a wife who would fulfill her role in the family as the woman and not want to have a career or look to fulfill herself in any other way. Lois, on the other hand, was not predisposed to Leo's way of seeing anything. As a middle child, not able to draw attention to herself in any way other than to disobey, she had defined herself as the family rebel. She disappeared in the family, except when calling attention to herself with her misbehavior. The only self she knew was the one she had found in opposition to something else.

Despite this somewhat basic difference in orientation, Lois began married life happily enough. She described herself as delighted to become head of her own household. After so many years of being a middle nobody, she was now a Mrs. somebody. She did, however, retain the edge of rebel isolation about her, somewhat in the same defiant way she had done with her parents. Even though Leo had a conservative, formal, and exacting preference about everything from how his shirts were folded to how the bed was made, Lois went to extreme measures to ensure that everything was done her way, which is to say in a helter-skelter fashion and damn the details. She found little reward in compromising with her husband and did not feel uneasy when he was exasperated with her. Indeed, in her marriage, she kept an emotional stance that was familiar to her.

In the early years of their marriage, they fought the same way any couple fights when married to someone with opposing habits. Leo began by trying to be the teacher, but Lois remained a delinquent student. Her description of their interaction painted a portrait of a couple destined to go their separate ways, even if continuing to live together. And that was really all right with Lois. She didn't mind the lack of intimacy. She characterized it as giving her the "space" she needed.

With the birth of their first child, Lois soon found herself in—from what I could see from my perspective in the present—a deep postpartum depression. The depression lasted through her second pregnancy, which came within the year. Lois felt that not until the second child was nearly two years old did she emerge from the fugue state of early motherhood. She remembered the first ten years of her marriage as a time when she was in a constant state of pregnancy. Between miscarriages, abortions, and the later arrival of a third child, it was nearly ten years before she emerged from what she termed "the milk years."

By the time the children, two girls and a boy, were of school age, Lois and Leo's sex life had become somewhat inactive. Never a lusty pair, the presence of three children had put a damper on an already restrained and somewhat shy Leo. Despite his adherence to very masculine and gender-specific roles, Leo was uncomfortable in his sexual skin. And Lois, more uninhibited and characteristically less emotionally mature, was unable to see this tender spot. In her usual style, she became resentful instead. She remembers feeling angry at Leo for his lack of enthusiasm and conservative sexual style.

Many of us who place the burden of feeling sexually desirable upon our spouse's initiation and performance in sex become angry when this wish is not fulfilled. A solid sense of sexual desirability enables us to share and help nurture our mate's sexuality to complement our own in a more constructive way than becoming angry or resentful. Lois did not have the emotional strength to help build sexual intimacy with her husband. This sexual isolation combined with her more comfortable emotional stance of keeping Leo the parent in the relationship. Unfortunately, the adult in the relationship is sometimes desexualized because of the unconscious fear of incestuous wishes, and the sexual relationship becomes impoverished.

For Lois and Leo, sexuality was not on their short list of issues to discuss. Problem solving was not their strength, and the issue was tabled indefinitely. As a result, their sex life continued to decline. Lois's need to feel sexually affirmed as well as sexually satisfied smoldered but never set the marriage papers on fire. Except for outbursts of anger from Lois, and cold retaliation by Leo, the emotional climate of Lois as a delinquent adolescent and Leo as the exasperated parent fed the lack of communication in the marriage. Despite what some might call a chasm in the relationship, Lois never had any intention of ending her marriage. She never toyed with the idea of separation, considered a divorce, or ever seriously thought about having a lover.

Did you ever consider seeking treatment?
That would have been seeking a solution. I liked living with the problem.
Because . . .
I found someone who had the same problem, too.

Lois eventually met a man who was to become her lover. She and Tom were members of the same carpool. Not only were they neighbors whose children knew each other, but Lois's husband and Tom's wife were both employees of the same large insurance company. The similarities were too hard to escape. It turned out they lived the exact same life, only not with each other. What began as a carpool with picking up each other's children ended up as a fifteen-year love affair that stabilized both of their marriages.

Tom was a carbon copy of Lois, or so she liked to think. The feeling of having an ally legitimized Lois's relationship with Tom from the very start. Their affair began as most relationships do, with shared confidences. Secrets. Telling each other things they didn't tell their spouses. At first the confidences were nonpersonal. They lived in the same neighborhood with the same problems. They commiserated. They knew the same people. They had the same concerns about their kids' teachers. They attended the soccer games of their kids. Most important, both the spouses were busy and always working.

As the similarities in their lives grew, the confidences mounted. They found themselves pinch hitting for each other, and the conversations at places where they found themselves together stretched longer and longer. Eventually, when Tom suggested they go have some coffee, Lois found it the simplest and easiest thing in the world to do. Unlike the more stilted conversations Lois had with Leo, she found herself jabbering away with Tom. He jabbered back. They were very open about their relationship, calling each other at home and talking freely in front of their spouses. They were acknowledged buddies. Half the time Lois felt that Leo was relieved when Tom dragged her out to a movie.

Predictably, in time their confidences became more personal. They found out that in their marital relationships, they each played the same role: They were the playful ones; their spouses, the more serious, formal "adults." Lois learned that Tom functioned in his marriage much the same way she did in hers. They were each the "wife" in the marriage, and their mates functioned as the "husband." The "wives" were involved in the traditional roles associated with women who stayed home to take care of children, and the "husbands" were career driven.

The term *wife* by no means denigrates or implies passivity. Quite the opposite. Most of the work of maintaining the family falls to the wife. If there was a vacation, not only did Lois and Tom function as the plotters and planners, but they loaded the car as well. Whether it was a ship to sail, a trailer to hitch, or a horse to saddle, both Lois and Tom discovered that it fell to each of them to do everything for the family. They were not only the chief cooks and bottle washers who took also out the trash, but each of them carried a large portion of the emotional burden of the family. While the family breadwinners were often preoccupied and remote, these two "wives" nurtured the family and saw to it that the family unit felt like a good place to be.

The curious cross-matching of similarities became a basis for their friendship. What Lois found endearing about Tom was that he was her "girlfriend." He was the first househusband she had ever met, and their friendship blossomed as she found an ally for the first time, in a man. His emotional style, while much like her own, needed the structure his wife lent to his life. He had little interest in a career, and his halfhearted stabs at writing did not earn enough for his family to live on. He enjoyed his status in the family as the sensitive artist and, much as Lois did with her husband, relegated the mundane facts of living in the adult world to his wife.

Lois found Tom engaging both emotionally and physically. The alliance was heightened by their sexual chemistry. The attunement only strengthened their bond. Like everything else about her relationship with Tom, this sexual attraction was a similarity Lois seized upon easily. Rather than become a distressing outcome of an otherwise uncomplicated friendship, it was easily integrated. There was no angst over it. They bantered about how well matched they were, but their relationship never became laced with the kind of romantic passion that would endanger their marriages. There was no pressure or what ifs. Lois felt quite grounded in her marriage, along with its problems, and had no wish or intention of changing that status.

Like Lois, Tom seemed devoted to his wife, even if his marital sexual union seemed cool. Tom felt that his wife never really liked sex. Without actually ever discussing it, each knew that breaking up their families was unthinkable. Tom would never leave the primary parenting responsibilities he had toward his children, nor could Lois imagine taking her children away from their father, shattering the family unit and leaving the safe harbor of her life. The easy bonding and camaraderie Lois shared with Tom helped them form a sexual relationship quite easily, and oil was cast over the troubled waters of each of their marriages.

Over the years, Lois and her lover Tom continued to make decisions about their lives that would ensure the stability of their affair. Lois dissuaded her husband from making any change in his career that might rock the boat. Transfers to another office were avoided. Vacations were planned to coincide with the school year, and both families ended up taking the same amount of time away. The status quo was remarkably easy to keep all through the years, and even increased when the children were away at college. Because both families were so similar in so many ways, this stability was easy to accomplish. They shared financial status and goals, and had similar ways of dealing with their inner lives and marital conflicts. The trouble came when Tom's wife became ill.

In affairs that serve to help maintain the status quo in marriage, everything that happens usually has the implicit if not explicit participation or approval of the spouse, even if it is as seemingly passive an act as ignoring what is going on. When Tom's wife's mammogram changed, so did their lives. Up until then, sickness, holidays, and scheduling all presented inconveniences that Lois and Tom worked around until everything wobbled back to the sameness upon which they built their affair. When Tom's wife's illness took on catastrophic proportions, facing the crisis in their lives caused disruption in Lois's life as well.

A series of costly surgeries and inadequate insurance forced Tom out of his artistic retirement and into the job market. He took a teaching position some distance away. His job and the burden of caring for his wife during her illness left less time to be with Lois. For her part, Lois could only watch the drama onstage in Tom's life. She could not change or control the events that transpired and could only feel helpless in the grip of the turn fate had taken. Lois continued to see Tom even after he and his wife moved to a smaller home an hour away, closer to his work and the medical center where she was undergoing treatment, but the affair underwent drastic change.

Had Lois or Tom, either individually or collectively, been stronger, they might have decided to try and make a life together. The fragmented pieces of both their personalities were made more whole by their respective partners, however, and each was reluctant to leave or change anything. Events conspired to make a decision for them.

When change entered their lives, it created an unstable situation that offered much less emotional satisfaction. Lois found it unrewarding to be an empathic bystander to Tom and his wife's distress. Tom, busy trying to hold his life together, could relate much less to the now seemingly trivial issues that made up Lois's life.

Eventually change took its toll. The time between meetings lengthened. Days turned into weeks, weeks into months. Each regretted the absence and void that filled their lives yet could not and would not do anything that would change the new state of affairs in which they now found themselves. Clearly, Tom could not leave his wife or any longer be the "girlfriend" Lois had enjoyed. Lois, for her part, did not want to join Tom in his new and tragically altered world.

Lois considered herself fortunate to have a loving husband and stable marriage. They still had a youngster at home, and she did not want to leave Leo. But she mourned the loss of Tom. She wanted to know what to do now. The affair was over. So I ventured into hallowed marital ground. It was time for Lois and Leo to work on their marriage.

Don't you think it's time you gave Leo a turn?
For what?
To be the child.
Is that what you think I've been?
What do you think?

The silence stretched.

So what do I do now?
Make a friend of your husband.
You mean I have to deal with who he is?
No. Accept who he is.
And me?
Become what and who you want to be and share it with him.

You mean it might change him?
No, but it will change you.

More silence.

You mean we could work on being friends?
Something like that.
And that will improve our marriage?
Friends make good marriage partners.

PART THREE

Finale

Chapter Fourteen

❦❧

The Aftermath

> Love is an ideal thing; marriage a real thing.
> A confusion of the real with the ideal
> never goes unpunished.
>
> —GOETHE

The aftermath of an affair begins with the discovery of betrayal. And while the affair and the marriage may continue for a good deal of time, discovery of an infidelity is the beginning of the end. I have witnessed the lives of many of my patients over the arc of their entire dramas. Life in the wake of an affair brings pain, anguish, and heartbreak, but it punctuates the end of illusion. As tumultuous as it is for both partners, the aftermath is the start of a new beginning. Whether it heralds the end of the affair, the end of the marriage, or the end of both, it can usher in an age of enlightenment, restoration, and rebirth.

The Discovery of an Affair

Whether it takes weeks, months, or years, eventually an affair will be exposed. Some affairs get exposed inadvertently in unusual ways. We read about them, we are told about them, we get diseases from them, we even walk in on them. The most common method of discovery is confession, with confrontation close behind. After the truth is revealed, the laborious job of rebuilding, either with the partner in marriage, the partner in the affair, or alone, needs to be undertaken. In the wake of an affair, we have the opportunity to uncover our personal cover stories and learn to communicate our inner truths. I'm not saying this is easy. There is no painless exit on the route of a sexual detour.

What happens in the wake of an affair basically reflects a desire to preserve the marriage or dissolve it. The beauty of the aftermath is that there are simple answers to complicated situations. One of the two paths available before the affair started is open to both partners again, only this time much more obviously. There is a fork in the road. The third alternative, which was presented by the introduction of a secret lover, is no longer an option. The marriage is now back where it started when it had only two alternatives:

> *improve the marriage*
> *or*
> *end the marriage*

If an affair is not revealed consciously, it will be detected unconsciously. An affair, like a cough, cannot be kept hidden. What keeps us from knowing the truth, no matter how fail-safe the secret, is our own denial. What makes us unconsciously reveal betrayal, no matter how cunning the deceit, is this same denial. Unknowingly, no matter how cleverly we think our tracks have been covered, we leave traces. We may believe that the truth about an affair is buried in cement, but this is simply our own denial, which is an illusion lighter than air that can float away to reveal an affair with one breath of reality.

In whatever method the affair is exposed, the discovery of betrayal is experienced as a catastrophe. An affair sits us down on an emotional roller coaster where we rocket from denial to obsession, rage to sorrow, self-pity to blame. Worst nightmares come true. Long-held assumptions are in doubt. Trust is shattered, and the age of innocence is formally declared dead. The last shred of romantic love is drowned by the flood of knowledge about an affair. We often think of love as a safe harbor, but in truth we are as vulnerable as if in a storm. If we have been betrayed and love has proved to be an unsafe passage, surviving the journey may be the greatest challenge of our lives. *Regardless of which side of an affair we find ourselves on, in the aftermath, we are faced with nothing less than restoration of the self.*

The burden of truth does not rest lightly upon the shoulders of any marriage. The marital union, if not shattered by the disclosure of an affair, undergoes severe stress. For both partners, there is an abundance of fear, terror, and emotional (sometimes even physical) trauma. Inner worlds collide upon the discovery of an affair because problems we sought to deny are brought out into the open. Feelings long buried and forced underground come boiling up. Emotions not only surface, but come armed in defense.

In the aftermath, we face each other with problems not just

magnified, but multiplied. Each partner in the marital union experiences disclosure of an affair differently. A woman well out of the marriage, and a man devastated by loss, have distinctly different experiences about the same event. The resolution of two individual sets of emotions (and perhaps two separate goals) is what we deal with in the aftermath. The likelihood is that whether the truth fountains out in a confession or is squeezed like blood out of a turnip, the effect is devastating.

For those of us on the other end of betrayal, discovery uncovers more than just infidelity. There are painful insights and hard choices. Nancy tearfully recognized the quandary she was in. I had helped her to see Ned for who he was. But who Ned was meant he could continue to have affairs. For the moment, at least until I helped her regain some strength and clearer emotional vision, she desperately wanted to remain married but knew that staying married to the same person who had been sexually unfaithful meant she would be betrayed again. As it turned out, because trust was dead, it was impossible to continue the marriage. Her feelings of hopelessness were eased by her recognition of the part she played in the affair. And while I helped her to see that a marital relationship is something for which two people are responsible and that nothing happens in a vacuum, especially not an affair, it also revealed how incapable her partner was of change. It gave her strength to feel she had control over the future.

THE ROLE OF JEALOUSY IN DISCOVERY

Jealousy plays a major role in the discovery of an affair. It is an archaic emotion and represents a fear of loss. It has its roots in the separation anxiety of infancy. Like a passionate lover, a baby's attachment to his mother is a possessive one. A baby acts as if his mother's body belongs to him. This is so complete and natural that the baby never wants his mother to leave. In fact, in anticipation of this dreaded eventuality, the baby develops an eagle eye. If the mother so much as thinks of leaving, the baby becomes piteously inconsolable. There is no better picture of misery and despair than a baby's face. Unless, of course, it is the face of the bereft, betrayed adult lover.

Many romantics mistakenly define jealousy as proof of love. Jealousy, like territorial response, is a protective instinct and has more to do with that primal fear than with love. The fear of loss is felt as if there cannot be any replacement. The loss of a love object is a threatening feeling fraught with abandonment and rejection. The fear of loss, nourished by low self-esteem, can be easily provoked. Jealousy may inflate a suspected relationship out of proportion. Or not. Good self-esteem guards against jealous overreactions.

Jealousy is like the smoke alarm of the unconscious and usually indicates the presence of something lurking below the surface. If nothing else, jealousy suggests that there is some distance in the marriage. Usually, where there is smoke, there is fire. Smoke may come from ourselves or from the reality of an affair. A suspicious partner may feel pangs of jealousy because he or she has good reason. Usually, most husbands or wives allay reasonable fears. Unreasonable jealousy is something even a faithful marriage partner cannot cure. Conversely, a guilty partner can rarely set at ease an astute partner's suspicion. Guilt often provokes defensiveness and, in turn, increases suspicion.

The Role of Denial

Suspicions about an affair are sometimes hidden under a blanket of denial. Often, even when reality points a finger, we don't want to see. Our senses, however, continue to operate in defiance of our denial. Pieces of evidence are filed away in the unconscious until further notice. Discrepancies, which in retrospect may pop out like a bumper crop of freckles, go unrecognized. Later, we put together pieces of this unconscious puzzle and are surprised we didn't know all along. But, of course, we did.

Our senses are never fooled. Blatant evidence may stare us in the face and we still refuse to notice. Later, we discover what we knew already. We may overhear bits of conversation where the same name comes up one too many times for comfort. Our mate may have a drastic new look. Weight alters dramatically. Workouts at the gym increase. New hairstyles. Sexier new clothes. Even the scent of lotion or perfume may linger. We may sense an emotional difference. Distance and tension stalk a sexual detour like shadows. In these ways, we know without asking, all along.

Gerty had been married for more than twenty years when she came to see me. She painted a portrait of a marriage pockmarked by obvious deceit. The excuses her husband had given her for one kind of behavior or another had as many holes as Swiss cheese. Gerty didn't see that. Instead she saw a curtain that had been drawn over a truth too painful to bear. She hoped, as many of us do, that whatever it was would blow over. Of course, it never does. Most of us are afraid to directly confront the question of a spouse having an affair. Suspicions are hard to live with, but they often are easier to tolerate than the truth. To ask or not to ask. To tell or not to tell haunts sexual detours.

The Opportunity to Take Action

The discovery of an affair ushers in real action. It removes us from the comfortable place of ennui where we don't have to do anything. Discovery of an affair makes something happen. Suddenly, we can no longer deny the truth. An emotional imperative exists to take stock of ourselves for a marriage to redefine itself, or for an affair to become part of a new reality. Uncovering a secret betrayal forces both marriage partners to consider the options, to take a stand, to make a decision. Issues are forced. Change has broken free from the entangling web of an affair and is once again on the march.

What I tell patients who have suffered betrayal, especially the ones on the brink of despair, is that the real hope of resolution lies in the aftermath. I remind them that the only way out of the pain is through resolution. Either with or without the partner, hope lies ahead. With honesty, the future becomes real. The illusory world we have constructed about ourselves or our marriage evaporates like white-hot steam when the lid is lifted off an affair, but the truth is not easy to bear. For ourselves, for our marriage, even for an affair, honesty can feel like a terrible curse. We know too much. Sometimes we may feel unable to bear the burden. There is too much to process, too much to alter. The mountain of truth may seem insurmountable, simply too hard a climb.

Even more daunting than the burden of truth is the reward that honesty holds forth: intimacy. For those of us who have fled in fear from this threat, it is difficult to suddenly embrace it. Both partners in a marriage where infidelity has occurred have colluded to some degree in legitimizing distance. For Jennifer, the aftermath of betrayal forced her to accept some truths about herself that she would rather have avoided. Her husband, Bob, had taken to staying at work later and later, until some nights he didn't come home at all. Jennifer had accepted his explanations more easily than even Bob would have liked. The truth was that Jennifer didn't mind being alone. She enjoyed the perks of Bob's dedication to his career. She found interaction more difficult than being alone. When Bob was home, more often than not Jennifer was involved in a solitary pursuit. She needed emotional distance more than Bob. It was by no means easy for Jennifer, this business of honesty, of facing inner truths. We are all so adept at running away.

HOW TO AVOID TRANSFERENCE
AND REGAIN INTIMACY

Under the influence of transference, we run away from the role we have cast upon our partner. The person from whom we run and hide may not be our wife but the grandfather of responsibility wagging his finger at us. We frequently try to outrun the demands of our own adulthood by fleeing from what the partner in our marriage represents. We have no clear picture of who a husband or wife indeed really is unless we penetrate the veil of transference by developing intimacy with our inner selves.

With the discovery of an affair, we can no longer hide from our marriage partner. We are free to leave, but we can no longer hide. When secrets are no longer present, distance disappears. After disclosure of an affair, feelings perilously close to intimacy can exist. Strange as it may seem, *in the aftermath of an affair, marital partners often have a more intimate relationship than they did before.*

An affair suffers from its own baptism by fire once the secret is revealed. Once the cocoon has been punctured and some air is let in, metamorphosis must occur. Something has to change. Change is necessary in order for an affair to transform into a real relationship. An affair must develop the ability to live in truth, breathe reality, and fulfill needs. For a relationship steeped in fantasy and overt lies, the demands of truth can be overwhelming. Marriage, on the other hand, must improve to survive.

Two Methods of Revealing the Truth

When we are suspicious and want to know the truth, instead of creating a forum for discussion, we often set traps and seek to ensnare the enemy. We do this, of course, not because we really want the truth but because, above all, we want to be right. I chide my patients about this universal condition. When we are suspicious, in order to prove our suspicions correct, instead of asking, we assault. This is not the best way to go about dealing with the question of an affair. This question, whether coming from the side of confrontation or confession, should be approached with as much preparation as possible.

CONFRONTATION

The thought of confrontation usually makes our blood run cold. Questions about an affair are ones we are afraid to ask out loud because we dread the answer. This fear buys us exactly what we need: time. Time to think. If we are going to ask, it is imperative that we think first. Confrontation about an affair needs to be carefully thought out. Any negotiation demands rehearsal and preparation in order to achieve emotional control and our emotional comfort zone. We must sift through inner chaos to find a uniquely personal goal for our marriage. This is not to say that we need time to scamper back to hide in some fantasy or wishful thinking, but time to discern a reasonable outcome and path for the future of our marriage.

I tell my patients who want to confront husbands or wives about their suspicions to take enough time to prepare themselves for all the possibilities of what the truth may reveal. Before blurting out questions and levying accusations, they need time to envision all the possible scenarios. They need to go through it in their heads, and with me, before it comes out of their mouths. They need time to figure out what is realistic for them. To figure out what is unacceptable or acceptable. To know how to go about negotiating the future. Then, and only then, after enough soul searching, do I tell them to go ahead. Ask.

Asking for the truth about an affair can be like pouring kerosene on a fire. Often, the one suspected of being on a sexual detour resorts to a defensive, indignant, angry offense. The truth may be denied to the bitter end. The besieged partner may act as if heinous and outrageous accusations have been made.

In another scenario, when confrontation is met by the admission that the accusation is true, the same detonation can occur. In the ensuing explosion, sane human beings are wiped out and only furious animals remain. Like mad dogs we go at each other, shredding what is already torn asunder. Pain, rage, and fear exist in both marital partners, for different reasons and in varying degrees. What seems most important is to gnash each other to bits.

Ask me no questions and I'll tell you no lies. We shouldn't ask if we can't accept the answer. When we ask about infidelity, we must be prepared to deal with infidelity. There is a crucial difference between being able and willing to handle what the truth reveals and simply fishing for an answer to allay the anxiety and dread knotted in the belly of the question. Revelations will be shocking. Hurtful. Painful. Maybe even shameful and humiliating. Problems that have been put on hold will be brought out into the open. Answers will demand action, whether it includes forgiveness and restoration or acceptance and separation. Bear in mind that asking will not bring an affair to an end. It will reveal the problems that need to be dealt with.

Confrontation can be an excuse to shift the blame onto an affair. Affairs can get blamed when, in reality, the marriage is over for another reason. Lorraine badgered her husband, Dennis, who was my patient, with her accusations. She was angry, critical, and suspicious. She went from one accusation to the next, obsessed with her rights. After a particularly heavy round of artillery fire, where she demanded to know whether he was having an affair, Dennis told her the truth. He felt confused and anxious about their marriage. He had sought out his old girlfriend, seeking solace. He couldn't remember if they had sex once or twice. Lorraine went berserk. She was not prepared to understand or offer second chances. She jumped at the chance to righteously end the marriage. The truth is that the affair provided Lorraine with an excuse to end the marriage. Dennis had sought my help precisely because he feared she was going to leave him. And she did.

Rita and Derek presented a totally different picture. They came to me because Rita suspected that something was going on and she wanted to give their marriage the best chance to survive. Rita felt sympathetic to Derek's distress. He seemed miserable, and his angst was a physical presence that seemed to eat away at him. Sex was tense, the distance between them palpable.

Something was going on. Rita was very clear about what she wanted. She wanted to know what was wrong, and no matter what was going on, she wanted to hold onto her marriage. When she confronted Derek, it was in my presence in an empathic manner and with a calm and organized plan she had forged out of an exhaustive inner struggle with her own emotions. Derek confessed to an affair, but Rita was prepared to ask him to stay in marital therapy with her. As it turned out, he did, and in doing so they gave their marriage the best chance to survive. With or without professional help, this is possible. Forgiveness and empathy are not unique to a therapist's office and are found within ourselves.

In the wake of an affair, the storm of emotions makes it difficult to hold onto what we really want. Many marriages are thrown away simply because we don't know how to overcome the challenges presented by infidelity. More marriages are destroyed by the response to betrayal than by the affair itself. Trust can be rebuilt. Wounds do heal. We cannot undo the reality of a sexual detour, but we can shape our future. When faced with the reality of confronting an affair, what we strive for should be grounded in the bedrock of an inner truth as well as an external reality.

How to Confront

Plan when to confront the issue of an affair. Choose the time and place carefully. Asking the question nonchalantly on the way out the door, or just as our mate is dozing off to sleep, is guaranteed not to bring about an answer, but a catastrophe.

Ask calmly.
Listen empathetically, thoughtfully, patiently.

Be prepared to experience disbelief, shock, humiliation, rage, self-pity, and blame.

Allow yourself to feel pain, sadness, and loss, as well as grief.

Rehearse. Practice the scenario as if it were a drama. It will be.

Do not expect anything to be resolved as yet.

Do not use alcohol or drugs.

Do not use threats.

Do not employ punitive, angry, or damaging words or deeds.

Do not be a judge or a jury.

Do not wield the sword of righteousness.

Do not take any negative action.

Do not act on your feelings of anger.

CONFESSION

Truth is a strange beast. As slippery as an eel for many. A chimera to some. Often, especially to those of us who choose a sexual detour, truth can be elusive. Truth with the trappings of illusion and the firmament of denial attached may feel more acceptable. Before we unload a confession upon a partner, it is incumbent upon us first and foremost to discover an unadorned inner truth about ourselves. Unless we are able to see ourselves and accept responsibility for our actions, confession will only complicate our lives.

Confession is by far the most common way for the truth about an affair to surface. With confession, secrecy is brought to a close. Bear in mind that telling may not bring about an easy end to entanglements, especially if an affair is still in progress. Confession will not cure the problems that helped pave the road to a sexual detour. What confession will do is provide an opportunity to wrestle with real issues and deal with problems in ourselves and in our marriage. Revealing an affair, especially one over and done with, will change the nature of the marriage relationship. However lightly an indiscretion is undertaken, it will be felt more heavily by the betrayed marital partner. Ideally, a confession will reflect a desire to save the marriage and be made in order to bring about that specific goal.

Diana came to me as the result of her husband Harvey's confession about his affair. Harvey had finally decided to tell Diana the truth. Harvey had spent most of their married life involved in affairs, and Diana had spent it hiding from the truth. He was still involved in the affair when Diana came to see me. I was pessimistic about the marriage because she couldn't convince Harvey to come with her. Harvey didn't know if he wanted a divorce or not. He wasn't particularly interested in therapy. He was tired of subterfuge and was really feeling quite sorry for himself. When he told Diana of his affair, he exploded at her reaction. He was resentful of Diana's pain, unwilling to face the consequence of his actions, and reluctant to undertake the hard work of rebuilding a marriage.

I helped Diana understand that he wanted her to fix it. His confession was a bid for Diana to do the work of the marriage for him. Make life easier for him. He wanted someone to alleviate his doubts, fill his emptiness. In short, to be the self he was unable to become.

It didn't take long for me to help Diana face the question she had been avoiding most of her married life. Diana thanked him for sharing and left the marriage. She couldn't make his life work for him. Luckily for Diana, childless, it was easy to leave. For others with more complications and unable to leave, living with Harvey would have been like being slowly sawed in half.

Christy was lucky to have come for help before it was too late. She had allowed herself to be abused not only physically but emotionally as well. When her husband, Kevin, decided to tell her about his affair, what he called a confession turned into an accusation. Kevin couldn't begin to fathom that he had cast Christy into a complicated mother role. Moreover, a mother toward whom he felt great resentment. Like a child, he had run from Christy's (his mother's) control, yet blamed Christy (his mother) for everything in his discontented life. He threw out a hundred and fifty excuses for his behavior. Most of them landed on Christy's broad shoulders, until excuse one hundred fifty-one. That was when Kevin made the unfortunate mistake of using the "you drove me to it" ploy. His assaultive stance dropped the nickel for Christy. Kevin's issues were siphoning off her self-esteem, blame by blame. The answer was clear to me and, fortunately, to Christy as well. Her decision to leave restored a sense of the self that had been eroded.

After nearly twenty years of marriage, Henry and Justine came to see me. For some inexplicable reason, Henry told Justine about an affair that had ended five years earlier. He confessed to an affair that occurred during a turbulent period in their lives. He and a coworker had been lovers. He had been in a midlife crisis, his future at work was clouded, and the affair served as a crutch. The affair ended when his crisis resolved. Henry even went so far as to describe the details to Justine.

It was at this point that Justine and Henry came to see me. Justine was distraught and confused. The confession had no point. Justine couldn't get over it, couldn't get under it. There was nothing that would assuage her hurt, restore her belief system, or put Humpty-Dumpty back together again. Justine confided that she rues the day she asked, recognizing that she was asking for reassurance, not truth. Henry curses himself. Not for the affair. For telling. For wanting absolution. This couple did not need my help beyond a few sessions of commiseration and helpful hints. Time and their own long-established empathic union would do the rest.

Goal of Confession

We need to search for truth before we confess, both in the interest of preserving a marriage or ending one. Endings need to be undertaken with as clear a view as beginnings. In order to do this, we must turn our attention, sometimes uncomfortably so, to an inner self we have long avoided and see what truths are reflected in the cover story of an affair. What were we *really* looking for? What truths have we discovered? What truth is being reflected by a wish to confess? In the final analysis, what we confess to should reflect what we want, for we certainly will get more of it than we bargained for.

There is no reason to believe that denial, which has played such a prominent role in the architecture of the sexual detour, will dissipate with the wish to confess. When a decision to tell the truth is reached, we must assume that denial continues to grease our psychological operations. It is imperative to take a second look at where denial may camouflage the real reasons for wishing to disclose an affair. A wish to confess an affair may be due to guilt, or a need to seek forgiveness and gain approval, or a need to end subterfuge—or it may simply be a way of getting rid of a burden. But to what end? We must assess the practicality and purpose of confession. Sometimes the most positive action we can take in the wake of an affair is to shoulder what is past alone.

Confession works best when an affair is over. It's plain and simple. The most constructive reason for confessing is to reinvest in the marriage in a committed, restorative way. When we confess to an affair, the burden is upon us to make an effort toward emotional repair of the damage that betrayal has inflicted. The degree of this effort should not depend on how much we want to continue the marriage. This burden falls upon the marital escape artist, and it is not always successfully undertaken. The perilous job of dealing with the fallout is shouldered by the one least able to do so. It's hazardous to assume that revealing an affair is not going to require attending to our partner's needs, no matter what course we want the marriage to take.

Confessing to a sexual detour should include compassion, because presumably a person about whom we care or cared in the past has been hurt. It is our responsibility to display sensitivity and tenderness. To be kind. Being kind does not mean we capitulate to demands or suffer abuse. It simply means being a friend. Being kind does not mean we have to pay with our lives or be responsible for another person's life. We do not have to give up ourselves in order to care for another's pain. Very simply, we should take responsibility for our actions, without displacing it onto blame, or causing unnecessary wounds. Do not make a confession without displaying empathy or offering some solace.

For those coming off the path of a sexual detour, confession may be a relief. Often a sexual detour is experienced as if the affair were a hole we tripped into and needed a hand out of. *Embroiled* is a word often used. The truth is that sometimes sex still just happens. And sometimes one thing does lead to another. And before we know it, we're in deeper than we want to be or intended to be. When this is the case, and when the marital partner is forgiving, confession can be a light in the window, leading the way home.

How to Confess

It is imperative to have a specific goal. We should not confess in order to relieve tension, or because we expect our mate to offer a solution. We should not confess in order to displace the responsibility of having to make a decision and force our spouse to make one for us.

If the goal is to save the marriage, that objective must be stated first, foremost, and repeatedly. The marital partner needs to be aware of our love and intentions. Problems can be addressed later. Not while confessing.

If our goal is to end the marriage, or we are not sure where the marriage is headed, we must be kind and patient. Confession in this instance can be used as a springboard for a recovery. Over time, the future of the marital relationship can be addressed as we decide our priorities.

Keep the truth simple. Speak calmly. After saying what needs to be said, be available to empathetically hear a response. Empathy means stepping outside of ourselves and walking in someone else's shoes. Above all, recognize that:

> Confessing to an affair is not blaming the other person.
> Confessing to an affair is not telling the other person
> what is wrong with him or her.

Plan when to confess an affair after you've come up with a good reason why you should confess. Choose an appropriate place, where you will be able to speak uninterruptedly, without pressure of time or hindrance of emotional availability.

> Recognize the legitimacy of your spouse's injured feelings.
>
> Empathize with your spouse's pain, fear, and sorrow.
>
> Display tolerance of his or her reaction.
>
> Listen patiently.
>
> Help your spouse understand what happened.
>
> Behave like a friend.
>
> Accept responsibility for your actions and choices.
>
> Ask for forgiveness for the pain inflicted.
>
> Do not use alcohol or drugs.
>
> Do not talk about your lover.
>
> Do not under any conditions become defensive or accusatory.
>
> Do not reveal sexual details.
>
> Do not criticize your spouse.
>
> Do not blame your spouse.
>
> Do not lie.
>
> Do not frighten or threaten your spouse.
>
> Do not defend or justify your actions.

After you have revealed your affair, remain focused on your spouse's feelings and reactions. This is no longer about you but about his or her reaction to what you have said. Remember, it was your affair, your spouse's betrayal.

In the aftermath of a confession or confrontation, we can be certain of one thing: *Something will happen*. The end of secrecy brings options to the table. It may mean that the affair will end and the marriage will survive. It may reveal the end of the marriage, or it is entirely possible that both the marriage and the affair will end. Whatever the result, in the aftermath we have the opportunity to become familiar with the key players in our lives. We can finally come face to face with not only the marital partner from whom we desire to escape, but ourselves. Finally and irrevocably, it's about who we really are, what we really want, and why.

Chapter Fifteen

Endings

Perhaps they were right in putting love into books. . . .
Perhaps it could not live anywhere else.

—WILLIAM FAULKNER,

LIGHT IN AUGUST

Endings have existed since the beginning. The oldest divorce document in the world dates from about 1200 B.C. It is written on limestone in hieroglyphs. The ending of a marriage in divorce rarely passes without leaving something behind. Somewhere, somehow, however insignificant the marriage may have been, endings leave their mark.

Endings, in the natural state, mean that something has gone wrong. Perhaps because endings reflect the state of our own mortality, when the life of a relationship ends there is pain and loss and we feel sadness and grief. Emotions run the gamut. For some, the ending of a relationship is a simple gasp. For others, the ordeal is like dying. When this is the case, the feelings are vivid and extreme, holding great consequence. We go through the same stages of grief that Elisabeth Kübler-Ross found in terminally ill patients: denial (disbelief), anger (rage), bargaining (promises), depression (loss and loneliness), and acceptance (believing, understanding).

During my career as a therapist I have witnessed the ending of many marriages. Some endings trailed off into the mist, a barely decipherable whisper of reality causing hardly a ripple, as if what ended had never existed at all. Other endings were surrounded by pomp and circumstance and created a great commotion, as if the existence of what ended warranted the observance of nothing less than a state funeral. The lives of some of my patients have been devastated by explosive endings, which have left their emotional lives as bare, burned, and haunted as a nuclear wasteland. Yet other patients had marriages and divorces where the endings stretch out like a thin filament of silk, growing longer and stronger, seeming to go on forever. And even other endings provided fertile ground for the beginning of another deep, rich emotional life.

Ending a marriage is a more profound event than ending an affair, not just because the marriage is the primary relationship, but also because of the emotional state of marital beginnings. Marriage, unlike an affair, is entered into with lavish hope. Unconscious wishes for reunion and the state of infantile bliss are alive. More than a marriage dies when a couple decides to divorce. Their hopes die, dreams die. Marriage is our investment in a future, while an affair represents an escape from the past. When an affair ends, the end is almost always self-explanatory because of the complex nature of the triangle. When a marriage ends, we mournfully ask why.

Reasons for divorce are not always clearly defined. Certainly when infidelity has occurred, the underlying factors leading to a sexual detour play a prominent role. The triangle can wedge a marriage so far as to crack it wide open. We stumble into a divorce as a consequence; we go too far, and before we know it, we are there.

Other couples fight incessantly and tear themselves apart with no sign of infidelity.

Greg and Priscilla were desperately ill matched. Their differences were so marked they could not find any common ground upon which to meet. They had drifted too far apart, and I could not help them find any way of anchoring themselves to each other. Their only hope was in individual rescue. For them, the only prevailing wind that would carry them to salvation was divorce.

Divorce

The enormous escalation of divorce statistics reflects an alarming trend. Every ten to thirteen seconds someone gets divorced. The families that experience divorce number in the millions. Interestingly, statistics reflect the same duration of marriage today as a century ago. A century ago, single-parent households were commonplace. A century ago, marriage ended at an early stage. A century ago, single parenthood resulted in extreme economic catastrophe. The difference is that today the mechanism that accounts for the same statistics is no longer death but divorce.

People hold different values on fidelity and marriage. People divorce because the shock, anger, and incredulity of betrayal are impossible to deal with; because illusions run high; because we have unfulfilled expectations and no hope of repair. Even in so-called happy marriages, disappointment, unrealistic expectations, and exaggerated demands can leave a marital partner subject to the emotions that push us toward affairs and divorce.

Marriage, when begun with illusion, ends with disillusion. The spell romantic love weaves is one of enchantment. Enchantment and disenchantment are ongoing forces in our lives. The process of belief and disbelief, illusion and disillusion escalates into one of growth. The child's world of fantasy stretches through the long, hard pull of adolescence and on into adulthood. It is difficult to let go of the myths of childhood fairy tales and illusion. Sometimes divorce presents a new illusion and is preferable to working through a marital relationship. Marriage, after all, is a fairy tale born of a day when we believed that:

> *marriage would last forever . . . no matter what.*
> we would be happy forever.
> our partner would fulfill all our needs.
> marriage would bring everlasting comfort and security.
> our partner would never be attracted to anyone else.
> we would never be attracted to anyone else.
> there would be no problems.
> sex would solve all the problems.
> love meant great sex.
> great sex meant love.
> love meant never having to communicate clearly.
> our mate would change.
> we would change.
> things would change.
> *things would never change . . . no matter what.*

We believed that this would all occur without any effort on our part. Divorce is the result of the fracture of these unrealistic expectations, unreasonable ideals, and mythological beliefs as much as anything else.

There are many reasons why a marriage could end, should end; however, divorce should never be promoted as a means of growth. Divorce *can* result in growth, but divorce is a sad court of last resort. Sometimes, instead of undertaking the hard work of change and growth, divorce is easier. All too often we make what feels like the hard choice of divorce, but we do it because it is an easier task than making a marriage work. Like an affair, many divorces are built on fantasy, on wishful thinking, and on the desire to escape. This is especially true when an intensely romantic affair is in progress and steaming forward under the engine of romance. When divorce is connected to ongoing infidelity, the fantasy is always that the future will be better and our problems solved by Joe, or David, or June, or . . . That old devil illusion helps us along.

There are many couples who have divorced and have gone on to lead successful lives with other partners. But most have not. The statistics tell the story. Seventy-three to 90 percent of both men and women suffer a lower standard of living. Women usually suffer more economic distress. Fifty percent of women and 33 percent of men remain angry ten years after divorce. Ten years. A decade of distress.

CHILDREN AND DIVORCE

The statistics for children involved in divorce are even more dismal. Eighty-eight percent of children of divorce see one parent sustain long-term emotional damage. Fifty percent are less successful than intact family counterparts. Fifty percent quit college. More than fifty percent see yet a second or third divorce.

The disintegration of the family, if not nudged along by

divorce, is definitely pushed. When divorce occurs with children involved, the family suffers. Unless extreme measures are employed to mitigate the impact on a child, an intact family dies and it is left to the divorce-shocked child to learn to live with that fact. Parenting is not an easy job and is one for which we are never fully prepared. Divorcing parents, emotionally and financially bankrupt, have a harder time being parents to their children. Often, they need to be parented themselves.

Divorce poses the question of personal fulfillment versus parental responsibility. While parents go off in search of their own destiny and get lost in the sexual jungle of adulthood, a child is left to emotionally wander . . . and wonder . . . alone. It is distressing for children to look after their own childhood while the adults are busy trying to find a life of their own. Not surprisingly, then, there is a significantly higher rate of emotional distress among children of divorce. Surveys reveal that more than twice the number of children from divorced families seek help from mental health professionals. It is a fact that children with divorced parents have more difficulty in attaining the socioeconomic or educational level of their divorced parents.

EMOTIONAL DIVORCE

Divorce ends the legal union, but if we have been significantly married for any length of time, especially when children are involved, divorce rarely cuts the emotional cord. The rhythm that characterized the union is reflected in the music of divorce. People hang on. Especially to anger. To the wish for reconciliation. To the desire for punishment. If we argued in the marriage, we will continue fighting after the divorce. Especially about whose fault it was. Divorce does nothing—I repeat, nothing—to stop the emotional drama from continuing. The beat goes on.

Assuredly there is a place for divorce. Divorce is often a necessary step for some of us who have grown so far beyond our marriage that there can be no reunion. But quite often I see dismal results, chancy futures, and more complicated lives. The future, while different, is not necessarily better. In divorce, regret becomes a sad companion traveling with us in a hauntingly familiar way.

Divorce is disorienting. Divorces, like deaths, major illnesses, and similar dramatic changes, remove us from the context in which we have identified ourselves. We are separated from a familiar place in our emotional and social context. We lose a familiar and identifying trademark when we divorce. We are not quite sure who we are anymore. Without moorings we feel confused, lost.

I could see this quite clearly and immediately with a patient referred to me because of her problem dealing with her divorce. Paula was without a context. Her problem was obvious in the message she left on my exchange when requesting to see me. The message ended with her married name as Mrs. John Miller and left no doubt as to where I would have to begin. Together we would have to discover where Paula was, the woman who had been so badly hurt and buried within the context of her marriage.

When we are no longer a wife, or husband, we lose a piece of our inner landscape. Who we are and how we think about ourselves are very much connected to being someone's wife or husband. And it is this fabric of our lives, when ripped apart by divorce, that needs to be repaired and be rewoven into a new context. When we work through the anger and ambivalence surrounding divorce, we are more likely to be *divorced*. Until then, the question *Should I have . . .* lurks.

ABUSE AND DIVORCE

I can say with certainty that relationships that are physically or emotionally abusive should end. *Immediately*. When the sense we have of ourselves is being attacked by an emotionally abusive spouse who is either unable or unwilling to love, we should end the relationship or seek help in order to do so. It goes without saying that if the marriage is punitive, a threat to children, or in any way damaging to our well-being, we need to get out and get out fast.

There should be a very distinct line between emotional or physical abuse at the hands of another and the often hard work involved in maintaining a marital relationship. A marriage, hallmarked by fears and tears, filled with angry outbursts of physical abuse, is not to be confused with the more ordinary conflict of marriage. Weekend seminars where we learn how to communicate are a far different story from weekends spent hiding out from a raging drunk or an angry, drug-abusing spouse. The lines should never blur. We should never confuse abuse with anything else.

GENDER DIFFERENCES

Men appear to suffer fewer emotional consequences, but that is likely to be only in appearance. Contrary to widespread belief, statistics indicate that divorce causes more emotional upheaval for men. This belief is supported by the fact that women usually initiate divorce proceedings. They therefore process the emotional knowledge a bit sooner. Men are less likely to have close friends and less likely to seek counseling. They usually lose their house, their neighborhood, and most of the time with their kids. They frequently increase their workload to support two households and to escape from the emotional stress of divorce.

Women have more trouble starting new relationships than divorced men. Women suffer much greater economic strain in divorce. Generally speaking, an average woman's standard of living declines more than 30 percent upon divorce. Unless a woman has initiated the divorce, she is less likely to make peace with the outcome. Most women rid themselves of their marriage in order to make a statement about what was never offered to them—intimacy and closeness. Often, the unexpressed anger and hurt are what the divorce is seeking to communicate. Instead, they find themselves having to deal with this anger that leaves them lonely. Women have never had an easy time expressing their real needs and anger because our culture does not regard it as feminine. What a pity.

The Role of an Affair in Divorce

Divorce seldom occurs without an infidelity taking place first, especially in long-term marriages. More than 90 percent of divorces in long-standing marriages involve infidelities at some time during the marriage. More than 50 percent may be involved in a current affair, yet only about 25 percent cite an affair as an actual reason for divorce. Technically, divorces are due to irreconcilable differences. What does that mean in the language of a sexual detour? It means that if we've had an affair, we probably lied, torpedoed the relationship, then blamed it on the husband or wife. The legal term *incompatibility* is another way of saying that maturity, infidelity, and lack of communication ended the marriage.

Despite the negative influence of infidelity on a marriage, affairs do not cause divorce. An affair is the cover story. The underlying issues bring about divorce. Nevertheless, sexual detours complicate marriage and lessen the chance for a marriage to succeed. Emotional alienation is a major reason behind divorce, and affairs intensify emotional distance.

Affairs increase our emotional and physical alienation because they allow us slowly to integrate being separate as our identity instead of being part of a married couple. Intensely romantic affairs, versus lighter sexual affairs, damage the chances for the marriage's success because of the distance that fantasy creates. We are less inclined to seek remedy for the marriage when romance fills our heads. When we invest in the fantasy of a deeply romantic love affair, we have little regard for consequences, and we have difficulty ending the affair. When we do, the endings are painful and often lingering, for we have to give up our illusions. Fantasies die hard.

A F F A I R S   A N D   S E P A R A T I O N S

The lure of continuing an affair may be strong, yet we may be afraid to make a decision to end the marriage, so we ask for a separation. When an affair is still going on and a separation is sought, it usually means we want to continue to see a lover more freely. A separation while an affair is in progress only helps the marriage roll down the primrose path to divorce.

On the other hand, separation, if an affair is no longer in

progress, can be a legitimate way of sorting out feelings, cooling off anger, containing rage. The hope is that being separate will pave the way for constructive change to occur in the marriage. The best outcome of separation is that we begin to understand that we have to let go of our illusions and come to grips with what is real in ourselves and in our lives.

Reasons for the End of an Affair

Affairs usually end because they don't represent well-thought-out choices at the right time or place in our lives. Statistics show that 80 percent of those who divorce during an affair regret the decision, and over 75 percent who marry partners in an affair eventually divorce. The divorce rate and the ratio of infidelity are much higher among marriages to partners in an affair.

The reason for the dismal chance of success in remarriage to partners in an affair lies not only in the primary issues that interfere with intimacy but also in the impoverished selection process. Our method for "choosing" a person with whom we have an affair differs dramatically from how we "choose" a mate. Because we often end up in an affair with someone who was in the right place at the wrong time, the affair usually ends. When it does, it does so for one of three reasons: The third party wants out; the affair dies a natural death; or the affair is sacrificed for the sake of the marriage.

THE THIRD PARTY

Ending an affair is a complicated piece of business. It is simpler, although not less painful, for a third party to end an affair because he or she usually has the pressure of wanting a change in the status of the affair relationship on his or her side. The third party is the person outside the marital union. For example, even if two lovers in an affair are married to other people, individually each is the "third party" to the other's marital relationship. The premise for this is that the marital relationship is always the primary relationship.

When, in effect, the third party gets tired of being the third party, he or she usually ends the relationship because he or she realizes that the lover is not going to end the marriage. He or she is tired of having a secondary role in his or her lover's life. The third party wants to be married to the lover, but perhaps the lover is too ambivalent or reluctant to give up the marriage. This is the most common reason why an affair ends. Someone wants something *more*.

At one point in my practice I had three patients, each ending an affair for different reasons. June was the unmarried third party in an affair. She was starting to get wise to her situation, and I hoped she would do what most people do in an affair when they get smart: end the affair. Getting June to recognize that she was in the least primary position was difficult because she did not want to give up an illusion she desperately wanted to believe—that of being most important to her married lover. Her therapy would have to deliver the painful message of a different reality.

NATURAL DEATH

Hal was ending an affair that exemplified the second most common reason why affairs end. In effect, the affair dies a natural death. This occurs when reality takes a toll. Affairs with a low emotional attachment are usually kept secret and end in their time. This was the case with Hal. His secret lover wanted more than he did and accused him of losing interest. Continuing the affair was extracting an enormous price.

He came to see me for the express purpose of getting support to end his affair. He didn't want to do what his lover urged, which was to take the affair public and confess to his wife. He wanted to do what he felt was a heel's way out. To keep it a secret, end it, and get back to his life. He had lost the zest for the affair. He felt guilty and feared that his lover's accusation reflected a shallow and rotten aspect of his personality.

My job was to show him that being a heel was being human and that if he let his lover down as gently as possible, it was okay to do so. He was entitled to find his way back to the life he wanted to lead. What was not okay was to disappear in an inhumane way without an explanation or a good-bye. At least that was my definition of a heel. Losing interest was not as accurate a description of his feelings about the affair as the fantasy was losing steam. When reality punctures the illusions in an affair, some of the hot air escapes.

When an affair isn't worth what it costs, on an emotional level or in reality, it dies. When exposed to time and reality, most affairs do just that. Of course, the discovery of an affair by a marital partner is a sure way to introduce reality, but that kind of reality carries with it an inherent risk: Knowledge may end the marriage. Usually, exposing the relationship is avoided at all costs because on a sexual detour what we are seeking is escape, not confrontation or confession.

SAVING THE MARRIAGE

This brings us to the third reason an affair ends. Sometimes an affair is sacrificed in order to save the marriage. This is done either at the request of the marriage partner, or voluntarily, "for the sake of the marriage," which usually means children are involved. Family ties are treasured and binding and difficult to sever.

In basically good marriages, there may be enough common sense to end the affair. Affairs occur even in good marriages. Sometimes a glitch in the emotional road trips someone in a good marriage into an affair. It happens. And when it does, the recognition that the marriage is worth saving often runs headlong into the emotional entanglements of the affair. This collision makes ending an affair for this reason the most difficult.

Sacrificing an ongoing passionate affair for the sake of the marriage is by far the hardest decision to reach and to implement because there is so much fantasy and illusion present. Sometimes, the very notion of separation heats up the affair. Any attempt by the star-crossed lovers to end the affair still in full session not only fails, but fuels the drama. Very potent realism is necessary to stop an affair in its tracks for the sake of the marriage.

Giving up an affair in order for a marriage to survive is difficult to go through. Lovers miss each other for months and years. Berta was in the painful process of ending the affair. Step by painful step. She worked in an office where her lover was one of the managing partners. She couldn't face giving up the daily life of her children and, for her, this would have been a reality. Her husband, Jeff, an earnest, hard-working engineer, would have demanded full or equal custody had she continued the affair and left him. Berta also had trouble giving up the fantasy of what life might have to offer as the wife of a more flamboyant lover. The fantasy provided a life she would rather live. The key word being *fantasy*.

Berta's lover had been in a long-term relationship more than once before his marriage and had been in several relationships, even affairs, before he became involved with Berta. Her fears that her lover was an unstable relationship risk were not ill founded, but her other wishes continued to overwhelm her. The affair represented a secret second life to Berta, one she fantasied about greatly. To end the affair meant that Berta would have to give up the fantasy of a new identity. Therapy was crucial in helping Berta end the affair. She went to great lengths to do so. I encouraged her to change jobs, even her neighborhood, so that her lifestyle would keep her away from the lure of continuing her affair, which can be as powerful as any drug.

It is hard to give up an affair while it is in full swing because it means we have to trade escape for problem solving, fantasy and illusion for reality. This is not an even trade. When disillusion has not yet set in and the affair is our drug of choice, it fills unmet needs. The trappings of an affair are usually such that the day-to-day objective reality of marital life doesn't have much of a chance. Giving up an affair to save a marriage may mean renouncing what we yearn for and tackling the job of making life work with what we have. We may do so, but with reluctance. Could've been, would've been, and should've been continue to haunt. Ending an affair means trading in snake oil for some real medicine. No one wants real medicine.

Giving up an affair completely is almost always the only way to save a marriage. Fidelity is a conscious choice. It means taking the long-term view instead of short-term gratification. It is a commitment. There can be no recovery of restoration of the marriage until the affair is over. Honesty and openness, the rebuilding of trust, cannot be partners to an affair. Giving up an affair to save the marriage must be treated as an emergency. In order to do so successfully, the affair must be treated like a drug and given up just as stringently. And in so doing, we will suffer the pangs of withdrawal.

There is only one time to end an affair: sooner rather than later. Often the betrayed spouse knows better than anyone else how necessary permanent separation from the partner in the affair is as a first step to restoring trust. Sometimes families go to extreme measures to assure that this separation is effective. Careers are sacrificed, friendships ended, and schools changed in the interest of ending an affair and preserving a marriage.

L E T T I N G   G O

Ending an affair is one act. Letting go is another. Sometimes it is harder to let go of something on an emotional level than to end it in reality. Divorce often reflects the fact that the emotional reality is different from the legal one. Whether it is a marriage or an affair, the difficulty in letting go reminds me of a story a patient told me:

> Two priests were traveling through the forest. They came to a river where stood a lovely woman. She asked to be carried across the river. One of the priests willingly picked her up and ferried her across. He put her down on the opposite bank where she gratefully thanked him. Days passed as the priests continued traveling, but one of the priests had grown strangely silent. As they were nearing the end of their journey, the quiet priest confided what had been troubling him. "We are sworn not to touch women, yet you held that woman very close to you when crossing the river." The other priest thought for a moment before he replied, "How strange, I only carried the woman across the river. You are carrying her still."

In grasping the opportunity presented by the crisis of the endings in our lives, and then in letting go, we can prepare for a new start. It is only when we finally let go of the hopes, the dreams, and the anger that we are able to have a beginning. In the book *Transitions,* William Bridges makes the wonderful observation that the sine qua nons of beginnings are endings. It is very true that going through the end of a relationship, we learn it isn't the end at all, simply the beginning of transition.

Chapter Sixteen

Beginnings

*Things don't change,
but by and by our wishes change.*

—MARCEL PROUST

Beginnings, unlike new chapters, rarely happen neatly. Turning over a new leaf is not as easy as turning a page. Rarely do we wake up with the cheery thought of how great it is that we get an opportunity to rise like a phoenix out of the ashes of our lives. No one gives thanks for the chance to embark on a painful journey within. At least not in the beginning.

Beginnings are tricky. We rarely have them firmly in our grasp. Endings leave so many ragged edges that the end of one phase of our lives and the beginning of another blur and flow into each other like watercolors. By definition, beginnings are the end of something—and that end lingers on into the new phase of our life. Between the old and the new, the past and the future, lies an emotionally scarred landscape that to some feels like a valley of despair they cannot cross. To others, a new beginning is a far simpler journey. Whether the bridge is long or short, we usually make the crossing in a state of emotional flux, sometimes without even knowing where we are or what we are doing.

The best way to navigate the space between old and new, past and present, endings and beginnings is simply to allow our feelings to exist. To feel our way through. We must lose ourselves to our particular loss, great or small. We must allow the emotional field to lie fallow. This might mean we don't do much of anything. We are in a state of limbo. This comes quite naturally with the shock of endings. Maybe we stare into space. Or wander aimlessly. Even feel numb. We flounder. We sleep. Or we don't sleep. We work. Or we don't work. We see without seeing. We hear without hearing. We eat without tasting. We feel disconnected from the past and not yet emotionally secure in the present. Thus with the help of a ritualized passage of ordinary routine, without even knowing it, we heal.

I learned the lesson of healing from a friend of mine. I watched her go through several misfortunes, one after another. The death of a parent, her own illness, her husband's affair, and their subsequent divorce. Through it all she kept her routine as intact as possible. She got up each morning, did her daily jog or some physical activity, went to work, kept her appointments, continued the evening schedule, and dropped into bed promptly at nine.

I felt frantic watching her. I hollered that she should crash, weep for a month, scream every night. There should be some change, I ranted, foolish child that I was. I would declare all sorts of hysteria. She looked at me in horror and explained that her routine was like a strand of pearls. Routine was the knot that held each pearl together. She was going from knot to knot so that she could stay intact. The hardest part of all was enduring and going on. Falling apart was easy. The hard work of change had to take place under an emotional scab. Routine held everything together long enough for scabs to form so that she could heal.

We can spend our time in the overlap between endings and beginnings, trying to understand ourselves. This foundation of better knowing our inner needs lends shape to the action of a new beginning as the disintegration of the old becomes reintegrated in a new identity. This "trying to understand" is an activity, but it is an internal one not obvious to the naked eye.

The wake of an affair presents us with a demarcation line between the old and new. With an ending, the past and the future are clearly spelled out for us. We don't have to muddle through years of not knowing what or where we are. In the wake of an affair we become the divorced, the reunited, the remarried, or even the single again. We may be in the external context of a new identity before we emotionally catch up, but at least we know what world we will have to operate in.

Forgiveness

The transition from endings to beginnings takes time. It takes time to recover from having an affair or from the betrayal of one. We need time to go from the end of a marriage to the beginning of a new one. We need time to adjust to being alone. Whether our course is that of rebuilding the marriage, ending the marriage, building a relationship with a new partner, or even living single, the tasks left to us are relatively the same and involve restoring a sense of self-worth. Beginnings start with the forgiveness of ourselves and of others.

Recovery from betrayal, from the end of the affair, and from divorce requires that we let go of anger and resentment, illusion and disappointment. In each case we must take responsibility for our actions, forgive ourselves, and make a new start. The recovery of a marriage after an affair depends upon the restoration and rebuilding of trust. It is crucial. We need to forgive ourselves for being who we are, flawed and imperfect, and we need our partners to forgive us and accept us as well. Anger is corrosive. And anger turned inward becomes depression.

Forgiveness is giving up resentment or the desire to punish. The dictionary characterizes forgiveness as giving up a right and a claim. Forgiveness is something we must ask for in words, consciously and often. It is helpful and healing to ask for it repeatedly. That doesn't mean we apologize forever, but we demonstrate our sincerity by asking instead of expecting. An appeal for forgiveness demonstrates an intention of honesty and our commitment. Marriage has a better chance if we stand united against a common enemy, the enemy being the one outside the marriage. Forgiveness, like trust, doesn't happen overnight or on a weekend. It takes time. The person asking for forgiveness and the one giving it are both responsible for healing.

Forgiveness does not apply only when there is a wish to restore a marriage. Forgiveness plays a crucial part whether we are going to be single or build a relationship with another. Hurt, bitterness, and resentment keep us attached to the past in a way that precludes building the future. We have to forgive ourselves for the role we played in the end of a relationship, however large or small, by recognizing our contribution to the failure of the relationship. We also have to forgive our partner, or we will remain bound to him or her forever. Taking responsibility for our role in an affair does not mean taking the blame. It simply means acknowledging our part, then forgiving ourselves for it and learning from it. When we are able to look inward, accept ourselves, and acknowledge our own mistakes, we can build a better future.

Even when we are hurt and forgiveness is difficult, it is crucial if we want to rebuild a marriage. Can you imagine how hard it would be to restore a marriage if the spouse wouldn't agree to forgive and forget? I constantly reminded Cindy of the roadblocks she was throwing into the path of restoring her marriage. She had the memory of an elephant. She insisted that she forgave, but wouldn't. She couldn't forget one moment of her husband's affair. Even while she swore to me that she forgave him, she rehashed every little crime he had committed. I gently reminded her that forgiveness meant putting something away. As in *forget*. But Cindy could not let go. She drew each action out to be examined, questioned, looked at, and turned over like a moon rock. She insisted that she wasn't passing judgment. Of course I knew her husband couldn't possibly feel forgiven. Her husband's trial was still in active session, and Cindy's verdict was not yet really in.

Forgiving includes reshaping our expectations about the partner in our life. Forgiveness requires that we recognize that a partner cannot fulfill all our needs or do for us what we can or should be doing for ourselves. Our partner cannot function for what it is that we hide from or are afraid to develop in ourselves. When we are too ashamed of ourselves, or feel ashamed by what we perceive has happened to us, we can restore a sense of power and reshape our destiny by forgiving ourselves. This forgiveness allows us to share ourselves more readily. It restores hope and allows us to take constructive action.

Communication

The way people forge a lasting, intimate relationship is a complicated piece of work. The word *relationship* reveals a clue as to how we go about it:

> *Relationship means to reconnect.*

A relationship means a coming together again and again of two different individuals, psychically distinct from each other. A relationship isn't forged and forgotten. It must be a constant reenaction.

The burden in marriage of maintaining this relationship, of promoting this ongoing reconnection, falls not to mind reading or romantic union but to communication. The ability to communicate determines the success of a relationship. In marriage, where a relationship is paramount, behavior comes first. The behavior in this case is the way we communicate.

In relationships old or new, this means learning how to communicate in a way that builds intimacy. This is not done just with a leap of faith, but by putting into action that which we have set as a new priority. We learn a new process in word and by deed. Women are more likely than men to identify intimacy as communication and set this as a priority. Males might groan at a process approach to relating with its rules and guidelines, but they actually love the idea of simple and clear communication. Mostly, they like the fact that learning how to communicate a new way will mean no arguing.

A beginning requires developing the ability to relate differently and to communicate honestly and openly. We can learn how to do this by designating communication as a priority. We need to set aside time to give that priority our individual attention and use the process outlined in the following pages. This needs the commitment and undivided attention of two people. It requires time, energy, willingness, honesty, and enthusiasm. One cannot do it for the other. We are each responsible for bringing about the conditions of our own satisfaction. By setting aside time to talk about specific problems and listen to each other, we allow communication to become an emotionally safe place where we can reveal our feelings and air our differences without damaging the marriage.

Communication is a process that is both verbal and nonverbal. Sexuality, as a primary form of nonverbal communication, is an important part of marriage. However, problems in relationships cannot be addressed nonverbally. They must be addressed verbally in order to be solved.

Nonverbal communication is always present in nuances. The trouble, however, is that when we have a problem in the relationship, nothing can solve the problem except talking. In order to solve problems, we have to learn how to communicate. Our hopes and dreams do not reside in another's eyes but in the way we handle conflict, the way we communicate with each other.

Communication has an added benefit because it not only builds intimacy with another but it also helps us to discover ourselves. One of the most profound ways we can discover ourselves is by talking to our partner in a relationship. In the process of relating that discovery, and in being accepted and understood, we find validation and self-esteem. Therapy relies on this method. When we listen to someone else express himself or herself, we return this feeling. Intimacy in marriage is built on this exchange.

The more we speak to someone who listens, the more we feel understood. Many call the feeling of being *empathetically* understood being loved. Being empathetic means that we step outside of ourselves and try to put ourselves in someone else's shoes. The job of the therapist, to empathetically understand, is something every marriage partner must learn. In therapy, the therapist listens and the patient talks. In relationships, we trade off these jobs. Each partner in a marriage should learn how to function as the therapist for the other so that they are able to solve problems. There is no other way to resolve conflicts.

Problem solving is really about communication. It's the way we not only make a decision about what to do but also how we negotiate our differences and go about having our needs met. Often when we try to solve problems, emotions get stirred up. An argument starts. The fight, no matter what the content, is always about blaming each other. Fundamental issues are not addressed in a constructive way. Bonds and ties are not forged because we do not really listen to each other. We have no way of being intimate.

Relationships are fraught with pitfalls. Marriages are made up of terribly fragile, vulnerable people. Studies on divorce have found that the likelihood of divorce can be predicted by how couples handle their personal conflicts. There are many methods of communication that resolve conflict and are designed to build enduring and intimate relationships. They are simple and, most of all, effective. No matter what they are called or how many steps they have, they all operate on the principles designed to improve the way we listen and talk to each other.

Story Telling and Story Listening

We all have styles of communicating. Very few of us are able verbally to address our differences and needs, offer understanding and acceptance, and negotiate a compromise when needed.

Most of us grew up thinking that talking about feelings meant blaming the other person and complaining about what he or she has done to us. As adults, we carry this notion into relationships. Most of us express our feelings by criticizing the other person.

When we communicate, we become a patient and a therapist. We take turns telling a story about ourselves. The story teller is the patient who tells a story about his or her inner world, and the listener is the therapist, the audience. Like a good audience, the story listener is receptive and responsible for positive feedback.

Story telling reveals an inner world and tells how we feel inside. We can do this ourselves, by talking to a therapist or a friend. Even by talking to ourselves. The fact that we are social animals means that the most natural place to do this is within the context of our relationships. We build intimacy in a relationship by taking turns telling stories about how we feel inside.

Telling our personal stories is the paramount exchange of intimacy. When we find someone to listen to us tell about who we are as a person, it helps us discover who we are, what we need, and what we want. It helps fill the emptiness inside. It helps us gain a good sense of ourselves and build intimacy. We are less likely to go outside a marriage to find ourselves, or to find acceptance and validation.

Unlike conversations or arguments, story telling sessions are structured, and there are rules to follow: Set aside a story telling time. No more than twenty minutes. Take turns being a story teller and a story listener.

The rules are simple:

1. The story teller "tells a story" by relating a feeling about a problem. Use *I* to express your feelings and refrain from using *you*.
2. The story listener listens in a nice, empathic way. If *you* pops up, it is up to the story listener to bring the story teller back to *I*.
3. Do not continue when anger crops up.

Do this several times a week until the method of talking and listening to a story becomes a familiar and comfortable way of communicating.

TELLING A STORY

Story telling means telling about yourself, telling what you feel inside. You can even relate your feelings to your own personal history. Story telling in this way tells the other person about yourself. Use *I* instead of *you*. When we use *you*, we are not revealing an inner self but sending out blame. It also displaces responsibility, in effect making the other person responsible for our emotions.

Telling a story means revealing how you feel inside and then speculating upon where those feelings might have existed in our early life in order to gain insight.

The need to communicate an inner self is not easy. More often than not we want our mate to intuitively know what we need. We all yearn for our partner to be responsible for fixing us, for making us feel whole. For knowing what is wrong without our having to say it in words. For giving us good self-esteem. For fulfilling the needs within. But no one can be responsible for healing the wounds within, for making us feel separate yet strong. In the keen disappointment we feel when a marriage partner does not fill the emptiness inside, instead of finding a way to like what we are and where we are, instead of working on ourselves and the relationship, we run away. We withdraw. We escape into distance. We seek gratification. We go on a sexual detour.

LISTENING TO A STORY

The other half of the communication equation is story listening. Hearing the story our partner tells us is difficult because we are personally involved. We hear things that arouse our emotions in a primitive way. Listening is the professional art of therapy. Becoming a therapist in addition to becoming a husband or wife is not something we think of when we take our wedding vows, but it is in fact exactly what each of us needs to do once we take those vows.

Story listening means we listen to the story being told, and instead of taking it personally, instead of disputing whether the story is right or wrong, we just listen. We try to put ourselves in another's place. We may hear stories we don't like. We may hear facts or feelings we disagree with, and we may long to shout out in anger, but the difference in story listening is that we don't react. That does not mean we deny or change our thinking, but when we listen to the story, the only comments we make are ones that help the story teller tell us more of his or her own unique and personal story.

Like any good audience, story listeners should not act bored, angry, or barely tolerant. Simple expressions of responsiveness and understanding help the story teller reveal his or her own personal drama. Encouragement takes the form of a nod, a look, or a comment:

> *Go on.*
> *Oh?*
> *That's interesting.*
> *Really!*
> *Tell me more.*
> *I understand.*

Constructive questions help the story teller go into his or her inner life and explore what lies there in order to gain self-understanding.

> *Did you ever feel that way a long time ago?*
> *What does it feel like?*
> *How did you feel then?*
> *How does it feel now?*

In this way of listening, we don't fight about what we hear. We just listen. By listening to each other in this way, marital partners build intimacy.

The Sexual Connection

Restoring a sexual relationship that has been damaged or interrupted by an affair requires a recommitment to equality and trust. Both partners must acknowledge their role in the affair, as well as take the responsibility for rebuilding the sexual trust that has been shattered.

REESTABLISHING SEXUAL TRUST

The single most important element in reestablishing a sexual connection is overcoming the emotional *trauma* of sexual rejection. Sexual betrayal hits us at the core of who we are as sexual beings. Usually there are enough disturbances in the emotional relationship of a couple where one partner is involved in an affair to have put the other on edge. Anxiety, fear, and feelings of rejection so keenly interfere in our ability to enjoy a sexual relationship that unless these feelings are attended to, the sexual relationship suffers long after the affair is over.

What usually helps people who have been caught up in sexual betrayal is reassurance. Over and over and over again. I cannot stress this enough. Frequently the partner who has had the affair complains that he or she has already reassured. Already apologized. Already asked for forgiveness. I tell one and all the same thing: Do it again. The trauma of sexual rejection needs the soothing balm of good intentions, loving feelings, reassurance as to desirability, applied over and over to the sexual wound.

Time is a great healer. One of the ways sexual trust is reestablished is through the passage of time. Time that includes generous heapings of love, attention, and verbalization of our remorse and good intentions goes a long way. What goes even farther is the recognition that sexual fidelity is something that is demonstrated. When an affair is over, it has to be over. Any suspicion or cause for suspicion on the part of a partner undermines sexual security and sexual trust. The task of the partner who has taken a sexual detour is to establish a secure zone in which the marriage may thrive.

The task of those who have faced betrayal lies in learning to trust again. Forgiveness plays a key part. If we have truly forgiven our partner, we stop blaming and start picking up our share of building an intimate relationship that includes sexuality. Leaving the burden of our sexual insecurity forever on the back of a partner who engaged in an affair, as another facet of blame, only breaks the back of the marriage. Sexual affairs are not proof of undesirability, nor is fidelity a measure of sexual desirability. Sexual intimacy is something we build into our lives by working at it.

Taking responsibility for our share of rebuilding our sexual security involves allowing ourselves to be vulnerable to our partner. Reestablishing sexual intimacy means we must take a risk. Allowing the sexual connection to be repaired requires a leap of faith. When we have decided to reinvest in our marriage, the only thing we can do to demonstrate this willingness is to reengage in a sexual relationship. Sexual intimacy is reinforced and rebuilt in much the same way as emotional trust is restored in a *trustworthy* relationship.

Reestablishing sexual trust is the most difficult aspect of repairing a marriage after betrayal because it requires us to be vulnerable. Allowing ourselves once again to become exposed, especially in the sexual arena, is made easier by the continued assurances of our partner. The act of rebuilding takes time. For some, it is a difficult and halting process, one that only time and continued fidelity will establish. For others, it is a more easily accomplished step. For all, it involves demonstrating in the most intimate sense of the words the hope, love, and courage it takes to rebuild a marriage after a sexual detour.

REESTABLISHING SEXUAL AND PHYSICAL INTIMACY

Reintegrating sexual intimacy is something that naturally follows the reestablishment of emotional intimacy. However, sometimes we remain shy and we are afraid. I tell my patients that learning how to reestablish sexual intimacy can be made easier by using a partnering approach to physical pleasure. I urge them to spend a weekend away from home. Take a vacation. Plan romantic interludes. Or treat themselves to a course in sexuality right in the comfort of their own home.

To enhance physical intimacy, we must learn to distinguish sensuality from sexuality and learn to communicate clearly our sexual wishes. This is difficult under most circumstances, and even harder in the aftermath of an affair. What makes it easier is to use the tried-and-true approach recommended by sex therapists: sensate focus exercises created by Masters and Johnson.

Sensate focus centers around physical exercises that teach couples how to take turns giving and receiving physical pleasure. Basically, what most sex therapists teach is the art of the caress. Tactile pleasure is recalled and relearned. The method is easy to understand and implement and helps ease fear of performance.

First of all, it is important to recognize that sexual functioning is a phenomenon of vasocongestion, an engorgement of blood vessels, tissues, and organs, and is not a measure of true love. This state of plumbing is the nature of physical sexual responsivity. It is triggered by erotic stimulation, whether touch, sight, sound, smell, memories, or fantasies.

During sex, the erotic trigger sends blood into the sexual tissues of the body. An erection occurs when more blood drains into the penis than can leave it. This allows the penis to penetrate the vagina. In females, arousal similarly prepares the vagina so that it becomes more receptive and can more easily accept penetration by the male organ.

Many things, both emotional and physical, can interfere with the process. Focus on performance interferes with arousal, and this is especially true when sexual infidelity has occurred and insecurities peak. Performance anxiety drains blood away from the genitals. An unhurried and loving manner helps ensure successful sex. Impulsive, spontaneous sex is fine if it works, but for most of us good planning and attention to every detail works better.

The first phase of sensate focus requires abstinence from actual sexual contact. This removes the performance anxiety from goal-oriented sex. In this exercise, we focus on sensuality. We are free to caress, massage, kiss—anything we want except touch the genital area. We take turns simply stroking the body of our partner, communicating what feels nice. The goal is not of sexual arousal or performance. The goal is simply to enjoy the pleasant sensation of touch.

In the second phase the same process is repeated, only now, sexual arousal of the genitals may be included. But no intercourse is *required*. There is nothing to worry about. Orgasm is not the end result. This phase is one of sexual stimulation with no goal other than that each partner take turns bringing sexual pleasure and excitement to the other. Somewhere along the way, sensate focus will help reinforce, enhance, and reestablish sexual trust and intimacy.

Chapter Seventeen

❦❧

Growing Whole

Oft-times nothing profits more
Than self-esteem, grounded on just and right
Well managed.
—JOHN MILTON,

PARADISE LOST

❦ While our development is most active in the formative years of infancy, childhood, and even adolescence, in adulthood we continue to grow. The rate is slower but the process is the same. In *The Empathic Imagination* by Albert Marguiles, Milan Kundera's notion of living on a Planet of Inexperience is marvelously explored. In this book, the idea that the creation of the world did not occur at the beginning of time, but occurs each day, is put forth. Every day we are faced with new dramas, new challenges, as infants, children, adults, partners, and parents. We even enter old age as children, not knowing what we face or what lies ahead.

The drama of living with the unforeseeable future is never felt more keenly than during the catastrophic events in our lives such as grave illness, death, and the end of an important relationship. The wake of a sexual detour represents, for some of us, this same kind of personal crisis. For all of us, it represents a crisis of opportunity. Rarely are we prepared for the forces that rock us, and we know little of how to achieve recovery. Crisis, however, because of the intense attention to the acute problem at hand, brings heightened awareness. Change blows into our lives, and old and new shift. One door closes and another opens. The emotional jolt of a personal crisis can motivate us to actively seek out new ways of understanding ourselves in order to ensure that the past does not repeat itself. Growth and maturity are often born of painful times.

Maturity is not, as the word may imply, age. Rather, it refers to a whole, intact, and separate person who can function as an individual capable of insight and of self-understanding. A mature adult can tolerate frustration and does not need to act out in self-destructive ways. When we are mature, key issues around abandonment and loss, or engulfment and control, are *under control*. These issues are not absent from our emotional lives, but they are under control. This means that we are capable of merging in a relationship where negotiation and compromise exist. Our expectations become more realistic. Our self-esteem is a palpable presence within ourselves and we are able to see our partners for who they are, not as the figures transference might make them into. We are better able to function as good partners when we grow more whole.

Emotional Vision

Growing whole requires purposeful action versus passive reaction. It is a process of gaining emotional vision, of opening up our inner selves, and revealing to ourselves not just what we want but also *why*.

Emotional vision reflects the capacity for knowing our problems and where they come from. As a whole, intact person, we have the ability to distinguish between problems coming from inside ourselves or from outside reality. One result of inner vision is that we are less likely to blame our partner for internal issues that interfere with feeling good about ourselves or for the problems that arise in our relationships. This responsibility for our self brings us closer to solving problems and getting what we want out of life, and farther from the kind of acting-out behavior that results in a sexual detour.

Many of my patients suffer from the mistaken notion that what ails and provokes anxiety comes from the outside and is dependent upon the action of others. Whether that is true or not is less of an issue than the fact that there are many things we cannot control. Blame is useless because we have limited control over certain realities, and we cannot change anyone else. We can change only ourselves and our reactions to situations and in this way attain a measure of balance and control.

We discard blame and accept responsibility by turning to an inner world. Becoming intimate with our inner world is a healing process. Self-awareness builds our self-esteem. When we acknowledge all our strengths and weaknesses, we no longer need to hide parts of ourselves in shame or out of fear. Shame hurts. We can't change if shame keeps us hidden from ourselves. The part of ourselves that needs to grow whole is this hidden part. One of the ways to let go of shame is to come to love the little child that you were shamed into believing wasn't *good enough* but really *is*. You have to raise that little child all over again. It is the part of yourself that you put away. Emotional vision frees us from the shame and gives us a self to share.

Accepting ourselves means taking responsibility for who we are, what we do, and the choices we make. This is the hallmark of an authentic person who demonstrates pride in himself or herself.

Becoming authentic, having a whole sense of ourselves, enables us to establish an *intimate communication* with ourselves and others. Revealing ourselves to another, who in turn accepts us for who we are, builds more strength and further increases our self-esteem. Intimacy helps us develop new skills, set goals, take risks, and fulfill our wishes. Self-knowledge and intimacy become a self-fulfilling prophecy by reinforcing positive skills.

I stress with my patients that an inner journey brings an achievement. The process itself is a victory of which they can feel proud. It is not easy to pierce the veil of an inner self. Some of us see ourselves only through rose-colored glasses. Others with a dark, somber, and critical eye. Some of us operate in total blindness. Sometimes it is only through a personal crisis that we are able to put ourselves into perspective. That is why a sexual detour represents such an important window of opportunity. The victory of engaging in the process and gaining emotional knowledge is restorative. It is a healing and hard-won gift.

Crisis is a fork in the road. No matter what the past has wrought or what the future holds, we cannot step into the same river twice. We will be able to move only as changed individuals in altered states. Our experiences will have impact upon us and those connected to us. We will have scars, but scar tissue is said to be stronger.

Finding Our Conscious Self

In order to move forward purposefully, to change anything in ourselves or in our lives, we have to tackle the job of growing whole by understanding ourselves first and then by translating the illuminating force of understanding *into a conscious act*. If we want to change anything, fix anything, we *have to do it consciously*. Only our conscious self can override the powerful motivation of our unconscious wishes and fears. When we gain the power of conscious choice, we flex an invisible muscle. This strength gives us the courage for free choice. When what we cannot see becomes visible, doors open. We reach a watershed. Transformation becomes possible with understanding when we know *why*.

Why has a peculiar power. It releases us from what we may have ordinarily thought, or even from the constraint of what we should be thinking or feeling. It allows us to explore our inner world in much the same way as we explored the world around us as children. Childhood is an endless chorus of whys. Why this. Why that. Why everything. My mother, either because she did not know the answers to my endless list of whys or simply couldn't be bothered, developed an easy answer for every why in the world:

Y is a crooked letter.

What that said to me was ultimately it didn't matter why. Why was a frivolous pastime. *What mattered was what I ended up doing.*

I've spent the better part of my adult life trying to help people discover the answer to their own whys and then helping them finally *do*. At the end of the day, the beginning of the journey, we have to stop asking and start doing. We have to go someplace. However, unless we know why, we won't know where we're going. Asking helps us discover who we are and thus gives us a road map. Unless we have the road map of knowing who we are, and what we really need and want, we may take the wrong turn and somehow find ourselves off the beaten path and once again in an obscure wood.

Having attainable hopes and finding fulfillment of dreams is the promise growing whole holds. The difference between growing whole and hiding on a sexual detour is knowing ourselves more honestly. It is a struggle to go through guilt and forgiveness, feel loneliness and fear, or experience our own weakness as we fight to grow whole. It is a process wherein we learn who we really are and what we need. We grow emotional muscle as we search ourselves. The painful process we go through in the aftermath of a sexual detour can be one of growth.

The process of growing whole takes place in three arenas of our lives:

EMOTIONAL ARENA

We experience ourselves most intensely in the emotional sphere. By looking at our relationships with others, we can see a picture of who we are and how others influence how we feel about ourselves. This examination of the emotional world is vital, both in childhood and throughout adulthood. A good sense of self-esteem reinforced in positive relationships allows us to feel vitality, creativity, and bonded to others. Self-esteem grows out of how we experience the world and how the world reflects our actions.

PHYSICAL ARENA

Physical movement and pleasure in our bodies are of paramount importance in feeling whole. When we can take care of our bodies, use our bodies creatively and for pleasure, we feel better about ourselves emotionally.

INTELLECTUAL ARENA

How we experience the world and function in the world vis-à-vis our interests and our careers can allow us to grow. Intellectual stimulation teaches us to grow in unexpected ways and helps us find avenues of change. The pursuit of interests uniquely our own can help us define ourselves and structure purpose into our lives.

Feeling whole involves two steps in all these three arenas of our lives. The two steps involve:

1. *Reflection:* taking a journey within
2. *Action:* to reinforce and establish what we have learned in reflection

Step 1: Reflection

EMOTIONAL ARENA

1. Make a commitment.

The first step is actively to commit to the pursuit of self-knowledge. Like other important commitments in our lives, this endeavor is not demonstrated in word, but in deed. The pursuit of self-awareness involves the commitment of:

t i m e

Set aside some time as if it were a bag of gold. The amount is up to you. It's your time. If you value your time, you will set aside more, not less, for this crucial journey. Nothing is more precious to us than time, and nothing is more important than to use some of it for ourselves. We can make the best use of our time if we can stretch it out and use it grain by grain, very deliberately. The amount of the time set aside, five minutes or fifty, matters less than a scrupulous adherence to the process. Every day, no matter where, no matter what, take out a measure of time and set it aside, as if on a shelf.

2. Focus.

The second step involves how we use the time set aside. This time should be used only for one deliberate purpose:

take the time to focus on your inner self

Let me distinguish between taking time for yourself and taking time for your self. Time for yourself might be reading the paper, shopping, taking a walk, hiking, exercising, taking a nap. It's a treat. Like a bubble bath. A quiet corner with a good book. Time for yourself is something to indulge in that feels enjoyable. Time for your *self*, on the other hand, is focusing on your inner self. It is a meeting of your minds. Your conscious mind connecting, insofar as that is possible, to your unconscious mind. The hardest sphere to reflect upon is this inner emotional world.

There are many ways we can focus on ourselves. We can think, look, talk, question, sort, or sift. Reflection reveals the fears, wishes, and dreams of our innermost self. We take out our hopes and dreams and think about what they are, where they came from, and why. We examine our fears in the same way. We think. And we rethink.

PHYSICAL ARENA

There are physical manifestations of exploring your emotional arena in a way that utilizes your physical gifts.

1. Write.

Many people find that one of the easiest and most rewarding ways to reflect is to write in a daily journal. Each day, the journal is used as the repository for thoughts and houses what we might glean from the rummaging we do in the basement of the self.

2. Look.

Use your sense of visual awareness. I tell many of my patients who are fortunate enough to have family photo albums or videos of their childhood to use them. Look and remember. Notice what feelings they evoke. Like music from a bygone day, these strike chords of nostalgia and provide missing pieces of an inner self we have drummed out of our awareness. When visual memory clicks in, it brings emotional memory and emotional knowledge. The people in the pictures are still alive within us, no matter how our appearance has changed. Noticing the similarities between the past and present gives us a clearer picture of the patterns of our feelings and behavior.

Another way to look inside is by looking outside. A patient of mine uses a hand mirror and studies her face every day for at least five minutes. She is drawn, she says, not so much into the lines on her face as into the crevices of the past. Memories come forth, feelings and experiences are evoked, as the face in the mirror becomes secondary to the thoughts about herself. She uses her mirror as a gateway into herself. It is almost as if the intense reflection operates as self-hypnosis. In self-hypnosis, any device that focuses the mind and sets us free from external distraction gives us a ticket to time travel.

3. Talk.

Improve your ability to communicate verbally. Talking is a good vehicle to use for a journey within. We can uncover our cover stories and discover who we really are by talking to someone about ourselves. And no, it does not need to be a therapist. Needless to say, it is an expensive situation to set up enough time for this project with a professional listener. Talking to someone each and every day is complicated, even with a partner who is willing to lend an ear and a nod now and then. What that leaves us with is talking to ourselves. Not a bad idea. For openers, talking out loud forces us to play two roles. When we talk, we become listeners. In listening to ourselves, we automatically turn the questions around and are forced to ponder ourselves a bit more. This may feel embarrassing at first, particularly if someone else is in the room or nearby. So try the shower, and instead of singing, talk to yourself.

4. Listen.

Practice what Theodore Reik called listening with the third ear—to others as well as yourself. Wake up to your sleep self and listen to what you are saying. An interesting route into the inner self is to write down what your sleep self is talking about. "A dream is a wish your heart makes when you're fast asleep." The Disney refrain echoes through our childhood, but although it's close, it's not quite correct. Dreams arise not from the heart, but from what is going on in our present-day lives and from unconscious yearnings, fears, and unresolved conflicts.

Dreams can tell us a great deal about ourselves because they are the unconscious representations of what is going on inside. The unconscious is creative, melodramatic, and accurate. Dreams give us instant, clear, and important information. The information is precise because we never dream about anything that applies to anyone else. Dreams are self-

centered and self-serving. No matter how small and insignificant the detail is, we dream about what is important to *us*.

The vividness of dreams feels as real as conscious life.
When horrors befall, and dreams are frightful, we usually
awaken with a start, heart pounding. Sometimes they are so
vivid we cannot tell the dream from reality, yet when we
awaken, dreams can evaporate like smoke. Usually, when we
try to grasp at the wisps of the dream with our conscious
mind they elude us, trailing back off into the unconscious
recesses of an inner world. Some are so strong that they stay
with us for hours. Most of us want to forget nightmares. And
why not? But they may articulate for us that which we are
unable to tell ourselves. They can let us know what we are
afraid of, and even why.

Dreams are the way the brain discharges, processes, and
translates the daytime data. Some dreams clearly reflect this
conscious daytime sensory input. We have snippets of dreams
countless times a night of which we are unaware as we rid
ourselves of daytime debris. We also have more lengthy, intri-
cate, complicated dreams wherein we solve problems or
replay them. Dreams can reoccur for years, echoing the key
problems and chronic anxieties of our lives.

In light of the fact that there is a performance nightly,
right in the comfort of your own bedroom, attend the show.
During this investigatory phase, keep regular sleep hours. A
bath before bed will relax your body. Keep a pad of paper and
a pen next to your bed. When you awaken from a dream, or in
the mornings, try to remember the fragments and quickly
write them down. Don't be dissuaded if you find that you've

written gibberish. Eventually, somewhere, a word or a phrase will bring back something from the dream that may enlighten your day journey as well.

5. Ask.

Connect yourself to others and to yourself. Growing whole is a lifetime affair. No one can be so presumptuous as to believe it ever stops, that we arrive at adulthood and are finished. Our growth continues, and ensuring our development requires our attention. All we have to do is look at the human body and our neurobiological interiors to bear witness to the complexities of existence. An inward journey helps us track another dimension of our growth and development.

One way to journey inward is to ask ourselves questions about ourselves and our relationships. These are questions that many of you will be able to answer in some detail and others only sketchily. If answers are not forthcoming, take the time over and over to ask again. You will need a paper and pencil or handy keyboard. Sit down and begin with a look at your family of origin. Here are some sample questions:

Family of Origin
How did your parents relate to you?
Were you allowed to develop a true inner sense of
    what you felt?
Did you grow up with the feeling that your parents
    communicated?
What was your mother's view of love?
What was your father's view of love?

Did you grow up believing in a prince in the guise of
a regular guy?

Did you grow up waiting for a princess to come
along?

Were you taught that love is chemistry?

Were you taught that love endures through daily action?

Marriage

When did you get married?

Why did you get married?

What was your life like before you married?

Did you want to escape your home?

Were you hoping that you would be rescued?

Can you answer these questions for your mate, and if
not why not?

What do you still like about your partner?

What do you still like about yourself?

Are you the parent or the child in your relationship?

Do you want to change?

How do you think you can change?

Sexual Detour

If an affair was hoped for or acted upon, what was
going on inside of you?

What was going on inside of your marital partner?

If you didn't know the answer to the above question,
why not?

Were you afraid to confront your fear? Hurt? Anger?

Did you choose a partner in an affair who had something you did not?

What was it that attracted you to the partner in an affair?

How did your affair make you feel about yourself?

Did your mate see you less favorably than did a partner in an affair?

What did you hope an affair would give you?

What can you do to give that to yourself?

INTELLECTUAL ARENA

1. *Take inventory.*

Somewhere in the middle of life, beset by measurements of everything down to grams and milligrams, we may get the notion that living would be done better under a whole different rule. Perhaps the error is in the concept. Measure is different somehow from measurement. Taking the measure of a life feels more whole than taking measurements. More lasting and worthwhile. More worth calculating. In taking stock of who and what we are, we may find out more about ourselves: characteristics, aspirations, talents, predispositions, inclinations. It is an inventory of what comprises the person we feel we are and think we are. It goes without saying that this inventory should be an honest self-appraisal as well as an exhaustive one. It should, in words, give a clear picture of the physical, emotional, and intellectual beings we are. We may be surprised at how many assets we have that we took as liabilities.

We may have mistaken ideas of the way we are perceived by those around us. We can use intimate friends, work partners, and casual acquaintances in our lives to help give us a picture of ourselves. If we check our inventory against theirs, we will discover more about who we are. Like a mosaic, these tiny fragments reflect part of the whole self. This is in some ways a reality check against our own denial. Remember, no right or wrong here. Simply information so that we can learn more about who we are and who we might want to become.

Ask the questions about yourself from a number of different people. Use the same type of questions. This is a personal survey. If a majority of people describe you as quiet and withdrawn and you don't perceive yourself that way, what does that mean? Perhaps it means you are afraid to admit you are shy. To hear any criticism may be too painful. Asking for a critique of yourself may mean taking an emotional risk, but we can garner very worthwhile information about ourselves in this way by creating a road map we can follow to find ourselves. Some questions to ask might be:

How would you describe me?
Do I seem easily irritated?
Am I friendly and sociable, or withdrawn?
What three characteristics describe me best?

2. Determine priorities and set goals.

In discarding what is unimportant and determining our priorities, we reveal more about who we are and what we represent. What is important to us defines who we are. Hone your self. Sort and sift through what you can do without and what is of real value. Discard what is not really important to you. We usually know what to trim with our physical selves. Fat applies not only to inches but to the dimensions of the inner world as well.

Emotional tone is as important as muscle tone. This sorting and sifting will bring into focus your priorities and values, and allow you to set reasonable goals and hold expectations of yourself that you can successfully accomplish. Some questions you might ask of yourself are:

> What do I want to build in myself?
> What strengths do I want to encourage?
> What do I want to discard?

There comes a point, which is different for each person, when what we learn has to be put into practice. Sitting and staring at our navel may bring about inner enlightenment and make our lives infinitely more peaceable, but the chances are, unless we *do something,* unless we put knowledge into action, nothing will change. The vehicle through which we change ourselves, or our lives, is *behavior.* After the first step of reflection, we arrive at the second step of growing whole: *action.*

Step 2: Action

With emotional knowledge we discover more potential in ourselves and our lives than we had ever hoped to find. Inevitably, this knowledge brings loss as well. Knowledge dispels fantasy. Self-knowledge, which reveals and enables an enriching and hopeful future, also uncovers the futility of fantasy. The loss is sad and painful when we discover that our wishes are not congruent with reality. We may want what is self-destructive. We may want things we cannot have. Wanting is easy. Giving up and growing whole is hard.

Growth not only involves learning but also requires shedding and reconciling ourselves to the losses real life demands of us. In the aftermath of an affair, we need to restore hope, rebuild strength, replace illusion, and employ methods to start anew. Change requires courage and an active change of behavior. Action and doing breed self-esteem. If you find yourself paralyzed and unable to take action, go back to Step 1 and search out what fears prevent you from taking action. Then, come back to Step 2 and push them through, being kind and accepting of yourself in the process. Change doesn't happen in a day. If you want to change, you will.

EMOTIONAL ARENA

1. Stop the behavior.

No matter what kind of destructive behavior plagues your life or hampers your recovery, GIVE IT UP. This is the starting point for any kind of change. Destructive behavior is anything that perpetuates situations in which we find ourselves abused or in which we are the abuser. Abuse is something we are addicted to, whether it is sexual acting out, alcohol, drugs, compulsive overeating, or rage reactions. Whatever the negative behavior, giving it up means just one thing: STOP. Stop the old behavior and begin a new one. The first step comes with the decision, but in order to solidify changed behavior, we need to understand its roots. Above all, we may need to have help from the outside.

2. *Reach out for support.*

To solidify change in behavior, reach out for support. The climb toward recovery from physical and emotional crisis is often hard and long, and we all need help. Friends and family can lend crucial help. If you prefer the kindness of strangers, they will become your extended family. Twelve-step support groups provide enormous help. I am an avid supporter of such groups. A support group helps you to see yourself without shame and without the prejudice of others' opinions. It helps you find a new, enlarged opinion of yourself. Support groups are made up of those who have been there, have been helped by others, and are eager to pass along what they have learned. When you reveal the shame you may feel about who you are, a supportive atmosphere where you are accepted can begin actively to raise your self-esteem. It helps you stop the behavior—for good.

The origin of self-esteem comes from the way we are seen. If we have suffered from emotional trauma—meaning more negative experiences than positive ones—we can become plagued by shame and keep that part of ourselves hidden, thereby preventing change. In order to like yourself with all your flaws so that transformation is possible, acceptance and understanding are crucial. Standing up in a support group and stating what makes you feel ashamed diminishes the shame. By sharing the secrets about yourself that you are ashamed of, you can evolve and thereby grow more whole. When we pass through the stages of accepting responsibility, blame, anger, and resentment give way to self-love and growth. We cannot love another if we cannot love ourselves.

There are support groups for every crisis imaginable, and many meetings are listed in the newspapers.

3. Take an emotional risk.

This does not mean *put yourself at risk*. Taking an emotional risk means challenging yourself to deal with your own particular personal issues. Revealing your vulnerabilities and engaging in an emotional life despite the disappointments and pain of the past are emotional risks. Fear of being hurt and feeling strongly should not stop you from embracing feelings. Risk passion. Employ trust. Express your vulnerabilities. Work out the emotional kinks by risking emotional change even though this may involve fear and loss. Giving up illusion is risking change. Resolve whatever your particular issue is. We all have painful personal issues we avoid. We may feel insecure and unsure. This might mean trusting again. This might mean allowing ourselves to feel vulnerable. This might mean redefining our feelings about expressing sexuality. We may want to hide emotionally for what we've convinced ourselves are a thousand good reasons. Don't. Do it. Be it.

4. Respect individuality.

Whatever your personal quotient is, feel it, be it, do it. Wear a suit and tie to sleep if you prefer. Cherish your individuality. This does not mean defending destructive, immature, or unkind behavior. It simply means appreciating your uniqueness and liking yourself. Along with respecting your own individuality comes an appreciation of the right of others to have a distinct and separate identity different from your own. We are all separate individuals, unique in our own way, and should both give and receive respect from those who share our lives. Therefore, if your mate wants to wear a suit or tie to sleep, respect it as you would wish your self to be respected as well.

5. Be intimate.

Intimacy is an active commitment. It requires an ongoing effort to build intimacy into a relationship. Intimacy insists that we know ourselves, respect ourselves, and demonstrate trustworthiness. When we take responsibility for our actions and eliminate blame from our lives, we both give and garner respect. Liking, love, and intimacy grow and require that we are willing to go the distance in order to establish them in our lives. Put intimacy into action. Intimacy as an active commitment may mean risking something in the face of fear. Defining what intimacy means to you and to your partner helps you build intimacy into your lives. Ask yourselves the following questions:

How is intimacy defined for you and your partner?
Is intimacy defined the same for both of you?
Is intimacy defined sexually?
Is intimacy defined by feelings of closeness or trust?

If you are confused as to what intimacy means, rethink the issue and then with your mate engage in the following exercise:

Reveal to each other the ways intimacy is present in the relationship.
Reveal to each other how the concept of intimacy has changed during the course of the marriage.

Reevaluate your definition of intimacy and how you are building it into your life. Remember, growing whole is a lifetime affair.

PHYSICAL ARENA

1. Move your body.

Engage in some form of regular exercise. Stretching counts. Do it alone or convince a buddy to motivate you. If that doesn't get your body moving, enroll in a class that requires you to move your body in some way, shape, or form. The list, from yoga to community sports, is endless.

2. Take care of your body.

It goes without saying that regular medical and dental care is important, but often in the crisis of our lives, we neglect the basics. Get the basics checked without delay no matter what else is going on in your life. If you abuse your body, get help from a support group so you can take better care of yourself.

3. Pamper your body.

Indulge your body in special ways that feel good to you. There is no better or more important time to pay special attention to yourself in a physical way than during an emotional crisis. Soaking baths, invigorating showers, massaging oils and lotions, and special attention to appearance give a sense of physical and emotional well-being.

4. *Play with your body.*

Do you have shame about your body that inhibits you from playfulness, either in bed, in clothes, in sports, or in secret? Broaden your perspectives and recognize that your body is the temple of your soul. Worship it . . . playfully.

INTELLECTUAL ARENA

1. *Play.*

We are social animals, and in the tumult of a fractured personal life, we may have ignored the boisterous flow of life that nourishes the human need for social contact. Renew and enrich friendships. Learn to play in whatever way works for you. Some blare rock music; others tune in to soft classical. Tap-dance or dig in your garden. Paint the walls. Read the newspapers. Listen to the news. Have a conversation. Engage in life in a manner that encourages social contact and play.

2. *Learn.*

Learning something new engenders stimulation, enrichment, and freedom. Whether it is knitting or a new language, the opportunities open to us through community education sources are infinite. Physical tasks or intellectual pursuits give us avenues of exploration that open up both inner and outer worlds.

3. *Help.*

Step outside of yourself and help someone else. The world is bigger than our own personal crisis. Some of the darkest hours can be brightened by the light we carry to others. The volunteer world is an honorable place to spend a few hours. It can be as simple as helping the elderly person next door or reading a book to a classroom of children.

Conclusion

This brings to a close the easy part. Mine. It's always easy telling people what to do. The hard part is actually doing it, and it is twofold.

First is the continuing struggle of trying to understand ourselves. It is an ongoing attempt to recognize that there are issues within us all that continue to thwart our desires and sabotage our efforts by providing us with cover stories instead of the real insights that make us whole. These inner wounds and the avoidance of feeling them are issues with which we all struggle. We all want soothing and a strong sense of self-identity. We all have to deal with the fear of closeness and intimacy and struggle with issues of abandonment and control. We all carry the emotional baggage of the past and unwittingly transfer it onto those in our present-day lives. We all suffer from the emotional wounds that interfere with self-esteem. Importantly, we all hold the elements of repair for one another in the understanding and empathy we can lend and in the ways we can learn to accept ourselves.

Second is the continuing effort of building an intimate relationship through both word and deed. We can enhance the course of our emotional lives with the vehicle of communication. Understanding ourselves and relating to one another as empathetic partners promise a path leading toward lasting intimacy, instead of sexual detours.

A sexual detour is a wake-up call telling us that something is going on inside of ourselves of which we are not aware. This alarm warns us that we are not following a line of emotional sight, but are deviating from a more direct route in an unconscious search to gain something we desperately need. If we heed this call and look deeply into ourselves, an affair can become a crisis of opportunity wherein we can develop the internal vision needed to grow whole and become capable of having enriching intimacy in our lives.

Love and grief are different sides of the same coin. It is only by doing the work of growing whole that we can understand and savor the bittersweet nature of our humanity. The greatest gift an effort to grow whole brings is allowing us to stretch and gain the inner vision that offers us potential for our future: the ability to become intimate.

The journey within and the intimate connection to another take courage and commitment. Dedication. Sexual detours may be enchanting. Divorce may prove easy. The road to intimacy is hard and long, but it leads to a place we all long for. It is coming home to the strength, peace, love, and security of an enduring intimate relationship. So go on, have an affair. With yourself.

Bibliography

Adler, Jerry. "Adultery, a New Furor over an Old Sin." *Newsweek*, September 30, 1996, 54–60.

Atcheson, Richard. "Oh, Such a Hungry Yearning." *Lear's*, February 1991, 55–57 +.

Bach, George R., and Ronald M. Deutsch. *Pairing: How to Achieve Genuine Intimacy*. New York: Avon Books, 1970.

Baumgold, Julie. "Why She, Personally, Won't." *Mirabella*, March/April 1996, 80.

Beattie, Melody. *Codependent No More: How to Stop Controlling Others and Start Caring for Yourself*. New York: Harper & Row, 1987.

Bennetts, Leslie. "Cheating." *Ladies' Home Journal*, September 1996, 76–80.

Broderick, Carlfred. *Couples: How to Confront Problems and Maintain Loving Relationships*. New York: Simon & Schuster, 1979.

Brzeczek, Richard, Elizabeth Brzeczek, and Sharon De Vita. *Addicted to Adultery: How We Saved Our Marriage/How You Can Save Yours*. New York: Bantam Books, 1989.

Campbell, Joseph. *The Power of Myth with Bill Moyers*. Edited by Betty Sue Flowers. New York: Doubleday, 1988.

Carter, Stephen L. "Falling Out of Love." *Mirabella*, March/April 1996, 79.

DeSalvo, Louise. "Fidelity—What's Sex Got to Do With It?" *Mirabella*, March/April 1996, 88.

Ehrenreich, Barbara. "Why It Might Be." *Mirabella*, March/April 1996, 78–79.

Farney, Dennis. "Today's Twentysomethings: Realistic, Living in Present." *The Wall Street Journal*, July 6, 1998, A26.

Flook, Maria. "Fidelity and the Long-Distance Marriage." *Mirabella*, March/April 1996, 85–86.

Gaylin, Willard, and Ethel Person, eds. *Passionate Attachments: Thinking About Love*. New York: The Free Press, 1988.

Glass, Shirley. "Vows." *Psychology Today*, July/August 1998, 35–42+.

Goldberg, Arnold, ed. *The Psychology of the Self: A Casebook*. Collaborated by Heinz Kohut, M.D. New York: International Universities Press, 1978.

Hempel, Amy. "Flirting With Disaster." *Mirabella*, March/April 1996, 81.

Hendrix, Harville. *Getting the Love You Want: A Guide For Couples*. New York: Harper & Row, 1988.

Heyn, Dalma. "Why Women Are Always to Blame." *Mirabella*, March/April 1996, 86–87.

Johnson, Robert A. *We: Understanding the Psychology of Romantic Love*. San Francisco: Harper & Row, 1983.

Jordan-Smith, Paul. "Epicycle I: Oedipus." *Parabola: Myth and the Quest for Meaning*, 2, no. 4 (1985): 46–48.

Krantzler, Mel. "The 6 Stages of Marriage." *Good Housekeeping*, June 1981, 24+.

Margulies, Alfred. *The Empathic Imagination*. New York: W. W. Norton, 1989.

Mark, Bonnie S., and James A. Incorvaia, eds. *The Handbook of Infant, Child, and Adolescent Psychotherapy: New Directions in Integrative Treatment, Reiss-David Child Study Center*. Volume 2. Northvale, NJ: Jason Aronson, 1997.

Marks, Jane. "I Had a Fling with My Boss." *Ladies' Home Journal*, July 1998, 15–16+.

McDevitt, John B., and Calvin F. Settlage, eds. *Separation-Individuation: Essays in Honor of Margaret S. Mahler*. New York: International Universities Press, 1971.

McKay, Matthew, and Patrick Fanning. *Self Esteem: The Ultimate Program for Self-Help*. New York: MJF Books, 1987.

Milkman, Harvey, and Stanley Sunderwith. *Craving for Ecstasy: The Consciousness and Chemistry of Escape*. New York: Free Press, 1987.

Miller, Alice. *The Drama of the Gifted Child: How Narcissistic Parents Form and Deform the Emotional Lives of Their Talented Children.* Translated by Ruth Ward. New York: Basic Books, 1981.

Miller, Sherod, Elam W. Nunnally, and Daniel B. Wackman. *Couple Communication I: Talking Together.* Littleton, CO: Interpersonal Communication Programs, 1979.

Myers, Michael F. "Residency and Marriage: Oil and Water?" *Medical Economics,* June 15, 1998, 152–56.

Nemiroff, Robert A., Alan Sugarman, and Alvin Robbins, eds. *On Loving, Hating, and Living Well: The Public Psychoanalytic Lectures of Ralph R. Greenson, M.D.* Monograph 2. Madison, CT: International Universities Press, 1992.

Owens, Michele, and Gerald Coble. "The Wandering Wife in Film." *Mirabella,* March/April 1996, 82–83.

Paul, Jordan, and Margaret Paul. *Do I Have to Give Up Me to Be Loved By You?* Minnesota: Compcare Publishers, 1983.

Person, Ethel Spector. *Dreams of Love and Fateful Encounters: The Power of Romantic Passion.* New York: W. W. Norton, 1988.

Pittman, Frank S. *Man Enough: Fathers, Sons, and the Search for Masculinity.* New York: Putnam, 1993.

———. *Private Lies: Infidelity and Betrayal of Intimacy.* New York: W. W. Norton, 1990.

Reik, Theodor. *The Need to Be Loved.* New York: Farrar, Straus, 1963.

Rose, Phyllis. "Anna Karenina, the Patron Saint of Adulteresses." *Mirabella,* March/April 1996, 82–83.

Ryan, Michael. "Why He Never Will Again." *Mirabella,* March/April 1996, 80–81.

Sagan, Dorion. "Gender Specifics: Why Women Aren't Men." *The New York Times,* June 21, 1998, pp. 1, 20.

Scarf, Maggie. *Intimate Partners: Patterns in Love and Marriage.* New York: Random House, 1987.

———. "What a Triangle Can Do for a Marriage." *Mirabella,* March/April 1996, 87–88.

Scharff, David E. *The Sexual Relationship: An Object Relations View of Sex and the Family*. Northvale, NJ: Jason Aronson, 1998.

Shapiro, Michael. "Q. Why Do We Fall in Love." *Mirabella*, November 1992, 32.

Sherven, Judith, and James Sniechowski. *The New Intimacy: Discovering the Magic at the Heart of Your Differences*. Deerfield Beach, FL: Health Communications, 1997.

Smiley, Jane. "Why It's Not Worth It." *Mirabella*, March/April 1996, 78–79.

Solomon, Marion F. *Narcissism and Intimacy: Love and Marriage in an Age of Confusion*. New York: W. W. Norton, Inc., 1989.

Spring, Janis Abrahms. *After the Affair: Healing the Pain and Rebuilding Trust When a Partner Has Been Unfaithful*. New York: HarperCollins, 1997.

Stern, Daniel N. *The Interpersonal World of the Infant: A View from Psychoanalysis and Developmental Psychology*. New York: Basic Books, 1985.

Tannen, Deborah. *Talking From 9 to 5, Women and Men in the Workplace: Language, Sex and Power*. New York: Avon Books, 1994.

Thurman, Judith. "Monogamy, the French Version." *Mirabella*, March/April 1996, 84–85.

Viorst, Judith. *Necessary Losses: The Loves, Illusions, Dependencies and Impossible Expectations That All of Us Have to Give Up in Order to Grow*. New York: Fawcett, 1986.

Viscott, David. *I Love You, Let's Work It Out*. New York: Simon & Schuster, 1987.

Weiner-Davis, Michele. *A Woman's Guide to Changing Her Man (Without His Even Knowing It)*. New York: Golden Books, 1998.

Wheelis, Allen. *How People Change*. New York: Harper & Row, 1973.

Wolfe, Linda. *Playing Around: Women and Extramarital Sex*. New York: William Morrow, 1975.

Yalom, Irvin D. *Love's Executioner & Other Tales of Psychotherapy*. New York: HarperCollins, 1989.

D1116137

J

Borrowed Summer

Marion Walker Doren

1 8 17

———— HARPER & ROW, PUBLISHERS ————

Cambridge, Philadelphia, San Francisco, London, Mexico City, São Paolo, Singapore, Sydney

———— NEW YORK ————

ATHENS REGIONAL LIBRARY
ATHENS, GEORGIA

289469

Lyrics from the song "Button Up Your Overcoat":
Copyright © 1928 by DeSylva, Brown & Henderson, Inc.
Copyright renewed, assigned to Chappell & Co., Inc.
International Copyright Secured.
ALL RIGHTS RESERVED.
Used by permission.

Borrowed Summer
Copyright © 1986 by Marion Doren

All rights reserved. No part of this book may be
used or reproduced in any manner whatsoever without
written permission except in the case of brief quotations
embodied in critical articles and reviews. Printed in
the United States of America. For information address
Harper & Row Junior Books, 10 East 53rd Street,
New York, N.Y. 10022. Published simultaneously in
Canada by Fitzhenry & Whiteside Limited, Toronto.
Designed by Joyce Hopkins
1 2 3 4 5 6 7 8 9 10
First Edition

Library of Congress Cataloging-in-Publication Data
Doren, Marion Walker.
  Borrowed summer.
  Summary: Upset that her beloved great-grandmother
and an elderly friend are dying of neglect in a grim
nursing home, eleven-year-old Jan and her Sunshine
Club concoct a plan to get them out secretly.
  [1. Grandmothers—Fiction.   2. Old age—Fiction.
3. Nursing homes—Fiction]   I. Title.
PZ7.D7274Bo 1986   [Fic]   85-45816
ISBN 0-06-021723-5
ISBN 0-06-021724-3 (lib. bdg.)

To Marion Walker, my mother,
waiting to be rescued,
and to my husband, George Doren,
who rescued me

Borrowed Summer

1

Sunday is a hushed day. In the limpid sunlight of spring, Gram and I walk around our yard. She carries a cane, but it is more to point things out than to lean on.

"Those with the little faces are Johnny-jump-ups. And here"— she pokes with her cane—"are white violets. I love them best."

I resolve in that minute to favor white violets over purple, but then Gram leans over and draws in great breaths.

"Paper narcissus, absolutely the most wonderful scent of all. My favorite flower."

Hastily I discard white violets, seeing immediately that thin-petaled narcissus are greatly superior. Changing my mind so often has made me lag and Gram is now moving at full steam. For an old lady, she sure gets around.

"Clouds of crab-apple blossoms! Is there anything so heavenly?"

I give up. I love Gram, and willingly do and believe anything she says, but I can't change my favorite flower three times in three minutes.

"White lilacs are pretty, spraying down," I venture.

"Why, Jan, you picked my favorite flower. It's amazing how much we're alike." She lays a hand on my shoulder, light as a butterfly, and we stand a breathless moment glorying in the world.

"Jan Robinson, come in and set the table," Mom calls from the kitchen. I love setting the table, but I never let Mom know this or I'll have a permanent job.

Sprinting across the greening grass, I leave Gram to examine each flower friend before she climbs two flights to her attic kingdom to "freshen up" for Sunday dinner. Gram makes her own way, as she always has. I leap the porch steps and enter the front hall, an echo of her butterfly touch lingering on my shoulder.

I set the silver out. Forks on the left, knives on the right, my mind humming a song to remind me. A place for "Mom," which is my new name for her. The little ones still cling to "Mommy," but, at ten-going-on-eleven, I find that too baby-ish. Mom is beautiful. Her eyes are the pale blue that hides deep in glacial crevasses, and her eyebrows wing together in the center like birds flying.

David is six and sits to Mom's left. Everyone gives me the same message: "Give my love to that adorable brother of yours." I never do. Who wants a brother who looks like a Gerber baby?

Sue-Sue sits on Mom's right. A two-year-old cherub whose dark, curly eyelashes sweep her cheeks, she sits in a high chair and nibbles French bread, after having eaten her own dinner in the kitchen.

Then there's me—Jan. The one without wings, neither beautiful nor a cherub. My knees have knobs instead of dimples, and my elbows are hardening in their old age.

Next to me sits Gram. Gram is my best friend. My very best. While other people are attracted by the charms of David and Sue-Sue, Gram cleaves to me. I love that word, "cleaves." It means to split apart and to hold together. That's the way we are, Gram and me—the eighty-year-old and the ten-year-old—split by years, but holding to-gether.

5

Dad sits at the head of the table, in the chair with arms on it. He's the strongest one, so why he needs to rest his arms on anything I can't figure out, unless it's because he works in the city and is tired on Sundays.

The silver is laid, and now I put out what Mom calls the amenities. Crystal saltcellars with tiny crystal spoons. Rolled napkins in their silver rings. Butter plates and butter knives. A silver and crystal ashtray for Dad's cigar when Sunday dinner is over. Dad deserves his cigar for keeping up this house and all of us who live in it.

I ring the little silver bell and it is time for dinner. Two P.M. on a Sunday afternoon. David and Sue-Sue climb into their chairs.

Gram makes her way down the stairs. She lives in what were once maid's quarters, on the third floor of this roomy, old stucco house. Of all my friends, I am the only one with a great-grandmother. Mom's mother, Gram's daughter, died a month before I was born, and Gram went so far into grief they had to give her shock treatments. She came from the hospital to live with us. She is eighty, which means that when I'm thirty she will be dead.

Around the corner on the stairs, Gram maneuvers slowly, her cane feeling for the next step, her other hand gripping the railing. I love her tiny, narrow feet, and the soft dress that whispers when she walks.

Sunday dinner is always either leg of lamb or roast chicken. Mom comes out of the kitchen carrying the platter of lamb, and Dad sharpens the carving knife.

Gram smiles at us from the last step. She plants her cane on the throw rug at the bottom of the stairs. Left foot down to the rug, and then her right foot lifts and moves forward, but so does the throw rug. Her cane clatters across the floor and thumps against the wall. Gram never lies down except at night, but at two o'clock on a Sunday afternoon she lies on the throw rug that glides to the dining-room door.

David laughs. Sue-Sue claps her pudgy hands and sends a crust of French bread flying.

Gram does not get up.

Sylvia is my best friend after Gram, and Sylvia's older brother, Ronald, drives the town ambulance. Ronald is usually not welcome in my house, because he teases me because I think I know everything. But today he is welcome. He comes in with his friend Frank, who is a paramedic, and they gently place Gram on a stretcher and carry her out the front door, across the porch, and down the concrete steps.

It is the first time I have been left alone with the younger generation. Dad tucks a fifty-cent piece into my hand. "It says, 'In God we trust,'" he says. "If you get frightened while we're gone, just read your coin."

The siren screams so loudly I hope Gram isn't scared. She shuts off loud music and turns pale when Sue-Sue has a tantrum. She likes me because I'm quiet as a mouse. I scream inside my head.

The throw rug is by the dining-room door, and I move it back to the foot of the stairs. Sue-Sue still pushes bread into her cupid mouth. David bangs on the table.

"Let's eat, Mrs. Robinson," he says. Our name is Robinson, and he loves that record about Mrs. Robinson.

I don't dare use Dad's carving knife, so I pull a little lamb off the bone and put it on his plate. A scoop of mashed potatoes and a spoonful of peas, and he's happy.

The lamb tastes like cardboard. I chew and swallow to show David and Sue-Sue that this is just any old Sunday dinner, even though there are three empty chairs at the table.

Is Gram hurting? Will she close her eyes and stop breathing?

Finally, at three o'clock in the afternoon, I take Sue-Sue up to the room we share and dump her on her bed. Her thumb creeps into her mouth, among the bread crumbs. I plunk David in his bedroom and close the door. I don't care if he builds a whole city of blocks, as long as he doesn't show his beautiful face.

I climb the stairs to Gram's world. It smells of her perfume. There are two big rooms, with a big bathroom in between. All of it is painted white, and it feels cooler than downstairs. There's a photograph of a girl Gram says is Mom. A Victrola you crank up. Hard, brown, translucent soap in the bathroom. A granny quilt lies on the chaise longue. I put my face in it and smell powder and soap, breathe in my own lamb breath, and fall asleep.

"Oh, Sue-Sue," Mom cries. "I love you, you little darling." They are home.

Dad carries David down on his shoulders. "Trot, trot to Boston," he chants as he hits the stairs, "trot, trot to Lynn."

I unwrap Gram's quilt and run down the stairs. "How is she?"

Mom is putting away the food, and I know by the way she doesn't yell at me for leaving it out that something is wrong.

"Oh, Jan," she cries, in a voice she uses when it's all my fault. "She's going to have to stay for a while. She has to have surgery. Her hip is broken."

Even I, at ten, know that's the beginning of the end. It's only five o'clock on a spring afternoon, and my best friend in all the world isn't coming home to say good night to me.

I go out on the big porch, which runs along two sides of the house, and pace around, sniffing the smell of dark earth and listening for the first peeper. "Don't let them stick tubes in you and suck out your life," I whisper fiercely. The world stays silent.

2

Monday at school everything is the same. Trixie Murphy and I go to the field next to her house after school and jump our imaginary horses over the makeshift jumps we set up. Ten laps around the field and we are melting.

"Come back tomorrow and we'll set those jumps up a notch," Trixie says. I always think of the Irish as having red hair and freckles, but Trixie has blue-black hair and pale skin. Her teeth are squared, like horse teeth.

"Can't. Tuesdays I play Giants and Pirates with Sylvia. Why don't you come, too?" Trixie will take some time thinking about it, but I know once she makes up her mind she never wavers.

All day, in the back of my mind, lurking behind decimals and in and out of state capitals, there has been a picture of what home will be like. No Gram on the wide front porch to ask how was my day. No Gram suggesting I might peel potatoes while she picks my mind for new facts and figures. She believes the mind rusts if you don't use it.

But when I get home there is no Gram anywhere. Just Mom, hobbling from sink to stove with Sue-Sue attached to one leg. "Unlatch her, Jan. Take her up and change her pants."

I drag a screaming Sue-Sue up to the bathroom and gingerly, with two fingers, strip off the wet panties. It's the first time in a year she's had an accident.

"You okay?"

Tears bubble through thick lashes. She shakes her head and hiccups a sob. I know exactly how she feels.

We slide into our usual seats on the high-backed kitchen benches. I am on the inside, next to Mom. David is opposite me and next to Dad. Sue-Sue sits at the end of the table in her high chair. Once David and I are in, we are locked in, until everyone is finished. While Mom doles out the food,

I begin my quest. "When can I go visit Gram?"

The serving spoon hesitates. "She's coming along, Jan, but I'm not sure it's wise for you to see her."

I don't give up. "She's going to think something's wrong if I don't come. Gram misses me."

Dad feeds Sue-Sue a spoonful and then feeds himself. "We need you to babysit, Jan."

"But I need Gram." I bend over my plate, but I feel their eyes meet and can almost feel their heads nodding.

"Tell you what, Jan." Mom is thinking her way through this. "If you stay tonight with the children, I'm sure your father will stay tomorrow night, and you can come with me."

The dinner is no longer tasteless. Tomorrow night. I'll wear my best dress. No, I'll wear the pink one. Gram's favorite color is pink.

Mom and Dad go out the door, and I am left with the urchins. I finally get them to bed and there seems no reason for me to stay up alone in the dark house. I slip into my bed and am comforted by Sue-Sue's soft breathing.

The next day Sylvia, Trixie, and I skip the mile from school to the Wyndhams' Tudor house. After cookies in the kitchen, doled out by Bessie, the cook, we run out under blossoming cherry trees to see the chicken coop in back. It was cleaned and is getting a coat of whitewash. We agree it will be a perfect clubhouse.

We sit under a cherry tree and name ourselves the Sunshine Club. Yellow is our color, and we're to do something nice for someone every day. Our meetings will be on Saturday mornings.

"Ronald kept chickens when he was in 4-H, but now he likes boats and cars better. The chickens used to fly out, and I ran around and chased them back."

Sylvia can outrun all of us. Since second grade she has always been picked first for races. I can just see her chasing chickens, her thick, reddish-gold braids flying straight back from her head.

"I'm glad Ronald gave up chickens," Trixie says. "I love the coop. It's so nice and clean and empty." Trixie's the oldest of six young Murphys, and there's not one empty space in her house.

Sylvia smiles, her eyes crinkling till they almost disappear. She stands up, and since she's slightly taller than the two of us, her shining head almost touches the cherry blossoms. "Race you to the garden. We can teach Trixie all about Giants and Pirates."

Her long legs churn, and Trixie and I are left to scramble behind her.

14

———

Mom and I do the dishes before we leave for the hospital, me wearing an apron over my pink dress. It seems as if Mom is going to wash the patterns off the plates, but finally we are finished. It is still light out when we get into the car, and a cool lake breeze blows my carefully combed hair as we drive to the hospital.

This is the first time I've been inside a hospital since I was born, but I walk bravely after Mom through the reception room and take the elevator to the fourth floor. In the hallway the floor tiles are white and the walls pale green. We stop at room 407, where a card on the wall says Mary Agnes Lowden. Gram has the bed nearest the door. A curtain hides the next bed. I can tell by the snoring that someone is there. Gram wears snakes of tubes that hang down from bags of liquid, and her long white hair is spread out on the pillow.

"Jan," she says. "Pink, pink, Jan."

There's no way I can put my arms around her, and I am afraid of jogging her hip, so I grab her hand and press it to my face.

"How do you feel, Gram?"

She wiggles her fingers and twists my hair. "Much, much better, now that you're here."

She looks straight into my eyes. "Ten days or

15

two weeks, at the most, and then I'll be home. It hurts a little, but I got up today. Taking all this with me." She waves at the tubes and bags. "Soon I'll be walking without them."

Why is it so hard to talk in the hospital? While I'm digging in my mind for things to say, she plays with my hair and runs a finger down my cheek. I tell her I miss her.

"I miss you, too. But I'll be back in the garden before the irises bloom."

I nod, and squinch my eyes so tears won't fall. Ten days is not so long. "We formed a Sunshine Club. Trixie, Sylvia, and I. We will meet in Sylvia's chicken coop. We're going to do something good for someone every day."

"What a splendid idea! You know what I want you to do for me?"

I shake my head.

"I want you to take care of the little ones and help your mother until I'm home. Will you do that?"

"And visit you again?" I venture.

"No, dear," she says gently. "I want you to see me walking in the garden. I want you to peel potatoes with me and teach me that trick with the nines tables. This is a terrible place for a child to visit."

16

I can see Gram is getting tired. I lean over and kiss her lightly. "I promise, Gram. I'll see you in ten days."

I wait for Mom in the hall while she whispers her good-night. We go home without saying a word.

The next night, while Mom and Dad are at the hospital, I make notebooks, covering cardboard with a yellow-flowered material and sewing in the pages. The books are for recording good deeds. Finally, the headlights of the car swing up the driveway, and Mom and Dad are home.

"How is she?" I yell the minute they come in the kitchen door.

Mom doesn't notice that I've mopped up spaghetti mess and washed the dishes. All she sees is David's road that he made out of cereal boxes. She sighs.

"Gram hates it there. Her stitches itch and her food is cold. Today she told a nurse to take her fat hands off her." Mom laughs in spite of her sadness.

I laugh, too, but underneath I am frightened. Gram is a lady who dresses with care, who always wears a hat and gloves when she leaves the house. A lady who smoothes ruffled feathers and speaks

nicely to everyone. Gram would never hurt someone's feelings by calling her fat.

"Fred, I think we have to talk." Mom's giving
me my clue to leave. I.wish I could drink coffee
and sit with them and decide things.

Dad sighs. Fred is the last name I would have
chosen for him. Of course, he's not Hercules, either.
He's almost six feet tall, and looks good in his
business suits. Weekdays he works in an advertising agency in the city. Weekends, he used to
play golf, but now he spends more and more time
mowing the lawn and fixing things around the
house. Lately he's been wrinkling his forehead
. and staring out the window. I think he's worried
about money.

They carry their cups to the kitchen table and
sit on the ends of the benches. No one else can
get in.

I push through the swinging kitchen door and
sit on the stairs, my feet on the throw rug that
threw Gram. I'm close enough to hear Mom's voice.

"This big, square, old house. So much room
and all in the wrong places."

Dad's voice rumbles out the door. "How about
the dining room? Put the table and chairs out in
the garage and move her bed in."

"The bathrooms are upstairs. The least little

18

thing makes me throw up. Can you imagine what carrying bedpans will do?"

I trace the Indian pattern on the rug with my toe. Mom does gag in the morning. She's been giving us cold cereal instead of hot oatmeal, the way she did before Sue-Sue was born. Mom is going to have another baby.

"Want some more hot coffee?" I hear Dad step to the stove. "You know she won't be able to manage stairs at all. If she goes upstairs she'll be a prisoner, and I won't have you running up and down stairs all day."

Someone clinks a spoon against a cup. I strain my ears, wishing the little sounds would stop. I have to hear the words.

"But she's my grandmother. What else can we do? She has to come here."

"When she's back on her feet, of course she will come home. But, for now, I think the best place for her is Dugan's Rest Home."

Suddenly I don't want to hear any more. Tiptoeing up the broad, shiny steps, I escape the discussion that will go on until the pot of coffee is empty. I am afraid of what the ending will be. I am afraid that Gram will not come home.

Up the dark stairs, into the lighted hall. David's room is on the left, and then the room where Sue-

Sue and I sleep. The hall ends at the bathroom, which has doors at either side. One bathroom door leads to my room, the other to Mom and Dad's. Their room is huge, stretching from the front of the house to the back. Sue-Sue's old crib still stands in the back of their room, waiting now for the new baby. The stairs to Gram's place are directly over the other stairs. All the rooms are big, but there are too few of them.

I slip into my white and yellow room and turn on the night-light, a little bulb behind a plastic shield. Sue-Sue, in her own twin bed, snorts and moves her thumb more securely into her mouth.

I can't read in bed or I'd wake her. I don't dare cry, because the huge wail inside me would set Sue-Sue to screaming. I force my feet into pajama legs instead of letting them kick through the walls the way they want to.

Rubbing the satin binding of the blanket against my cheek, I pretend it is my long-lost blankie, discarded years ago when I grew up. I let the rumble and honk of a diesel freight do my crying for me, and I escape into sleep.

The Sunshine Club meets officially for the first time on Saturday morning. Sun shines in the polished windows and hits the whitewashed walls of the chicken coop with such force that I slit my eyes. The brightness hits the darkness inside me. At breakfast Mom made the announcement that Gram will be going to Dugan's.

Now that we're having our first meeting, no one knows what to say. I fumble in my pocket. "Here are the books I made for us." Slim pencils are tucked in the bindings, courtesy of Phipp's Insurance Co.

"Thanks." Trixie opens hers with a flourish. "I wiped the blackboards for Mrs. Primrose yesterday."

"That's hardly a good deed," Sylvia scoffs. "She made you do it because you talked in class."

"Good deeds are hard to find. What little old ladies want to be helped across Lake Street, for gosh sakes?"

I picture Gram briskly crossing Lake Street, and a little sound leaks out. Both pairs of eyes turn to me. "Sorry. Gram's not coming home when she gets out of the hospital. She's going to Dugan's Rest Home."

"Oh, God," Sylvia says, and it's more a prayer than a swear. We sit in the sunlight and finger our books.

A power saw whines in the garage, telling us where Sylvia's brother, Ronald, is. He's building a boat that looks too big to get out the door.

Trixie snaps her book shut. "We don't have to

help little old ladies cross the street. We can do our good deeds at Dugan's."

I look at Trixie in surprise. "Aren't we too young?" I ask.

"Kitty Dugan is in our class, and she helps her parents in the Home. We just have to show the Dugans how mature we are."

Sylvia shakes her head. "Last week you had to empty the wastebaskets because you and Betty had a hair-pulling fight. Just how mature is that?"

"A person can change, you know."

I stand up and shake the dirt off my jeans. "Let's check with Kitty on Monday and tell her about our club and the good deeds. Gram's not going to be moved for another two weeks. If we work at Dugan's before she gets there it won't seem like we've gone just to help Gram."

"It may help us get a nursing badge in Girl Scouts." Sylvia is gung ho about Scouts because her mother is troop leader.

We tuck our books into pockets and gallop up to the garage.

"Jan, how's your grandmother?" Ronald walks around the shell of his boat.

We tell him about her move to Dugan's, and he looks worried. "She's an elegant lady. I hate to see her go there. But I know how tough it is to take care of someone in a wheelchair. Tell you what I can do. I'll swing her by your house on the way to Dugan's. That way you can talk to her."

If Ronald thinks of Gram as an elegant lady, he's no longer an enemy of mine. "Thank you," I say shyly. I mean it with all my heart.

Ronald goes back to his saw and we gallop to Trixie's field, where we jump the course until lunchtime.

The house is gloomier than usual, even with the sun shining. Homesickness seeps through me in my own home. Without Gram's lap there seems no place where I can sit for more than a minute or two. I find myself following Mom around the kitchen like a little chick follows the hen.

"When will they let her out of the hospital?"

"Ronald and his friend will pick her up in the ambulance and drive her to Dugan's, Saturday after next."

"Can I visit her at Dugan's?"

"I don't know, but I'll ask." Mom never asks, but she makes life easier for herself by saying she will. It doesn't matter. I know the Sunshine Club will be working in Dugan's before Gram gets there.

3

Saturday morning I stand at the closet, picking over my clothes. The shirts and pants are faded and soggy from going through the wash for a whole year. Nothing is ironed. We need more than a maid, we need a laundress. I need some new clothes.

Sue-Sue jumps on the bed and yells to get dressed. I pick out a lemon-colored shirt, and pants that have no known color at all.

"Up, up. Dress, dress." Like her name, every-thing comes in twos.

"No, no." I am certain I have ruined her day.

It is hard to be nice to everyone, and I am saving my niceness for Dugan's.

We meet at the corner. Trixie is all in blue, and Sylvia wears pink. We look like ice-cream cones, though I'm not sure if my pants are butter pecan or mocha.

"Kitty wants us to use the kitchen door," Trixie says importantly.

Sylvia looks worried. In her house Bessie rules the kitchen, and the only thing Sylvia knows how to do in a kitchen is eat.

Kitty meets us at the kitchen door and hands us our aprons. They are pink-checked with bibs, and look silly over our pants, but we put them on anyway.

Kitty walks in front of us, leading us through the hall and into the front sunroom. I stop to catch my breath. Gram is old, I suppose, but we are so close I just never pay attention. But these people are *old*, old. Maybe people shut the old here so they can't be reminded that this is what happens if you live long enough.

"Walk around and talk to them," Kitty directs us. "They love having someone to talk to. If anyone needs something real bad, ring that bell over there. A nurse will help you."

I want to run home. I'm too young for this. I'm

sure Mom and Dad would not want me to see old, old men and women. I turn toward the door, remembering that Mom doesn't know where I am.

"Don't go." A long, thin hand plucks at my apron. I look upward from the hand to the face and see two blue eyes under a thatch of white brows.

"I'm Carl," the man says. "Where's your name tag?"

"Kitty's having them made up. We're new here. I'm Jan."

The man is in a wheelchair and is covered by a plaid blanket. Trailing by a long tube, a plastic bag of yellow liquid hangs near the wheel of his chair. I press my fingers to my mouth to keep from throwing up over his blanket. Carl pretends not to notice.

"You got anyone in this horrible place?" he whispers. "A man, I hope. Too many old women here already."

I shake my head. "Not yet. Gram will be. My great-grandmother."

"Pull up a chair and talk to me."

I find a chair with a cane seat and drag it next to him. I can't smell anything from that plastic bag and my stomach relaxes.

"A lot of these people are crazy. I'm not. Is your great-grandmother crazy?"

"She wasn't the last time I saw her."

26

Carl leans toward me, so close I wonder if he's hard of hearing.

"If she isn't when she gets here, she soon will be," he whispers confidentially. "That's why I wanted to talk to you. You look sane."

"Oh, I am," I assure him. All of a sudden I feel better. He's nice.

"Well, keep it that way. We need some sane people around here. I ran my own business until a month ago. Then I had an operation and I'm staying here until I'm unhooked from all this." He waves at the bag. I would have hidden it if it were my bag, but it doesn't bother him.

I nod and dare a peek around the room to see how the other club members are getting on. Trixie is trying to straighten pillows behind a lady. Sylvia is combing a woman's hair. Her mother would die if she saw that.

Carl extends his thin legs to show me his muscles. "Jogged every day up to the operation. I'll be out of here in no time. Just you wait and see."

We chat, but in the back of my mind I think he's maybe a little crazy. No one gets out of Dugan's. Not walking, they don't. They are carried out in Dugan's hearse to Dugan's Funeral Home. Carl doesn't seem to know this.

"First thing I'm going to get me is a good cup of coffee. Dishwater is what they serve here."

I resolve to learn how to make a good cup of coffee, the kind Mom and Dad sit up half the night sipping. Strong black coffee would put Carl on his feet again.

When we walk out into the warm sunlight it is like coming out of a matinee at Loew's. The sun slaps our faces and pains our eyes. Our aprons are hanging back in the pantry, ready for next Saturday.

Sylvia pulls out her book. "This is a good deed if I ever heard of one." She sucks the end of her pencil, so it hardly makes a mark on the first blank page.

"Kind of fun, too," Trixie adds. "That Marie is funny. Kept telling me how she almost got married."

I tell them about Carl and how his son is going to pick him up. Thinking about Carl getting out of Dugan's gives me hope that Gram will get out, too. Gram will, I promise myself.

At the corner of Lake Street and Main we run in different directions. Trixie heads for her little house, which is so different from the big, old houses in the center of town. It's called a ranch, but does not look like the ranches in western movies. Mom and Dad make it sound shameful, living in a "ranch," but if we lived in one, Gram could come home and wheel herself to the bathroom.

Sylvia gallops to her big, old house with diamond-shaped panes in the windows, and I head up the hill to our square, stucco house with its empty third floor. Saturday is tomato-soup day, with the soup made with water instead of milk. Ugh. David leans down and snuffles in his soup like an elephant. Sue-Sue fills her bowl with crumbled crackers and picks up the soup in her fingers.

The last thing I did at Dugan's was feed a lady who couldn't use her hands. She opened and closed her mouth, but I was not a good judge about how much she could take in one bite, and half the food dribbled off her chin.

Eating with David and Sue-Sue isn't all that different. I drink the lukewarm soup straight from the bowl and try not to think about the old or the young.

Mom runs up and down the cellar steps with dirty wash, clean wash, stopping here to swipe Sue-Sue's chin, and there to soak the saucepan. Between her comings and goings, without looking at me, since I don't have tomato soup on my chin, she reminds me to be home early for supper so I can babysit while they go to the hospital.

4

The Sunshine Club gathers at Trixie's, and we decide it's too warm for steeplechase. Trixie's house and field are on the very edge of town.

"Let's explore," I say bravely. The outside edges of town fill me with terror. But three can dare to face the unknown.

"If we cross your field, then where?" Little bubbles froth at the corners of Sylvia's mouth when she gets excited.

Trixie leans against a jump. "Behind the field is one more road. The one the Hammers and the Carpenters live on. After that, I think, is the river."

Since I was a baby I have laughed at the idea

of the Hammers and Carpenters living next door to one another. I wheel Tony, my imaginary horse, and head across the field.

We lose ourselves in the running. Feet pound out our troubles into the grass and dirt. Each jar of heel and knee is one for Gram. The spring wind rushes through me, filling the empty spaces.

We cross the last road and plunge down a dark and overgrown path. Our horses pull up and carefully pick their way along the ruts.

"Forget the horses—let's follow the yellow brick road," Sylvia says.

Immediately the horses melt away. We link arms and sing "We're Off to See the Wizard," and with a hop and a skip we're mashing last year's leaves and ducking branches that reach out to grab us. The road twists and winds, slanting slightly downward. We are heading for the river. Even on a sunny day there is a smell of dankness.

Suddenly, on the right, a second small lane appears. We stop, as if waiting for the scarecrow to point the way.

"Try it," I say bravely, though I wouldn't dare if I were alone. "Wish we had a ball of string to follow back."

"Or bread crumbs," Sylvia says, laughing nervously.

It is a powerful shock, after the mention of

bread crumbs, to come upon a small house in a sunny clearing. Last year's yellow grass tickles the brick foundation. The front door is unpainted wood, set slightly aslant, and the black-shingled roof has a sway like an old horse, but otherwise it looks sturdy.

I feel an urge to nibble at its corners. We link damp hands, as if we are all one person.

Sylvia breathes out and manages a sound. "Well?"

"You think?" Trixie asks.

We are all one brain. Evil can't hurt us. Good deeds are written in the books in our pockets. No boogeyman would dare attack members of the Sunshine Club.

Down the leaf-coated path to the front door, which is level with the ground, three as one we push the door open and squeeze through together. The house smells of dead leaves and dark earth. Nothing scurries.

The door opens into a kitchen. A white-enameled sink with blue linoleum on the drain-board, a small white gas stove, and an old refrigerator with a circular motor on top all line the walls. In the center of the room is a rec-tangular table with a white-enameled top sur-rounded by four unmatched chairs painted white.

Between the stove and the refrigerator there is

a door that leads us into the parlor. The room has two windows in front and a window and door in the back.

The door opens onto a screened porch that stretches across the back of the house. There is no exit to let one down to the shed or out to the backyard sloping to the woods.

Cushionless wicker chairs and couch in the living room are thick with many coats of paint, the latest coat being a dark and dirty brown. There are two little twig tables, and one large kerosene lantern. Two smaller kerosene lamps are on the stone mantel of the fireplace.

There are two small bedrooms off the parlor, each with a closet and with two windows that look out to the surrounding oaks and maples. The metal camp beds have thin mattresses covered by dusty sheets.

"Where's the bathroom?" I ask.

Sylvia opens a door on the other side of the fireplace and there, behind the kitchen, is a rusty tub, and a toilet and basin.

"Wonder how long the house has been empty." Trixie's voice is hushed, as if the former owners were hiding in a closet.

I pick up a newspaper near the fireplace. It is dated ten years ago. "I think we're safe. No one's been here for a long time."

We prowl around the vacant rooms. There are some mouse droppings, but the ceilings have no water stains and the floors seem solid. "I wonder how you find out who owns it?"

Sylvia closes the porch door. "No problem. Dad's a lawyer. He has a tax map of the town and a book with the names of all the owners."

Trixie turns around in delight. "I love it. I'd like to live here. Could our club meet here?"

"I still want to have meetings in my coop."

I agree with Sylvia. This is too special to be a clubhouse. We'll have to find out about it first and find a use for it later.

When we leave we slam the door so the wind won't blow it open. We scurry, racing to the main path, hurrying through the trees, back to the road of the Hammers and the Carpenters, across the field, and scatter our separate ways.

"See you," I yell as I do my Olympic sprint toward home. Sylvia matches me stride for stride as she heads for her mansion. Trixie waves and ducks into her ranch house, where younger Murphys are tucked into closets or somewhere. I'm home in time to babysit.

5

The house gets grungier each day. Mom goes to the hospital in the afternoon and again in the evening with Dad. She leaves the minute I come home from school—and no dawdling on the way— and I am stuck with the monsters and no chance to do anything else. I see Trixie and Sylvia only in school and on our walks to and from.

Books lie unread on my desk. Cobwebs hang down from the ceilings and knit themselves into corners. Afternoons I swing with the urchins to keep Sue-Sue out of the weedy gardens and David away from the garage filled with deadly sprays. Our lives are falling apart.

On Wednesday night Mom cries right in front of us in the kitchen, not minding if we watch her face turn red and blotchy. I busy myself with those darn spaghetti dishes, but that doesn't keep me from hearing her.

"She's not my grandmother anymore," Mom says into her coffee cup. "She's some strange little old lady who refuses, absolutely refuses, to get up and walk."

My heart sinks to the bottom of the greasy water. Gram is not the same? Well, neither am I. I crack a cup.

"She hated her lunch today and sent it flying to the floor. My grandmother, throwing food around like a baby."

Baby. I glance at Mom and see a swelling beneath her wrinkled skirt.

"You've done the best you can," Dad comforts Mom. Now, if Dad could stay home and help, then Gram could come home. I know money is important, but so is keeping a family together.

Saturday creeps closer. I am torn. Do I want Saturday to hurry up or do I want to hold off Gram's trip to Dugan's? Friday I am given a dictionary page to copy—"To keep my mind from wandering." Mrs. Primrose knows there is something wrong.

Saturday morning I wake so early I can't tell what kind of a day it will be. I hope it's a blue day for Gram's sake. A day when she can look out the ambulance window and see the sky and some fluffy clouds. This may be her last ride, I think. My throat hurts, and I don't even have a cold.

I do a forbidden thing, at least I guess it's forbidden since it's never even been thought of. I go up the stairs to the third floor and run hot water into Gram's tub. If I'm going to break the law, I might as well go all the way. I pour some of Gram's bath oil into the water and take a fluffy pink towel out of the linen closet.

When the water is just right, I go into Gram's sitting room and pick out my favorite *National Geographic*, the one with the pride of lions on the cover, and carry it into the bathroom. I lock the door, slip into the water, and lie back and read. It's so lovely, it's sinful.

It would make Gram so happy, just lying here in the warm water on a Saturday morning, looking up at her white ceiling, or counting how many black and white tiles make a square on the cold, clean floor. I sink until the water tickles my earlobes, and the magazine slips down so the bottoms of the pages glue together in a sticky, colorful mess.

There is no such thing as a perfect heaven. Now

37

I'll never get those pages unstuck and I won't be able to read about the lioness teaching her cubs to hunt. I pull the rubber stopper out and watch the water swirl away. Clouds scud past the window and I know Gram will see nothing but gray today. I dress quickly, leaving wet footprints on the floor and a faint gray line around the tub. The way Mom isn't doing anything these days it will be months before she comes in to clean it. I don't care.

I dump the lions into the wastebasket, hang the towel on a rack, and tiptoe down to the worst day of Gram's life, and the worst, worst day of mine.

Mom is already feeding the urchins and hasn't missed me at all. "Ronald says he'll drive up this street on the way to Dugan's. We leave the hospital at nine-thirty. I want you three to be out in front so you can see her."

Mom talks as if we're all adults, when actually I am the only one who knows what's going on. "Are you sure, certain, positive, she can't come home? I'll take her food up to her and take care of her. I'll even give up going to school. I already know as much as Ronald and could probably get into Harvard right now."

"Nonsense. They'll take wonderful care of Gram at Dugan's. When she can walk again, she'll come home."

I swallow. That sore throat feels sorer and there's a lump growing there. If it's a tumor, maybe I can stay at Dugan's, too. Swallowing hard keeps me from telling Mom what everyone else knows. No one comes home from Dugan's.

I wash Sue-Sue's cereal mouth so hard that a red circle forms around her lips and she sniffles a bit. A car motor roars in the driveway and Mom drives off.

David wears his white sailor suit and sailor hat. I'm sure Mom didn't notice, because these are his summer dress-up clothes. Sue-Sue looks all right in wrinkled cotton, but she smells of urine. I, on the other hand, walk surrounded by waves of lavender.

We march through the front hall, out the heavy oak door, across the concrete porch, down the steps, and then slowly around the garden. I have no watch and there isn't any sun to give me an idea of the time. It's at least an hour before they leave the hospital and another twenty minutes for the ambulance to detour past our house.

I pick lilies of the valley. The stems squeak when I slip them out of the green leaves, and they dangle moistly from my fist. David pulls up a tulip in the same way before I can stop him. The petals are a rich, velvety black and suit this gray day.

We march once around the garden examining

the greening weeds. I pluck the yellow fists of dead daffodils, and Sue-Sue tries to do the same but succeeds only in scattering a few dried petals on the grass. The clock in the front hall could tell me the time, but if I dare enter the house the ambulance will surely speed by.

Whenever I think of spring, which is usually when purple shadows grow longer on the snow, I remember warm, sunny days. Today is neither warm nor sunny. A chill wind blows and then a cold drop lands in the middle of my forehead. One hits Sue-Sue's button nose, and she stands in shocked silence a moment before she cries, "Mommy, Mommy."

"It's okay," I whisper. But it isn't okay. I scoop her plump body up in my arms and try to pretend I don't notice she's wet. She was almost all trained, but now it seems she's back on square one. I set her down on the porch where only an occasional raindrop blows in on the wind.

David is still out there somewhere in the garden. If there is a puddle he will find it and step in it. I sink to the steps like a flat tire. Mom and Dad are right. Little children shouldn't worry their heads about things. Childhood is a happy time. The chill grayness seeps into my head and aches behind my eyes.

Then we hear it. Far away, like a lonely, dying

animal, it wheezes and moans. The wind snatches the engine sounds, then tosses them back again.

I grab Sue-Sue by a chubby hand and fly her down the steps too fast for her toes to touch. She sinks to her knees on the driveway and I jerk her up like a kite.

David runs down the driveway, and Sue-Sue and I follow, the roar of the engine drowning the crunch of feet on gravel. David waves his black tulip like a flag at a parade and the stem breaks. The tulip hangs upside down.

The ambulance slowly climbs our hill and stops directly between the two pillars that guard our entrance. Facing out the back of the ambulance there's a little old lady half sitting in a cranked-up bed. She lifts a thin arm that's nothing but strings covered with skin and then lets her fingers fall. I wave the lilies of the valley at this person whose white hair is strewed every which way on the pillow, but I can't hand the flowers over because the windows are closed tight.

Mom sits next to the stranger. She smiles a set-toothed smile that's a black look in disguise. It says, "You're wonderful children, and you made it to the end of the driveway on time, but why is David all muddy and couldn't you have kept Sue-Sue from looking like a bundle of wash?" The smile, of course, is directed at me.

The back door of the ambulance swings open and Frank grabs my arm and hoists me inside. I still have hold of Sue-Sue's hand, so she flies in, too. David climbs in by himself, smudging the front of his sailor suit.

"Gram?" I ask. I know it's Mom sitting beside her, so it must be Gram. "Gram?" I say again.

The little old lady looks at me, her eyes cloudy and wild. "Clara," she whispers, then turns to stare out the window.

"It's me. Jan." I put the limp lilies of the valley into her pale claw, but the fingers do not close and the flowers spray to the ambulance floor. "Your Jan."

Frank takes me by the shoulders and leads me out. "She's a little mixed up today. Wait'll she has her rest." He lowers David and Sue-Sue and gives David a quick Navy salute before he swings the door shut.

Ronald revs the engine and the ambulance paws the ground, then leaps forward and disappears over the hill. I wonder who that old lady was. I know it was Gram.

Rain pours down. The parade is over. David throws his tulip on the driveway and grinds it, a black ink spot, into the gravel. Sue-Sue cries with her mouth open and more water pours down her chin than comes out of the sky.

I herd the urchins back up the porch steps and into the dismal hall. It takes what seems like an hour to clothe them in soft, unmatched things, the last dry clothes in a sodden world. Finally I change my own clothes and notice that the scent of lavender is washed away. Only the ache behind my eyes and the lump in my throat are still there.

6

Mom comes home in time to make Saturday's tomato soup as if it's any old Saturday, only she makes it with milk instead of water and that means it's a celebration.

"How's Gram?"

"Poor dear, she hardly knows what's happening. She's so afraid someone will touch her hip, she just cries, 'Don't touch me, don't touch me.' " Mom stirs the soup, kisses Sue-Sue on the lips, and ruffles David's towhead. At least she talks to me.

"Sue-Sue wet her pants again." Is there one nice bone in my body? I hate tattletales.

"My little dumpling. Of course you did. Mommy's been away too much. But now I'm home again."

Sue-Sue dips her fingers in her soup and licks each fingertip.

"No, no, darling, use your spoon. Watch David. See how nicely he eats?"

I like to plop the soup back in the bowl and then pick out the bubbles, but today I do just what I did last Saturday. I tip the bowl and drink it down, almost before I taste it.

"Jan," Mom says, like I betrayed her.

No wonder I don't have wings. I feel mean and nasty. "Gram taught me my table manners. Now she's not here. Can I go?"

I jump up without waiting for an answer. I have had it up to here with doing those dishes. I wish I'd broken them all, not just that one cup.

"Where are you going?" Mom remembers she is still my mother.

"Out." I want to stick my tongue out at the soup-flecked urchins who sit and eat like this is any ordinary day. But I don't.

"Your friends were at the nursing home this morning. They were wearing the cutest little aprons. You ought to do something nice like that. Imagine little girls thinking of those unfortunate people."

I slam the door before the bubble inside grows so big it chokes me. Mom thinks it's cute. She doesn't mind. All week I've been worried sick about her finding out and now she's telling me I ought to be as thoughtful as my "little friends."

I put myself through my paces all the way to Dugan's Rest Home. Walk, trot, canter, gallop. Walk, trot, canter, gallop. Magnificent legs stretch out, and a well-muscled rump catches the rain. My raincoat is still hanging behind the cellar door back home, but that's all right. Horses don't wear raincoats.

Sixty-eight combinations of paces and I slip into the kitchen and take down my apron with last week's food in hard, dry patches down the front.

Kitty grabs my arm and we fly down the corridor like two aproned Mary Poppinses.

Room 106. The numbers are in raised copper on the door. On the wall there are two places for names. One says Marie Morgan. The other says Mary Agnes Lowden. Poor Gram, having to live fourscore years with a name like Mary Agnes. But if anyone can overcome, she can.

My breath leaves my body. She's in there. I can see a sheet rounded over a pair of feet. Good. Gram still has her legs. There is the clink of spoon to plate and the sound of someone pleading.

"There, there, Mrs. Lowden. No sense not eating. You had a long trip this morning. Open your mouth. That's a good girl."

It sounds like Mom coaxing Sue-Sue to eat. "Open the tunnel, here comes the train."

Kitty squeezes my arm gently and leaves. Marie Morgan's bed is empty and smoothly made. Her bedside table has a pitcher of stale water full of bubbles.

I enter, ready to do battle. Imagine that woman talking to Gram as if she were a baby. Elegant Gram, who once served dinner to an opera star. Gram, who taught me how to multiply in my head, and how to write a proper thank-you note.

"Kitty asked me to feed her," I say.

The nurse sniffs. Then she smiles a wide and toothy smile with a broad display of pink gums. She is not quite the enemy I was ready to battle with.

"Good. Maybe you can get some food into her, instead of on the tray." She squeezes past me. There isn't much room. Extra space is taken up by wheelchairs and guest chairs. I wait until her white shoes with thick, pink soles glide into the hall.

"Gram, Gram," I croon. I kiss her cheek, soft as David's tulip. A sour, unwashed smell reminds me of soggy Sue-Sue but doesn't turn my lips away.

"Watch the hip, watch the hip." It is no more than a little squeak. Maybe her throat is closed up like mine.

"Gram, do you know who I am?"

The blue eyes look at me slyly. "Clara?" she whispers with a hint of a smile.

"No, Mom is Clara. I'm me. Jan."

Her thin hands touch my hair, then circle my neck. I bend and press against her and we breathe together in sobby breaths. Through her rough hospital gown I feel her heart thudding against me. It is like rubbing a cat and feeling the rumbling starting up inside. My Gram isn't dead yet.

Sometime later I fumble for a box of tissues and we both give a blow and a dab at the eyes. Gram's blow is not as strong as my honk, but she knows what she's doing.

"Look at you. You're all wet. Did I do that?"

I laugh. "Some. But most of it is rain. I forgot my raincoat."

Gram's little voice sings, " 'Button up your overcoat when the wind is free.' "

I answer, " 'Take good care of yourself, you belong to me.' "

It's been a long time since I've smiled, but I find it very easy. Gram smiles at me. Then her eyes close and her breathing quiets to nothing.

I know she's dead. I panic and reach for the

call button, which has been placed out of Gram's reach. The nurse appears at the door.

"Is she . . ." I can't say the word out loud.

The woman bounces in on rubber soles, puts her ear to Gram's chest, then snorts. "What'd you do? Give her a sleeping pill? She's sleeping like a baby."

I watch the nurse's starched white rear swish out the door and then I settle into the visitor's chair and focus on the thin chest moving almost invisibly up and down. Gram's sleeping. I curl up and, no matter how I fight, my eyes close, too.

7

Mom is happy that I'm wearing the cute, cute apron, which I bring home to wash. She is happy that I see her grandmother. Mom is redirecting her life. She carries Sue-Sue around in her arms, takes David for long walks, washes hair, clothes, and windowsills, and caresses her stomach like some broody hen spreading her wings over the eggs. She touches everything and everybody but me. I guess I'm too big or too bony to be hugged.

Since no one notices me, it is very easy to slide into a life of crime. I pick one day a week to skip school. Always a different day, and usually one when we have gym or art or music so I won't fall too far behind. I practice Mom's signature and copy the slant of her handwriting. From the medical book she keeps in her bedroom I find a sickness. Asthma. It often flares up in the spring and there are no red spots or swellings to show you have it. Sitting on the floor, under the night-light, I write, "Dear Mrs. Primrose, Please excuse Jan's absence. She had another attack of asthma. Sincerely, Clara Robinson." Now I can see Gram three days a week instead of just Saturdays and Sundays.

Gram is not dumb, though she fools Mom and Dad and has most of Dugan's thinking she's ready for the loony bin. Her voice is strong when she talks to me, but when a nurse asks her a question she answers in a tiny little voice as if it's too much to ask of her aging body to open her mouth and speak.

It's the same with the physical therapy. They try to make her walk in the therapy room with mirrors on every wall. I think I know why she won't walk. She has been wearing this little Johnny robe that doesn't cover her bottom, and she can see herself in all the mirrors. Gram is too much a lady to show her withered bottom to anyone.

While I wait for Gram to be wheeled back from therapy, I check the closet. Mom's blue suitcase

51

ATHENS REGIONAL LIBRARY
ATHENS, GEORGIA

289469

is there. I drag it out and unpack. There are bed jackets and robes and little knit shoes like ballet slippers. Down in the bottom are some loose blouses and jumpers. I hang everything in the closet except for a pink blouse and a rose-colored jumper, and the ballet slippers.

The nurse reddens when she wheels Gram in. "Your mother brought those in the ambulance. I've just been too busy to unpack them."

Now that Gram is dressed and ready, I try to make up for all the exercise she's missed. First I get rid of Marie Morgan.

"There's this wonderful, handsome man down in the front hall," I tell Marie. She falls for it, and runs down to see if it's the man who asked her to marry him. Once the door is closed, Gram and I are alone.

"Lean on me, Gram." There is the moment of great suspense when she dangles her skinny legs off the bed and finally settles her feet firmly on the floor. It never scares me when I'm with her, but there are nights back home when I wake in a cold sweat. When her hands are firmly on the walker, I count and she moves. Clump, step, step. Rest. Clump, step, step. Past the window, down by the feet of the beds, touch the doorknob for good luck, then back to bed again before the nurse enters.

Gram is getting stronger, but I'm the only one who knows it. To the nursing staff she is the perfect picture of an old woman who has given up. Even dressed in her prettiest outfit, Gram acts like a kid in dancing school who refuses to dance. The nurse in therapy has to tell each of Gram's legs to move. Left by herself, Gram would go nowhere. She walks only when we're alone in the room. She eats only when I'm there, and then she tells the nurse that I ate her food. That's why I have to skip school. To keep her alive.

There are only two weeks left of school. I can't wait to spend all my days with Gram. Mrs. Primrose is very nice to me because I've been sick so often.

We're eating our usual Wednesday night spaghetti when Mom speaks up.

"I'm going to visit tomorrow. I think I'm ready to face my grandmother and see whether she's ready to come home."

This is such a shock I have to lay my fork down so I won't spray the clean kitchen with pasta.

David claps his hands. "Gram is coming home."

I feel like clapping, too. Once Mom sees how strong Gram is, there won't be any question about it. Gram might even be home for my birthday. I keep my eyes on my spaghetti to hide my excitement.

"Don't get your hopes up yet," Mom says. "I'll have to see for myself."

I race home after school the next day, completely forgetting my homework, the test in science that I got a C on, and all the other botched-up work in my desk. Could Gram be coming home? I could go back to playing Giants and Pirates with Sylvia and jumping Tony over Trixie's jumps.

The car is in the driveway. The old screened door bangs behind me, and my bubbled, "Hi, Mom," dies as it is said. The kitchen is empty. Through the swinging door, so are the hall, the dark, crouching dining room, and the living room waiting for someone to live in it. She must be upstairs, cleaning Gram's tub. I bound the gleaming steps, two at a time. "Mom?"

"Jan. In here." Her muffled voice comes from David's room.

I hardly ever go into his room but today it looks even more unfamiliar. Mom has pillows hanging out the window and she's draping a sheet over the mattress. One corner of the sheet is crumpled, and when she smooths it out there are large damp teary spots.

"What is it?" I want to leap across the room, pull the sheet from her hands and force whatever

54

is terrible out of her. Instead I stand at the doorway of this alien room and watch my mother fall apart.

"I want you to go next door and pick up the children. I should have, but I got busy."

I see how busy she is. She's changing David's bed. When is that important to a six-year-old? "But Gram? Did you see her walk? Isn't she so much stronger?" I wait for an answer. "Is she coming home?"

"That little old woman?" Mom pulls the sheet toward her and covers her face. "Did you know they cut her hair?"

"I know, I know. I don't know why you're crying."

"She's a sick, weak, little old lady. They tried propping her up with pillows, but she couldn't sit up. When they brought her tray, her hand shook so, she couldn't get the food to her mouth. I had to feed her."

Gram! She is playing games with Mom. I don't know why, because getting out of Dugan's depends on showing Mom how much she can do.

"You told me she was getting better."

"She is, Mom, she is. Just get her home and see how much better she is." I try not to plead. Begging never gets me anywhere.

The sheet is spread once again with an efficient snap of the wrists. "Well"—there is that decided tone I know too well—"she's not ready yet. We'll give it more time."

I am invisible to Mom. She tucks the sheets in and draws on the pillowcases. I go next door to get David and Sue-Sue, and to them I seem the same as always. But I'm not. Gram is not coming home.

The last Saturday before vacation I carry my clean apron and slap one foot after another on the hot sidewalk. I am so filled with anger, there's no room for delight at seeing Gram or the usual heart leap at having only one more week of school.

I approach Room 106 uncertainly. Should I stomp in and yell, "Why?" or should I tiptoe in, full of pity, because Mary Agnes Lowden seems to have had a relapse?

Marie is just back from the hairdresser and wears a fairy-tale cloud of blue hair on her pink scalp. She sits in a chair and looks at herself in a hand mirror.

Gram's bed seems to be empty and unmade, the sheet and blankets in a mound in the middle. I walk over and lean against the bed and wonder if she is in therapy or down in the crafts room making something out of paper plates. The mound of blankets moves.

I bend down. "Gram?" I whisper. I pull the

blankets down a little and find a few strands of white hair. Ever so gently I uncover Gram, her Johnny robe every which way, her legs curled up like one of those favors you blow at a birthday party, the kind that shoots out and then curls back up.

"Gram?"

Blue eyes open and a translucent pearl rolls to her nose. "Clara?" Her little-old-lady voice is back.

"Jan."

"I'm sorry."

"You should be." I see shock in her blue eyes. "Why did you play helpless with Mom?"

"Afraid," she says faintly.

I can't imagine what she has to be afraid of. Growing old? She's already done that. Dying? That I can understand. I'm afraid of that, too. But Mom was her only chance of life outside of Dugan's.

"Afraid of Clara's eyes. They told me not to come home. They said don't make me take care of you."

I nod. Gram is absolutely right. She can see what I see. Mom wants to hug Sue-Sue and take care of David and clean the house. She doesn't want to be responsible for Gram anymore. Gram would be less trouble if she died right here.

Gram's lips are moving and I bend over to hear

her. "This is a living death, child. Help me end it. Daffodil bulbs are poisonous. Dig one up and I'll mix it in my tea."

This is so sad I burst out laughing, loud enough to make Marie put down her mirror. Whenever something is really sad, I laugh. "Tomorrow, Gram, I promise."

Tears are still running off her nose, but now she is laughing, too. "I do hope daffodil bulbs are not bitter," she whispers.

8

The last day of school is very hot and no one wants to hug Mrs. Primrose, who has a large, wet circle under each arm. We hug her anyway for being so nice to us, and then burst out the door when the noon bell shrills.

Later, as our first official vacation expedition, the Sunshine Club walks down the dirt road, cool now under summer's leaves. The secret house looks the same as it did in early spring.

"I had Dad look it up," Sylvia informs us as we walk into the kitchen. "Some New York man bought it and pays the taxes, but he never comes here."

I turn on the tap and get a burp of air. There

is no water, which means no toilet. In my mind that makes the house unlivable.

In the living room we sit on the wooden floor and I search for words in the jumble of thoughts in my head.

"This idea I have," I begin slowly, "comes to me when I'm in this house. I know it won't work, but I think today I'll pretend that it can work, even though it's impossible."

I stretch out my legs and lean back on my hands. Sylvia does the same, touching her sneakers to mine. Her freckles stand out on her pale face and cocoons of bubbles fizz at the corners of her mouth. "We all told Ronald it was impossible for a high-school boy to build a boat in the garage. Now it's just about finished."

Trixie unfolds her legs and her sneakers reach out to touch ours. "If you want something badly enough, you can get it. All my life I've wanted friends, and now look." She pushes her sneakers tight against mine and Sylvia's. We form a circle with our feet and now our fingers touch.

"If I could, I would bring Gram here. We could live in the same house together."

No one laughs at my outrageous idea.

Trixie says thoughtfully, "First let's talk about what we do have. Then we can talk about the things we can do ourselves. For one thing, there's space. And the house is all on one floor. And the doors look wide enough for a wheelchair."

Sylvia's feet twitch. "That New York man will probably never come here, so the house is as private as it can be."

They're so matter-of-fact that I worry even more. "But what if we hurt her or make her worse?"

Trixie pulls her feet back and stands up. "Jan Robinson, you'd never hurt your grandmother. Stop asking 'what if' and work on your idea."

We pull out our good-deed books and start writing down the things we need.

The first full day of vacation is a Saturday, which makes it seem more like any ordinary day. The early-rising sun lightly touches my face and soon I am dressed and out the door.

At Dugan's the surly cook is just setting a tray of bacon in the oven, and she barely grunts as I run by. The hall is dim and quiet. I poke my head into Gram's room and see that Marie is still asleep. I tiptoe past her bed to where Gram lies helplessly. She is wearing her sly look, as if she has done something naughty and is waiting for me to find out.

I try to make her smile. "Up and at 'em, rise and shine." These are the words she used every day to get me up. I don't mind getting up early if the sun is shining, but I hate rising in the dark and need much coaxing.

Gram groans and flips the sheet over her head. At home she would be fully dressed, including stockings and necklace. I stare at the sheet, not knowing what to do next.

The nurse rushes in and pushes me aside. "Good morning, Mrs. Lowden. It's time for our bath."

I sit in the visitor's chair and make myself as small as I can. Maybe I should run out into the hall. I plant my feet firmly on the floor and stay.

The nurse treats Gram as if she is a chicken about to go in the roasting pan. Plunk, turn the arms this way. Heave, sponge the back. Change the wrinkled Johnny robe for a clean blouse and pink jumper. Two passes of a brush to get that scraggly white hair out of Gram's eyes, and then a mighty swoop to prop her up against the pillows.

Gram lets herself be primped and prodded. Finally she is cleaned, trussed, basted with baby oil, and ready to be stuffed with breakfast. There is the rattle of dishes in the hall.

"Early start this morning?" Kitty, neat and shining, brings in a tray. My stomach rumbles at the smell of bacon and eggs. Gram's bed is cranked up and a table swiveled in front of her. She reaches for the juice and starts to spill it on the bed.

"Gram," I yell in a shocked voice. I take the

cup from her trembling hand and sip the orange juice.

"Jan. That is my juice." The voice is little, but I can understand her perfectly. She reaches for the cup and drinks greedily, the way Sue-Sue would if David threatened to take it away from her.

Gram puts all her attention on her food. When a bit of egg drops to the tray, she picks it up with thumb and forefinger, then neatly licks her fingers. She blows on her coffee and slurps it noisily.

Kitty brings me a piece of toast on a plate, and looks with surprise at Gram's empty plate. "Oh, Jan, you shouldn't have touched that food. The dietician judges how much your grandmother has eaten by what's left."

Gram laughs slyly. "I ate it all, young lady. And, if you don't mind, I'll have that piece of toast." She reaches over and grabs *my* toast.

Kitty laughs. "That's the first breakfast she's eaten since she got here. You'll have to come early every morning, Jan."

Maybe I will, but I'll eat before I leave the house. My stomach is not comforted by the promise of food tomorrow.

The morning is long and confusing. One minute Gram calls me Jan, and the next she calls me Clara. She absolutely refuses to wiggle so much as a toe.

At eleven I escape and run home to make a sandwich. At last my stomach is quiet. Mom and the urchins are out somewhere, so I pile David's red wagon with rags, paper towels, window spray, and jugs of water. Somehow I maneuver it to the corner of the dirt road where Trixie is sitting, bent over under a backpack and leaning on a broom. Sylvia joins us, carrying a basket containing detergents, cleanser, and dustpan and brush.

"Ronald and Frank are coming over this afternoon."

Trixie and I look at each other. I let the wagon handle drop to the dirt road. "How do they know where we'll be?"

Sylvia doesn't look at us. "Ronald came in while Dad was explaining the tax map. Then today I had to go out to the garage for this." She swung the basket up. "He said, 'I bet I know where you're going.' I didn't answer, just went back to get the cleaning things. But when I left, he called out from the garage and said he and Frank would see us later."

I want to cry. Our first secret ruined. We pick up our loads and start to walk, but the fun has gone out of it.

When we get to *our* house we feel better. Trixie sweeps the ceilings. Sylvia sprays the windows

64

and polishes them with paper towels. We slosh the walls with cold, soapy water, routing ants and wasps, cobwebs and mouse droppings. We scrub the kitchen and bathroom, sweep and wash the floors, and finally throw open windows and doors and let the warm June air dry everything.

We throw ourselves down on the freshly swept porch. "If Mom ever finds out I've done this house cleaning," I say, "she'll never let me out again. I'll be her slave forever."

Trixie smiles. "I thought it was great fun. I'd like to tip my house over on its side and dump everything out. Then I could clean it."

We lie on the warm wood and picture Trixie's ranch house tipped on its side with blocks and clothing spilled out the windows. The sound of a car breaks into our daydreams.

Sylvia stands up. "Well, here they are. I'm sorry about this, I really am." We walk into the living room just as Ronald and Frank come in through the kitchen.

Ronald is tall, almost six feet, and wears his brown hair shorter than other high-school boys. In fact, he is a little out of step in everything he does. Most things he does alone, like his boat in the garage, stargazing through his telescope, and writing all over the world for stamps. About the only thing he does with someone else is drive the ambulance with Frank.

Frank is shorter and slighter, and his black hair is curly. Besides being trained as a paramedic, he is editor of the school paper, and loved from afar by most of the girls, I think.

Ordinarily, we would not dare talk to older men, but it's hard to avoid Sylvia's brother when I'm over there so often. Besides, they both took care of Gram, and that makes them special.

Ronald stands and looks around the room. "You've done a good job of cleaning. What will you do if the owner shows up?"

Sylvia shrugs. "We haven't done anything except clean it. He couldn't be too mad about that, could he?"

Frank smiles, showing white teeth and a dimple on each cheek. It isn't fair that a boy has curly black hair as well as dimples. I would gladly trade my wispy light hair for his. "Don't scare them, Ron," he says. "The owner would probably thank them."

Ronald turns to me with a worried look. "How's your grandmother? She didn't look so good when we took her to Dugan's."

"Gram? She's not doing very well. It's hard to get her to move. She has to get strong, but she's so stubborn."

Frank nods. "Dugan's isn't the most inspiring place. We don't often get a call to take someone out of there."

Sylvia groans. "Never?"

"Not true," Ronald says quickly. "We take some of the old folks to the dentist or just for a drive. Some of them go home for weekends."

"Right, right," Frank agrees, too heartily. "This would be a great place for a party." The boys begin a thorough tour of the house.

"Oh, no you don't," Sylvia bursts out. "We found this place, and we have other plans." The Sunshine Club goes back to sit on the porch.

Finally the boys stop walking around and join us on the floor. I can't understand why two almost college men would want to sit with three girls our age. The boys fold their legs so their knees wing out widely making one half of a circle, three girls inscribing the other half. It is an uncomfortable circle.

Surely Sylvia will think of something to say, but her mouth stays closed. Frank breaks the silence. "This is a nice, clean floor. What did you do for water?"

"Brought it," Sylvia says.

"This house doesn't have water?" Ronald asks.

"Why would we need water?" Sylvia snaps. The

67

boys' questions are bothering her, but that does not stop them.

"Might be nice to have a drink of water after working so hard. Let's check around, Frank, and see what we can find."

Frank unfolds upward. "If you're not going to have a party, what are you going to do with the house?"

"I plan to sit and do a lot of thinking," Trixie says. Everyone knows that is the truth and the air lightens.

We watch the boys go around the house and down the back slope. "There are some things we need," I say when the boys can't hear us, "and one of them is water. Can Ronald keep a secret?"

Sylvia smiles. "In all the ten years I've known him, he's never told me anything, so he must be full of secrets."

That makes some kind of sense. We think it over.

"There are lots of things we need," Trixie says. "Most of them are things we can't get ourselves. You can't count on me for anything except what I can do with my hands." She spreads her fingers out in a kind of offering.

It is important. Too important to mess up. It is Gram's life. "I vote we tell them."

"I second the motion."

"Me, too."

We join hands and wait for the boys to come back.

Ronald carries a covered jar. "You do have water. There's a well out back, a good old-fashioned wishing well with a peaked roof and a bucket on a rope. Frank can get this tested to see if it's drinkable, if you think you'll need water to drink."

We break our circle and let them in. "Sylvia says you can keep a secret, Ronald. Can Frank?" I ask boldly.

Frank's face colors. "I could tell you things about Ronald that would curl your hair. But I won't."

Ronald looks worried. "Just what are you girls planning? You're not going to get into trouble, are you?"

"Sometimes you have to get into trouble to get out of it," Sylvia says stoutly. "What's worse, to let someone die or to borrow a house?"

"We're all for helping people live," Frank says. "That's why we've been running the ambulance. Look, we're older than you. I think you should let us know how much trouble you're going to get into."

"And we're not about to tell you until we're sure you'll help and not tell on us. Why would you want to help three kids?" Trixie doesn't fool around with words.

69

Ronald puts down the jar. "To make sure my sister doesn't get into a big mess."

"Pooh," Sylvia says. "You never helped me out before."

"True. I guess I really mean this summer is going to be a drag. The boat is almost finished and we haven't gotten too many ambulance calls. This is a little town and there's not much to do."

"If you don't want this house, there's loads we could do with it." Frank looks straight at me. "It would be like the tree house I always wanted."

David is begging for a tree house. He's the only boy I know well. Maybe everyone needs a secret place. "Oh, we want it, all right. We want it for Gram. She's going to die at Dugan's unless we save her."

Now Ronald looks more worried than ever. "You're crazy, you know. All of you. You can't just kidnap someone and take care of her in this house in the woods."

"Yes, we can. If you'll help us." Sylvia jumps to her feet. "She'll have peace and quiet and fresh air and a chance to get better."

"Hey, wait a minute, Sylvia. I'm not sure if you're right or not, but she's a great lady and if anyone needs rescuing, she does. I don't know, Frank, what do you think?"

"Water," Frank says, "and electricity." We all

70

stand up because it's a very important moment. The two boys look at each other and smile. "I say go for it," Frank says.

Ronald smiles. "Count me in."

"Consider yourselves members of the Sunshine Club," Sylvia announces.

The boys do not look too happy about that. Sunshine Club sounds sissy to them.

Outside, we pack up the cleaning things. "Today's my birthday," I say shyly.

"Congrats," Trixie says over the straps of her backpack. "Are you going to have a party?"

"This was my party. A splash party. I haven't had so much fun with soap and water in my whole life. Scrubbing the house was the best party I've ever had."

"Don't tell my mother that," Trixie says.

9

I'm tired when I get home.

"Enjoying your vacation?" Mom asks. I nod, too tired to open my mouth. "Set the table in the dining room, please. We'll have your birthday dinner there."

There ought to be some rule about not having chores on your birthday, especially one as important as eleven, which is almost in your teens. I go into the dark room and set out the crystal and silver. The last time I did this was the day Gram sailed past the door on the throw rug.

Everyone is jolly. Sue-Sue eats real food with the family for the first time and David wears his hardly-stained-at-all white pants. He keeps a matchbox on the table that I hope is not my present, because I can hear something scrabbling to get out.

Dad carves the roast chicken with a flourish and I'm pierced with a terrible pain. Someone is missing.

"How long before Gram comes home?" The table quiets and we can hear that thing in David's matchbox.

Mom smooths her hair with fingers greasy from Sue-Sue's chicken. "You've seen Gram, darling. You know what she's like now. Therapy hasn't made her stronger and she's as helpless as a baby. I can't take care of any more babies."

Dad puts down the carving knife and continues Mom's long, sad song. "It's just not practical, Jan," he says in his patient-father voice. "Your mother has enough to do in this big old house taking care of you and the little ones. And with the baby coming . . ." His voice trails off into a mouthful of chicken and gravy.

I eat quickly, the way I've been doing lately. It fills an empty hole somewhere. Practical, practical, my mind chants as I chew the rubbery chicken. Practical is a hard word. It's practical to keep Gram in that cramped little room with kooky Marie. Practical to cut Gram's hair so it's easier to wash, even though it falls into her eyes. Practical, practical.

My plate is clean but I never tasted a thing.

Mom piles the plates, something she tells me not to do, and comes back with a bakery cake with twelve candles. Eleven for the years and one to be good on. Or is it one to grow on?

I draw in a huge breath, enough to blow that word "practical" right out of me and fill up with one gigantic wish. On a load of hay, the first star, and twelve candles, I whoosh out my wish.

All out. My wish will come true. I sit back to enjoy my gifts. A horse book I haven't read yet and a pink shirt that will look great under my checkered apron. David gives me a handkerchief and looks surprised when he sees it. Usually he gives me glue, or a truck. Sue-Sue reluctantly hands over a gold mesh bag of chocolate coins. After I share the gold-covered money, there are still enough coins left to nibble while I read my horse book. The birthday party ends when David opens his matchbox and a cricket leaps across the table and into the frosting.

Being eleven does not help much. I am still too short to lift Gram into her wheelchair. The nurse does this, starting out with "Now, Mrs. Lowden, we're going for a nice ride in our chair."

I wince, and blurt out, "No."

The nurse stares, her mouth hanging open.

"I mean," thinking hard for the manners Gram taught me, "I don't know your name."

She smiles, and I see that she has forgotten to be angry. "Nona."

"Nona what?" We talk over Gram's bent head.

"Nona Kincaid."

"Well, Nona," I say softly, so she has to lean down to hear me, "did you know Gram once had an opera singer to her house for dinner? She even worked for the governor."

"But what . . . ?"

"It's just that she knows it's *her* wheelchair, not yours."

Nona does not seem upset. "It's just the way we talk here."

"I know. But Gram hates it. And if she hates something, she won't do it."

Nona thinks for a minute and then gives me a big smile. "You're right. We'll take a nice walk in *your* wheelchair."

It's not quite right, but I see a little smile on Gram's face.

I go to the kitchen for a glass of juice while Nona and Gram struggle with the wheelchair and pillows. Before I finish the last drop, Gram goes gliding past in her wheelchair like a pink sail. She waves a strong arm, not one of those hanging finger things. By the time I get to the therapy room, Gram is standing and holding her walker.

"Don't touch me. Watch out for the hip," she croaks, but I have the feeling it is all show. Her eyes keep going to the wall of mirrors and she shakes the shaggy white hair out of her eyes so she can see her beautiful pink reflection.

At the end of the morning I find Nona in the kitchen drinking a cup of tea, and I sit beside her.

"Gram's doing better, don't you think?"

Nona puts down her cup and looks at me. I can see by her eyes that she really cares about Gram.

"She should be at home and walking. Why isn't she?"

I shrug and blink a tear back. "Partly it's the house we live in. The bathrooms are upstairs. Gram would be trapped there. If she's on the first floor, then Mom has to carry bedpans up and down. Mom's going to have another baby and there are already three of us at home. Gram's the one extra thing Mom can't handle."

"I hate working here," Nona says quietly but with force. "It's such a dead end. Once people come in here, they seem to stay. You tell your mother that your grandmother is better off at home. There are nurses that come to the house. I'm beginning to think that's what I should do."

"I do tell her. But she and Dad think Dugan's is practical."

"It's a good place to finish you off." Nona stops and looks scared. "Forget I said that. Don't listen to me. If Mr. Dugan hears about this, I'll be fired."

I quickly promise not to tell, but now I feel worse than ever. Even the nurses think Dugan's is the last resort.

Sylvia and I walk home together. "How's Carl?" I never get into the dayroom, now that Gram's at Dugan's.

"Not so good." Sylvia's lips are dry and cracked. "He doesn't talk anymore. He just sits by the front window, waiting for his son to come and take him out of there."

"Does his son know Carl's ready to go home?"

"Kitty said her father called the son. The son said he was very busy, running his father's company. He would come when he could."

I brush Carl out of my mind. The day is too full of June for sadness. "Gram's better. She went to therapy today."

We are so caught up in thoughts of Gram getting stronger that we cartwheel the rest of the way home, completely forgetting that eleven-year-olds are too old for such antics.

———

Trixie escapes from whatever kept her in her crowded house all morning and the three of us sit on the floor of *our* living room.

My heart is as heavy as the two peanut-butter sandwiches I had for lunch. "We need kitchen stuff, gas for the stove, all kinds of things."

None of us has any ideas. Back home I have $1.19 in my metal horse bank. Sylvia has money, hundreds of dollars, but it's all in a bank account and her mother has to sign for it. We know Trixie has nothing.

It is a relief when Ronald and Frank show up. Frank has a piece of paper in his hand. "No harmful bacteria in that water at all. Perfectly safe to drink. I'm sure you girls can get water out of the well. Just don't fill the bucket too full. And don't fall in."

We groan. The boys still think of us as little kids.

We follow them, like David and Sue-Sue follow me, as they check around. Frank tests the fireplace by burning some of that ten-year-old newspaper, and then they go up on the roof to check the chimney while we stand below, looking up. Ronald leans over the eaves to tell us the chimney looks all right and the roof still has a few years to go. My toes uncurl and the heavy feeling leaves my stomach.

Out in back, next to the well, there is a locked shed. This is the only time we really break the law. Ronald takes out a screwdriver and works off the metal lock. Inside is a big motor, which Ronald calls a generator. The boys tinker and soon it's roaring. Ronald points to the wires leading from the shed to the house.

"You've got electricity. That will work the refrigerator and lights. Those kerosene lamps are too dangerous."

Back in the house, Sylvia has a proud look on her face. Ronald is turning out to be all right and she was wise to let him in on our secret.

"What's your timetable, Jan?"

One minute I've got this crazy, pie-in-the-sky dream, and the next minute Ronald is asking me what my timetable is, as if it's not a crazy dream, after all. My cheeks burn and I hold my hands in my lap so they won't shake.

"Gram's still in a wheelchair, but she can walk with a walker. I think she'd do more walking if she could go into the kitchen and make herself a cup of tea."

We look around. Everything is on one level, and the doors are wide enough for a wheelchair. Even the kitchen door to the outside is level with the ground. Things are moving more rapidly than I'd planned. What if Gram isn't ready? What if she has some medical problem we can't handle? I am afraid to stop, but my insides are going through a meat grinder.

Ronald grins and looks satisfied. "I ordered a tank of propane gas. The company will set it up outside the kitchen and run the line to the stove. Told them it was for a renter and no one questioned it."

"Who paid for the tank?" Sylvia asks. The boys exchange smiles.

"We did. We'll extract it from your allowance this summer, a little at a time."

The Sunshine Club is really full of sunshine. The house is not a home yet, though, since home means food and we are already starved. We close up and run home where the food is, very pleased with ourselves.

10

Sylvia and I made up our game of Giants and Pirates years ago when we first discovered each other in second grade. The lawn in the middle of Sylvia's garden was an imaginary island inhabited by either giants or pirates. It didn't matter who lived there, because we spent our time planning what we needed to take off the sinking ship. We would name books, clothes, and food, and when we had named all the cans of food, someone would finally think of a can opener. That was a winner. Without opened cans, no one could eat. I think of the game as I walk in the early morning to Dugan's.

This secret project with the house is very much like the planning part of Giants and Pirates, only the planning part is almost over and the rest of this game has to be played out.

This morning Nona puts Gram on a seat that swings over the edge of the tub and eases the patient down into the water. Gram fights every inch of the way.

"Watch the hip, the hip," she screams, her voice echoing thinly in the tile bathroom.

I sit in the visitor's chair and listen to her scream, wishing I had brought her lavender bath oil to soothe her fragile skin. It would take a lot of kettles to fill that tub in our house, but lavender oil might make the bath an occasion.

Later in the therapy room I ask Nona, "Will bath oil hurt her incision?"

"No. She healed before she left the hospital. The pin is in. There is no reason she can't walk. Just herself. She is the reason."

"No. Dugan's is," I say, and watch Nona jump as if she's been slapped.

"Stop looking at me," Gram says piteously. She is maneuvering her walker over a little bridge.

I stare at her because I'm trying to find out something. Is she a kooky old lady, or is she Gram?

"You're making me nervous," Gram scolds.

"Nonsense, Mrs. Lowden," the therapist says. "You're going to have to get used to people watching you once you go home."

Gram snorts and it is most unladylike. "Home? I'm going home like that Carl is going home. I will sit by Dugan's front door and wait. The way he does. All the rest of my life I'll share a room with Marie and listen to how she almost married."

I smile into the bib of my apron. Gram knows as well as I do that Mom will make one excuse after another not to bring her home.

Leaving Gram to her angry muttering, I go to the dayroom for the first time in weeks. Old people sit in wheelchairs around tables. The radio is on so low no one can hear it clearly even though the room is silent.

Trixie and Sylvia are near the door, talking to an old man in a wheelchair.

"You don't need that wheelchair," Sylvia coaxes. "Come, take a walk with us. They're making strawberry shortcake in the dining room."

Carl? I recognize him now. Everything about him has collapsed inward. His teeth are out and his mouth has pulled into a sour line. His head hangs to his chest and skinny hands dangle uselessly between his legs. He looks like a baby strapped in a stroller.

I remember my first day at Dugan's, when Carl

83

showed me his leg muscles, strong from jogging. He talked about running his own business and he was interested in me. Except for being in a wheelchair and attached to a yellow bag, there had not been a thing wrong with him. Now it is hard to find anything right.

"Let's get him out of here." Trixie and Sylvia look up with such startled looks, I laugh. "Not 'out,' just out of this room."

Carl's hands move up and clutch his chest as we race him to his room and make him put in his teeth. He glares fiercely at us and we feel better. Sylvia smiles and looks at me. Tell him we have a home for him where he'll get better, the look says.

I shake my head. I refuse to promise something that might not happen. His son has already broken one promise. Another broken promise might finish him off.

We stop at the door of the therapy room and watch Gram pull herself up the practice stairs.

"Would you like to work on your walking, Mr. Stringer? You should be in here at least twice a week." The therapist tries to coax him out of the chair.

Carl grits his false teeth and shakes his head. Nona leaves a patient and comes over.

"Mr. Stringer. If we're ever going to have that

dance you promised me when you first came here, you'd better get in shape. I don't like slow dances."

Carl almost smiles. "I remember that promise. It's just that I'm not in the mood. Some other day."

Sylvia and I wheel him into the dining room, where we spend the rest of the morning cutting strawberries with blunt butter knives.

At lunchtime, kooky Marie, Gram's roommate, eats her shortcake one layer at a time. First the whipped cream, then the strawberries gobbled greedily, then the shortcake, and finally she licks the empty plate. Again I am reminded of babies. Sue-Sue would eat her shortcake the same way Marie does.

11

A soft rain falls on our snug house. Sylvia unpacks a nested set of pots, pans, and tin cups once used for camping. We boil water on the gas stove, now hooked up to the propane tank, and drink hot cocoa out of tin cups, which are boiling hot and which we quickly put down on the enameled tabletop.

"I would love to live here." Sylvia blows on her cocoa. "No rules, stay up as late as you want, and no Ronald. Speaking of the devil . . ."

Ronald and Frank shake rainwater from their hair before making cocoa, which they drink standing up against the sink because there are no more chairs.

"You're just about set. The generator's hooked up and the gas is in."

"You guys are wonderful." Trixie flutters her dark eyelashes, but the effect is lost. She has a circle of cocoa around her lips.

"We may be just about set, but what happens when they're missed? Won't the police be called?" I can picture Mom if she gets a call from the police. She'd be frantic and that certainly would not be good for the unborn baby.

"How often does your mother visit Dugan's?"

I think Frank's question over carefully. "Well, she hasn't gone since vacation started. I see Gram every day and go home and tell them about her."

"Good. You can tell them about your grandmother whether she's here or in the nursing home."

"But surely, someday . . ." I trail off.

"Someday is not the question. If she has a chance to get better, we've got to make sure she has that chance."

Rain drums against the windowpanes and the kitchen suddenly turns cold. Sylvia looks at her brother. "We can't wait much longer. Carl looks like he's going to die of a broken heart."

Trixie puts a large yellow pad on the table.

"While we're waiting for answers to the big problem, let's make a list of all the little things we need."

Sylvia and I look at each other and smile. It is our old game of Giants and Pirates. "Can opener," we yell in unison.

"Gram's linen closet is full of sheets and towels."

Ronald snaps his fingers, yellow from boat varnish. "We have boxes of kitchen stuff Gloria used at school. I'll bring them over tomorrow." Gloria is Sylvia's older sister.

Trixie writes fast in large, neat handwriting. "I can slip out a few boxes of cereal and cans of soup."

The list grows. Sylvia and I have done this so many times that we remember the little things that make life bearable, like toilet paper and a portable radio.

We clean up and put the tin camping gear into empty cabinets. "Soap," Sylvia says.

"Kitchen towels," I add. Whoever cannot think of something ends the game and loses.

"I'll drive you girls to the corner, if you're ready to leave. That way you won't get too wet," Ronald says.

We close everything down and shut the door firmly behind us.

"Lock," Frank says.

"Shelf paper."

I search wildly, unready to end the game. "Buckets to fill the tub with." We hurry to Ronald's car, which is an old rust bucket with a fine-tuned engine. I love the mildewed smell of it.

At the corner Trixie and I get out. We stand in the pouring rain, waiting for a car to pass, only it doesn't. There's a squeal of brakes and the whine of a window cranking down.

"Janet Robinson, what are you doing here?" Mom's stomach rests against the steering wheel. Sue-Sue is in her baby seat in back and David is buckled up in front. "Get in this car this very minute. You, too, Trixie. I'll drive you home."

We scramble into the backseat, next to Sue-Sue.

"Who was that in that junk of a car?"

"Ronald and Sylvia."

"You weren't in his car, were you?"

My tongue sticks to the top of my mouth like when I eat peanut butter. If there's one thing I do not do well, it's lying.

Trixie opens her mouth before I blurt anything out. "We were just crossing that street when they came out. We talked awhile."

Mom is not going to let go. "What's down the road?"

"Ronald heard there was a dump down there. He's looking for parts for his car," Trixie explains.

I love Trixie. She leans over the front seat, her wide-open Irish face looking so honest I almost believe her.

"I'm not sure I approve of all this running around in the rain." Mom jerks the car to a stop, and oranges rain all over us. Trixie slips out the door and is halfway home before Mom can say a word.

"Maybe you ought to spend more time at home."

My heart pounds. Oh, not to be a babysitter again. Not with drippy David and sticky Sue-Sue. "Gram won't eat or try to walk when I'm not there." My voice is not quite steady.

"Well"—There is a long pause as the car climbs our hill—"I suppose." She really doesn't want me at home. She is playing "mama," and children can't have two mamas. She continues in a softer tone. "Just don't get your hopes up. Old people slide downhill. Once they break something, it never heals. Their minds go. Soon Gram won't know who you are."

We pull into the driveway, all but my stomach, which is back somewhere on the slick road. *Not true. Not true.* I squeeze an orange until my thumb bites through and the juice tracks to my elbow. Mom has lost the house key and shifts Sue-Sue into contortions while she fishes through her purse.

David steps into every puddle. I wrestle with the damp grocery bag and close the car door with a hip. The stucco on the house has darkened, as if the rain has soaked clear through. The gloom of the world seeps inside me.

No sooner are we in, than I'm up the stairs and up Gram's stairs, and I'm safe until supper. If I were in the kitchen there would be a thousand jobs to do, but once I disappear Mom does everything herself and never thinks twice about it. I should think she'd look around and say "Where did that girl go to?" but she never does.

In the morning the world is still soggy and low clouds hang dark against a gray sky. Gram complains that her hip hurts her and Carl once again refuses to wear his teeth.

Therapy is depressing. Whoever designed this room with no windows was not thinking about people. Fluorescent lights bounce angrily off mirrored walls. Gram's jumper, as blue as the blue of her eyes, does not cheer her. She refuses to look at herself in the mirror.

"You're all trying to kill me," Gram squeaks in her little-old-lady voice.

"Come on, Mrs. Lowden. Just a few steps and we'll take you to the hairdresser."

Gram's eyes gleam, then return to their blank

stare. She loves having her hair washed and brushed. She pretends to be fragile, but her legs are moving well and her arms do not shake when she holds the walker.

Carl sits all crumpled up in his wheelchair and seems to be staring into space, but his eyes are on the mirror and he is watching Gram walk.

Sylvia tries to get Carl up and moving. He looks at her calmly. "I can commit suicide if I want to." He says it in such a low, firm tone, there is no question that he means it. If he does, I'll have seventy years to think every day that it was our fault Carl died.

On my way out through the kitchen, I find Nona Kincaid with her head on the table, her fingers wrapped around a mug of steaming coffee.

"Are you all right?"

Nona lifts her head and tears stream down to her teeth. "No."

I pull up a chair and think of what to say, but there isn't much. I want to cry, too.

"These are people," Nona says thickly, "not bodies to wash and push around and stuff with food."

"Do you think Gram can be a person again?"

Nona looks at me with red eyes. "I think so. Yes. She is spunky and still has some fight in her."

I breathe a deep breath. "And Carl?"

"All Carl needs is to get out of this place. He has some good years left."

I sit and draw swirls on the table with a fork. "Would you like to help us save Gram and Carl?"

Nona blows her nose in a large paper napkin and nods. "While you're at it, do you think you can save me, too?"

12

There is no joy in the afternoon, even with the sky bluing and fleecy little clouds tripping over one another. While Mom does the wash, I tiptoe up and down the stairs carrying Gram's linens out to the red wagon. David decides he must have his wagon this very minute and he's getting louder and louder, so I jumble everything into cartons, load them onto the wagon, and run, before Mom hears him.

Going down the hill is no fun. The wagon hits my heels until blood runs warmly into my socks. Twice the cartons tip, and I stop to pile them up again. Sweat burns my eyes and trickles down my legs to mix with the blood.

There is no way I can keep that wagon horizontal on the dirt road. One set of wheels rides the center mound and the other is down in the rut. I walk backward, feeling my way with my feet while holding the cartons steady.

When I see the house I feel happier. Windows gleam in the sunlight, and the big tree in front has leafed out to make the yard a cool and shady place. Home.

Ronald drives in. *Now* he comes, I think as I wipe my heels. Frank jumps out and carries in the cartons.

I make the beds with hospital corners, the way Sylvia's mother taught us in Girl Scouts. I always thought it a silly thing to learn, when I really wanted to go camping, but now it comes in handy.

Ronald brings in dishes and kitchen things and then hands me two camp blankets and two ribbed spreads. The dark back bedroom will be Gram's, so I put on the yellow spread and hang paper curtains with yellow chrysanthemums blooming on them. The front bedroom has twining ivy on the curtains and a green spread. Now it truly looks like home.

In the living room we hang blue curtains with

white sailboats, and in the kitchen's one window we put up a curtain with blue-green herbs. Sylvia lines the kitchen cabinets with yellow shelf paper, and Trixie puts away cereal and soups. She proudly shows us a carton of light bulbs, which none of us thought of. We work so hard we don't have time to think of the real problems.

Sylvia, her head still in a cabinet, tells the boys that Carl said he could kill himself.

Frank frowns. "That's serious. Never ignore a suicide threat. We'll have to do something fast." I think of Gram and the daffodil bulb, but don't say anything.

Since no one knows what to do, we busy ourselves boiling water, taking tea bags out of a canister, and unpacking yellow cups with blueberries on them.

"Gram would love these." Suddenly the blueberries swim out of focus.

"People in Dugan's do get out, you know," Ronald says comfortingly. "Shopping, sight-seeing, a trip to the dentist. Some families take relatives home for visits of a weekend or more. I'm not sure just what has to happen to get someone out. Our job has always been to drive them in the ambulance."

"Nona told me she wants to get out of Dugan's. She said she would help us. And Kitty Dugan would know." The minute I say that, we all know it's the truth. We have two friends who are the keys to the whole puzzle. Trixie pours boiling water into the yellow cups and we toast one another.

"I'm the adult here," Ronald says, picking at a pimple that blooms on his chin. "I'll take full responsibility."

"Oh, no, you won't," I rage. "Gram's mine."

"I mean I'll be the one to go to jail if anything happens."

"Harvard would love to see that on your record," Sylvia says. Laughter fills the kitchen, and for a minute we forget to be afraid.

The next morning we meet in Dugan's kitchen and put on our limp aprons. Kitty pours juice into pitchers.

"When do you get out of work?" I ask as I try to tie a decent bow.

"I help out, I don't actually work here. Like you, I'm just a volunteer. What's up?"

"We've got something very important to show you," Sylvia says, sounding as breathless as if she's just run the marathon.

Trixie plants her feet solidly. "First we have to know how trustworthy you are. If you're going to run to mommy and daddy and tell everything, then we don't want you."

Kitty steps back. "If you don't trust me, I won't come. But I knew when my sister was secretly married, and even about the baby coming, and I never told a soul."

Trixie relaxes and drops her fists to her sides. "Meet us at one this afternoon in the field next to my house. Think we should blindfold her?" Trixie does get carried away. We drag her into the dayroom.

Toothless Carl droops by the front door. Gram's whispery old-lady voice draws me down the hall.

"You put something in that coffee. You can't make me drink it."

The battle is on, and I know who will win. If Gram decides not to eat, drink, or take a step, there is not much anyone can do.

I pull Nona out into the hall, and tell her about the afternoon meeting, and she agrees to come.

At one o'clock we hurry Kitty and Nona down the dirt road. Sylvia opens the door of our house with a key she wears around her neck, and Kitty and Nona walk in. They explore the rooms like little children in a candy store.

Back in the kitchen we tell them our plan. Kitty nods, frowns, explores the corners of her mouth with her tongue, and clasps her hands together. Nona listens and does not shake her head, which is encouraging.

When we finally finish, there is a silence that pains my ears. Say something, I shout silently.

"Well, there are forms," Kitty says so slowly it is like she's speaking another language. "The patient's family signs him out and promises to give him his medicine. No one checks to see if the signatures are forged."

We all yell "forged," as if we're shocked, but of course we knew we'd have to sign papers.

"How long do they usually spend at home?" I ask. I press my hands on the table to keep them from shaking. Now the table shakes.

"Usually for a day or a weekend, though we have had people go for as long as a week."

Of course we want forever. If we have to send Gram and Carl back, it will kill them.

"I think you are very wise to rescue your grandmother and Carl. But I have to know that nobody's going to mention my name." Nona looks right at Kitty. "If this gets on my record, I'll never get another job."

Kitty raises three fingers in the Scout promise, and we do the same. Nona smiles. "You can count on me."

"You'd better all do the same for me," Kitty says. "My father is not going to like this." So we give Kitty the salute, even Nona. "This looks like a real home to me. As long as there is a car here and someone here at all times, I'll get you the papers and the names to copy."

We stand and join hands, friends in a giant secret. When Nona and Kitty are gone we throw ourselves on the ground under the maple tree.

"I think I have the answer to the problem of having someone here at all times." Joy bubbles through my words. We have a short meeting of the Sunshine Club, and when the meeting is over, we feel much, much better.

13

Did you ever do a crossword puzzle where one whole section stays blank and then you find the key word and everything falls into place? Today this happens. Sun, sky, breezes, and birds all come together in one perfect picture, symphony, something. All the fears of the last weeks dissolve in one giant cup of joy.

I hate going to the nursing home. I am afraid my face will tell Gram our plans. Sylvia has bitten her lips till they're bleeding, and Trixie has no more fingernails. We make Carl wear his teeth and have Nona give Gram a bath. We pretend it is an ordinary day.

101

At noon we gallop to our little house and pick up food for lunch on the way. Kitty comes bouncing down the road, waving permission papers.

We spend two hours practicing writing "Leopold Stringer," the way it is written on the admission form. The honor finally goes to Trixie. I have no trouble signing "Clara Robinson." After all, I forged her name for months.

Kitty folds each paper into proper thirds and puts them in envelopes. "Tomorrow is Friday. Have Ronald and Frank come at one."

She picks up the envelopes and kisses us for luck. "Have you got someone who can stay here?"

We laugh and nod. No problem. Kitty dances down the road carrying our precious envelopes.

It is Thursday night at home. Wednesday is spaghetti night, and Thursday is nothing night. Tonight it is a tuna-fish casserole swimming in canned mushroom soup with drowned peas floating in it. I am too excited to throw up.

"You know about our club?" I ask after I have forced the first pea down.

"What club is that, dear?" Mom has taken to calling me "dear" all the time, now that I am taking care of Gram for her.

"The Sunshine Club. We do good deeds."

"What a nice idea," Dad says, washing a mouthful down with hot coffee.

"We need more meeting time, so we're going to stay over. Tomorrow night we'll be at Sylvia's. Some night they'll come here."

Mom sort of listens. "Sue-Sue has the other bed. How will you have room for more?"

"We've got Sylvia's sleeping bags. We'll sleep on the floor."

"I think it's a grand idea. Could you take care of breakfast when they're here, Jan? Even cold cereal turns my stomach."

I'm so relieved at the way my plan is working, I help with the dishes before I go up to bed. I almost have Gram in my arms.

In all my years of living I've never had trouble sleeping except maybe on Christmas Eve. But tonight the frogs chorus, and the late freight train shakes the room, and moonbeams land right on my eyelids. There are little things that crawl on my legs and make them itch, and when I doze, my body shocks awake. I barely close my eyes and it is light.

I pack a duffle with my night things, and pick up powdered milk, cheese, cans of beef stew, and a pound of coffee. Gram loves coffee.

My note is on the table. "See you tomorrow afternoon. I'm at Sylvia's. Love, J."

The duffle is light as a feather. I am a feather. I float on the June air with the butterflies.

Now, how can I keep Gram from knowing I've almost captured her? Kitty hides my duffle, and I put on my apron and fly down the hall. Gram looks at her breakfast with the eye of a spy who knows she's being poisoned.

"Eat up, Gram. You need your strength. Today we're taking you for a ride."

She gives me her sly look and I hold my breath. *Is* she as kooky as Marie?

"They're trying to kill me, Clara," she says. I hope we aren't too late.

"Eat your cereal," I croon. I put my arm around her thin neck and hug her to me. "Just one bite."

Usually I make her feed herself, but this day I don't care. I spoon cereal into her mouth, wipe her chin, with the little white hairs that sprout there, give her a sip of her favorite coffee, all the time holding her shoulder blades.

"It's June, Gram. The flowers are blooming and the sun is everywhere. You'll love it out there."

Gram chews noisily and burps. We just may be too late.

Somehow we get through the morning. I catch Sylvia's eye as I wheel Gram to therapy, and get a mixed signal from her. She is excited, but Carl is giving her the same trouble Gram is giving me.

We shrug like two old ladies and hope the afternoon will be better.

While Gram is still eating lunch, I take off my apron and grab my duffle. Sylvia, Trixie, and I meet under the rhododendrons. We have half an hour to kill.

"Ronald's got the sleeping bag in the ambulance." Sylvia is trying to be calm. "I packed Carl's clothes."

I gasp. "Be right back." I've been so full of plans I forgot about Gram's things. I run to her room and pack her clothes and toilet things into the suitcase from her closet. Gram isn't there and neither is her wheelchair. I wonder if she and Carl are sitting by the front door waiting for someone to rescue them. My heart is pounding. Somehow I carry the suitcase out, through the hall, out the kitchen door, and under the rhododendrons.

Trixie looks worried. I nod at her and smile and try to keep my heart from jumping out of my mouth.

Middays in June are quiet, hot with sun, heavy with scent, and musical with the sounds of birds and insects. In the midst of all that quiet the ambulance roars up the front driveway.

Gram and Carl are wheeled out the front entrance. Frank opens the back, puts down a ramp, and wheels each chair up. The doors close. The

105

ambulance pulls out, turns the corner and stops. The Sunshine Club hoists the luggage aboard, and we're off.

"I want to see the lake," Carl says. I know he and Gram are thinking the same thoughts. Their last ride on earth. I hold Gram's hand and Sylvia holds Carl's. Ronald drives all around the lake, past the swimming beach covered with people, around by the country club with its blue flag flying, up Lake Street to Main, and finally down the dirt road. There isn't a sound as the trees close in on us.

"Are you trying to kill us, Clara?" Gram says to me in a piteous voice. She looks confused. "We should have taken the road before this. This isn't the way to our house."

We are barely crawling now, and the limbs of trees scrape the top of the ambulance. Carl looks scared, too, despite Sylvia's hold on his hand.

The ambulance turns into the driveway of our house. The motor idles, then stops. In the terrible silence no one moves.

Frank runs around back and opens the door and sets the ramp. "Welcome home," he says, and unlocks Gram's chair and wheels it down. He leaves her on the grass and goes back for Carl. "Welcome home, sir."

The two of them sit in the sunshine and look

around dazedly. Nona drives up and parks beside the ambulance.

"Welcome home, Gram," I say.

She trembles and looks like a very, very old lady. "This isn't my home."

"Not mine, either," Carl says. I think he would stamp his foot if he wasn't in the wheelchair.

All the emotions we have been holding in so many weeks are bursting to get out. I cartwheel around the yard. "It is now," I shout.

Sylvia unlocks the door. Trixie wheels Carl into the kitchen and I push Gram. Frank and Ronald bring in the suitcases, and then Nona comes in with her medical bag.

"A stove," Gram says. "I want a cup of tea." Trixie fills the kettle and turns on the gas. We push the chairs into the living room, where Ronald opens the porch door to let in the breeze.

"A real fireplace. How about a fire?"

It must be ninety outside, so we all throw back our heads and laugh. Proudly we show them the bedrooms and the bathroom and the view from the porch.

Finally we wheel the chairs back into the kitchen where Trixie pours tea. Gram reaches out a frail finger and touches the blueberry cup, the saucer, runs her hands over the enamel of the table, reaches up and pushes her white hair out of her eyes.

"Home?" she quavers.

"Home," I answer firmly, much more firmly than I feel.

"You wouldn't kill me, would you, Clara?"

My heart leaps into my throat.

"No, you wouldn't," she answers herself. Her hand slips into mine.

To my dismay a tear runs down my cheek. I lean down and put my head on her shoulder. "I love you, Gram."

The tea is rich and fragrant. Absolutely the best tea of my life. I wonder if it could be the well water. I sniff and sip and listen to the talk around me. Gram uses her normal voice, and Carl tells Ronald and Frank how much he loves fishing. The sun moves sideways, slanting down.

Finally the girls get up from the table and I walk out with them. We are all tired, but smiling.

"I think it's going to work," Sylvia says.

"They seem to be okay," Trixie adds.

Ronald and Frank come out. "We'll be back tomorrow, and we'll bring some food with us. Come on, girls, we'll take you home."

The ambulance leaves. Dust settles on the quiet road.

14

Nona opens some cans and begins to heat up soup. I get out bowls and set the table.

"Aren't they going to miss you at Dugan's?" I knew that Nona was going to help, but I'm surprised she didn't leave when the ambulance went.

She gives me her broadest grin. "I told them my sister is ill. I saved two weeks vacation and decided it might as well be here and now. I put off taking a vacation because I never had anywhere to go."

I sigh with relief. We won't be doing this alone.

"Look at them," Nona whispers. "They look better already. You kids may be crazy, but I think you're doing the right thing."

When I tell Carl the soup is ready, he's staring sadly out the kitchen window.

"Leopold never did come to get me."

"Nope. And he probably never will."

"Absolutely right, young lady."

After supper we wheel them out onto the porch. There are shrill sounds and chunking sounds and the chugarums of bullfrogs, and all kinds of night music. "Wish I had my flute," Carl muses.

"And how would you play with those false teeth?" Gram is feeling better.

"Do you mind, Gram? That we kidnapped you and brought you here, I mean."

Gram sinks her head to her chest and thinks awhile. "I miss my own bathroom and my own bed and my place in the family."

How many times in the last few days have I been close to tears? Isn't there any pleasing anybody?

"Now, Mary Agnes, give the girl her due. She only saved our lives, that's all."

Gram looks up and smiles. "You know, I haven't heard such night noises since I got in that infernal place."

We sit and listen to the choruses of the night. The sweet air is getting to me. I find myself jerk-

110

ing my chin up and pretending I've been awake all the time.

Nona comes to the porch door, the white of her uniform showing in the darkness. "It's time you children were in bed."

Gram snorts. "If this is my house, I should be able to stay up as late as I want. I'm older than you."

"Any other day, once you're stronger. But you had a big trip today and you need your rest."

Nona wheels her to the bathroom and then to the bedroom. We hear Gram protesting she can do it herself and Nona's voice loudly saying that tomorrow she can do just that, but not tonight. When Gram is quiet, Nona comes back for Carl.

"None of your nonsense with me," he growls. "If I need help I'll call for it." He wheels himself in.

Nona sits down on the wicker chair, which creaks and groans and finally decides to hold her.

"Where are you going to sleep?" I wonder aloud. "I've got Sylvia's sleeping bag, but we didn't bring anything for you."

"I sat up last night planning this thing. I brought an air mattress, which I'll blow up in a few minutes. Also brought a pillow and some old blankets. If you don't mind, I'll use the porch."

I would give Nona the world if she asked for it.

Nona bustles around and soon is kneeling on the porch floor, blowing up her mattress. After she is settled I turn out the lights, unroll my bed-roll, and sleep.

My eyes hood over. I know the floor is hard and don't understand why it is so comfortable. I open my eyes. The doors to the bedrooms are black rectangles. If I stop breathing can I hear them breathe? I force my lids down, but something, a noise, makes them fly open.

Slithering out of the warm cocoon, I stand and sharpen all my senses. Is it coming from Gram's room? My feet slide over the bare wood, warm from the summer day and clean from all our scrubbing. A disembodied ghost, I move toward Gram's room.

There it is again. A mewling sound. I force myself into the solid blackness of the open door.

"Gram?" I whisper.

I edge around the bed and find Gram's hand, warm and pulsing. Her faint voice floats in the dark. "Are you there, Jan?"

She calls me Jan, not Clara. Clean, fresh air and a good supper have cleared up some confusion.

"I love you, Gram." I lay my cheek against her hand, and there is a rustle and her other hand creeps across the sheet and strokes my hair.

"Stay with me, child." I nod against her hand and then walk without fear back into the other room, gather up my sleeping bag and unroll it next to Gram's bed. We squeeze hands lightly. Blood seems to course from one body to the other. I lie down. That much I remember. When I check to see if I am asleep, sun slants in the open door.

Gram's bed is empty. I should have known. Someone, Dugan or Nurse Nona, has taken her back, unless she died in the night and they have taken her body away.

I shuffle through the empty living room not caring to look in Carl's room to see if he's there, not willing to think about what they'll do to me for killing my great-grandmother, just biting my teeth to keep the hollowness inside me.

"Best food I've eaten in months." It's a man's voice, and not anyone I recognize. I walk into the kitchen prepared for the worst.

Carl is sitting in his wheelchair at the enameled table in front of a plate piled high with what looks like cat food. And Gram is in her wheelchair, her robe on backward.

The sun is shining in from the east, but even in full sunlight I don't believe my eyes.

"Jan, I need some water. Couldn't make coffee."

I'm still so frightened I hardly hear Gram. "How did you get out of bed?"

"I never thought you'd sleep through all my groaning," Gram says. "I inched it. Used my arms to pull myself up, swung my feet over the bed, backed into the wheelchair, and here I am." She waves a triumphant arm.

I have to get out of the kitchen and pull myself together. I grab the water jug and take it out and around back to the well. A robin sings joyously and there's a carpet of bluets at my feet. I dip the bucket with a splash and watch the muscles of my arms as I winch it up. No one at Dugan's would believe that pitiful little lady got out of bed and into a chair all by herself, I think, as I hoist, pour, carry back again.

A sleepy Nona takes the water and fills the coffeepot. The cat food turns out to be hash out of a can. "Carl opened it, but I heated it up," Gram says proudly. She waves to me to help myself. Carl is wearing his teeth and chews noisily, but this morning Gram is so pleased with herself she doesn't even notice.

We eat the whole can of hash and wish for more. I hope Ronald and Frank have found a source of food for us.

Nona is dressed up, and not in her usual white uniform. "Everything's under control, Jan. I'm going out to put my name in some of those agencies that supply nurses for home care. Then I'll pick up something for dinner. See you about noon."

I watch her drive off and realize this is the first time the three of us, Carl, Gram, and I, have been alone.

15

The morning is busy. I can see why the nursing home is always rush, rush, rush. Just getting dressed takes hours. I heat water in the kettle and fill a pan. Gram sits at the table and washes her face, arms, anyplace she can reach. Her hands are not strong enough to wring out the washcloth and her robe is soaked. Carl is lucky—he can put his teeth in a glass, but Gram must brush hers and lean her head over the sink so she can spit.

Getting dressed in a wheelchair is no joke. "I forget which is front and which is back," Gram confides to me.

"Well, sitting down like this, it's best to wear

the jumper backward. Leave the back open."

When she is dressed, she leans her head back and sleeps, snoring. I finish the job, pulling on socks and tying her sneakers. She is no help at all. It's like putting Sue-Sue's boots on.

Carl dresses himself, and that's good. I have no wish to see a man's body. I leave Gram to her snoring and find Carl tugging at the kitchen door. I open it and he wheels himself away.

This gives me time for the dishes, but first I have to get more water. The bathroom water has been used for flushing, and the kitchen water for coffee and washing up. I bring in two pails. Dishwashing could be a full-time job. First, heat the kettle for the wash water, and then heat up rinse water. Soon the blueberry dishes shine on the yellow shelf paper.

I look longingly at the beds when I smooth them out. If I could just lie down for a minute . . . Gram snorts herself awake.

"Where am I?" she asks, all bewildered. "Oh, Jan. For a minute there I thought I was back at Dugan's." She laughs and her crazy sly look comes back. "I think we're the only two who ever took a ride out of there and lived to tell about it."

This makes me feel better. She doesn't miss therapy or those goofy crafts they do to pass time.

Gram straightens her shoulders. "Time for my

therapy." I help her out the door. It is then I see the empty wheelchair and terror shoots through me. Carl must have fallen.

"Carl," I scream.

Carl steps out of the shadows under the tree. Steps might not be the best word. One foot moves slowly across the grass, and when it's firmly in place, the other foot slides past it. He is upright, he is moving, and I remember to breathe again.

"Oh, how lovely." Gram clasps her thin white hands together. "Get me my walker, Jan. Please," she adds softly. She can see I'm afraid. This ground is bumpy, and I am the only one here. She is older than I am and I usually do what she says, so I get her walker. For a little old lady who a few days ago screamed with fright whenever anyone touched her, she is suddenly too brave.

I lock the wheels of her chair and Carl and I offer steadying arms. She holds the walker. Triumphant, she stands a minute, and then Carl and I chant a cadence and she moves, ever so slowly, toward the tree. The rubber-tipped legs of the walker grip the ground, and she is more confident than she ever was on the shiny vinyl tiles in the therapy room.

"A red maple. See the keys flying?"

I pick one up, split it, and stick it on my nose

the way she taught me when I was little.

"Oh, Jan," she giggles. Then, "Get me my chair."

She sinks back and pulls up her feet. Carl gets into his chair, and the last I see when I go into the house is the two of them sitting in the sun, chatting comfortably.

At noon Nona drives back with Sylvia and Trixie. They help her carry in bags of groceries. I've never been so glad to see food before. While we put it away, Sylvia tells us about her morning.

"We went to Dugan's like we usually do, so no one would think it strange that all the volunteers didn't show up. We met Mr. Dugan in the hall and explained that you were staying home because your great-grandmother was visiting." She and Trixie start giggling.

"Then I told him my mother needs me to help her the rest of the summer, and Sylvia said that her family was going on vacation. Now we can come here every day and not split our time."

Nona has brought roast-beef sandwiches, and we all sit around the table and eat, and then she shoos Gram and Carl off for naps.

"How'd it go?" Sylvia asks, her blue eyes squinched up with concern.

"Okay, okay." My words sort of hang there. "They seem fine. Did some walking today. Gram even

119

made Carl hash this morning. It's just that— I don't know, it seems so"—I grope for words in my tired brain—"so endless."

"I'll be here today and Trixie tomorrow. You'll have two days to do what you want."

I look down at the table. What do I want? Suddenly, overwhelmingly, I just want to sleep.

Trixie nods. "Exactly right. Go home and take a nap. Your mother expects it."

"She does?"

"Sure. The mothers think we're having slumber parties. You know, sitting up and playing records and telling stories. My mother is always telling me about her slumber parties. They think we're not getting any sleep at all."

When I'm ready to go, Gram grabs my hand and gives me a searching look. The kind she used to give me when she was trying to find out who ate the last piece of cake or left a wet towel on the bathroom floor. Today she is not ready to ask questions, but it won't be long. We exchange kisses, and I know she is watching my back go down the road.

"I knew it," Mom greets me at the door. "You are exhausted, you naughty girl. You didn't sleep a wink last night. Go upstairs and close your door. I'll keep the little ones out of your hair." Trixie was right. Mom is delighted that I was up all night at a slumber party. She has also blossomed into a full shirt I haven't seen since before Sue-Sue was born.

I lie on the bed, counting corned-beef-hash and soup cans, and rubbing my arm muscles so knotted from carrying buckets of water, but then my eyes close and I burrow my face in the scratchiness of the bedspread and fall asleep.

16

When I wake I'm not sure if it's night or day, but then a hint of red shows in the east and I know it is early on a summer Sunday. Sue-Sue lies in the next bed, thumb tucked near her mouth, her dark hair a mass of sweaty ringlets. I stretch and breathe quietly, finding my skin pocked with marks from the spread. Gram's all right. I'll see her in a few hours.

By seven I'm bathed and full after an enormous breakfast, and out on the familiar trail to Gram's, carrying a bag of goodies, including Gram's lavender oil. The world is so fresh, every step is a delight, and I marvel at a bleeding heart plant and bearded irises and dew-glistened spider webs.

Our house is silent when I get there. I leave my bag by the door and walk around back, certain that Sylvia and Nona will sleep awhile longer. Walking softly in the grass, I almost scream aloud when I see Carl walking by the well.

"That forsythia needs trimming," he says in greeting. "Think your contacts in the outside world can get hold of some clippers for me?"

His eyes under their white sprouts of eyebrows twinkle with life. The sunken man who sat by the door waiting for his son is gone for good.

Nona raises her head and peers out through the screen. "You keep on like this, you'll be asking for more than clippers. Next it'll be dancing girls and nights on the town." She sounds pleased with Carl and with herself.

In the kitchen I find that Ronald and Frank had delivered a load of groceries the afternoon before. I try my hand at cooking bacon in the big iron frying pan. Carl brings in a bucket of water and pours some in the jug, so I can make coffee, and takes the rest to the bathroom. I wonder if he should be raising buckets from the well, but decide he's older than I am and should know what he's doing.

The bacon takes most of my attention, but I am struck with a terrible thought. What if Carl gets too well? Would he leave?

As if reading my thoughts, he sits at the table and peels one of Nona's oranges. "Don't look so downcast, little one, I won't desert you yet. First I'll work on these muscles, and then I'll beard old Leopold in his den."

We smile, like two old friends.

Sylvia grumbles when she comes in. "I can't cook," she says flatly. Babies in the family never can. They miss a lot of fun. The smells of bacon and bubbling coffee raise Gram and she wheels in, robe on backward again.

I ask Nona when she will start nursing in homes. "This is my vacation, Jan. I'm having a good time right here. I would never leave patients who needed baths."

"Oh, no," Carl groans, "I'm tired just from carrying one bucket. We'd better wait till the boys get here."

Sylvia and I start lugging water and heating it up for dishes. Frank and Ronald arrive near noon and the bucket brigade is on. Buckets of water go into the tub and then are heated by water poured from the stove. When the first bath is finally ready, Nona takes Gram and the lavender bath oil.

We start again, collecting and heating water.

How wonderful it would be just to turn a faucet and have hot water pour out.

Nona wheels Gram past us. She is perky in her favorite pink, and as she rides by we sniff the clean scent of lavender.

Ronald and Frank take over Carl's bath, and Sylvia and I go out to sit on the grass. Gram is around the corner, catching a little sun.

Sylvia makes a whistle out of a flat blade of grass. "Ronald thinks there's money somewhere. Money is being sent to Dugan's, and Carl and your grandmother aren't getting any of it."

"Gram gets a social security check once a month, but I don't know what happens to it." Money talk makes me squirm, but we could use some grocery money.

"When Carl gets stronger he'll be able to handle things."

A vibrant voice is singing opera in the bathroom. I ask Sylvia if Ronald sings, and she rolls laughing on the grass. It must be Carl. We're so busy listening we don't hear Trixie come up.

"Thought I'd never get away. First church, then Sunday dinner, then I had to explain again why I was going to your house, Jan. Where's everybody?"

We tell her to listen to Carl. Then we hear something else. The sound of a car on our road. The boys and Nona are already here, their cars parked in the driveway, so it is someone else. I grab Trixie's bag and run, the other two hot on my heels. We close the kitchen door and peer out from behind the herb-patterned curtains.

It is a blue and white patrol car that slows down and stops out front. The policeman is Billy Sullivan, who has known us since first grade. He steps out and we panic.

His hand on his revolver, he walks slowly across the grass and tries to see in the open windows. We duck back and cling to one another.

Then we hear Nona's, "May I help you, officer?" It is hard to hear through Carl's aria.

"No one's ever lived here as long as I've been patrolling, which is nine years now."

Nona laughs. She's enjoying herself. "It's my cousin's house. He lives in New York and never uses it. I rented it for the summer."

"Just you, ma'am?"

Carl is singing up a storm and water is draining.

"Just me and my husband. I'd invite you in, but he's taking a bath."

"Really enjoys it, doesn't he? Well, it's nice to meet you, Mrs. . . . Mrs. . . . ."

"Mrs. Stringer." We cling to one another in a spasm of silent giggles.

"I'll come down this way every now and then

to check on you folks. You're kind of off the beaten path."

We hear their voices grow fainter as they walk to the patrol car, and just as we're about to burst, the car door slams, and the patrolman drives off. Nona comes in, her finger to her lips. "He's got to go down to the river and turn around and will pass us in a minute." Now we cling to Nona and her shoulders shake, too. It seems five minutes before the patrol car slowly passes and goes down the dirt road.

"You were great, Nona."

We all hug. It's hard to believe I used to dislike this wonderful person.

Carl is shaven and clean. "I'd forgotten what a pleasure a bath is. If it weren't for that water-carrying, I'd spend my afternoons in there."

"You sing beautifully," Sylvia says, and we all giggle.

Ronald wants to know what's so funny so we tell him about Nona being Mrs. Stringer, and Carl claps her on the back. "Welcome to my family," he says and bows graciously.

17

It is Monday morning and my turn to stay with Gram again, and as I pack my duffle, Mom calls, "Phone for you."

Kitty is on the line and she is whispering. "Just wanted you to know that I heard Dr. Cronin asking about two of his patients this morning. He said that when they come back your great-grandmother needs more medication to help her sleep, and that Carl should have a shot of vitamins, since his strength is going so fast."

I thank her, grab some cans of food, thinking it won't be long before Mom thinks she's being robbed, and start on my way.

The day is grayer, but still no rain, and I laugh as I walk, thinking of Gram sleeping the nights through and Carl pruning the forsythia. Kitty's warning makes me realize the stay at our house could be over any minute, but that it's doing some good.

Ronald and Frank are already at the house. I ask Ronald how his boat is, and he smiles at me. "Just about finished. Another coat of varnish and she'll be ready to launch." Then he turns to Frank and Carl, and I can see they're cooking something up.

"Fishing," Carl gloats. "We're going fishing tomorrow in the river. When I'm stronger we'll go out on Ronald's boat. This is sure a great bunch of friends you've got, Jan."

The morning hassle is easier, though we are tired of carrying buckets. Gram sits at the kitchen table with a pan of warm, soapy water, swishing their clothes and wringing them out. It is a sloppy business, but it strengthens her hands and she enjoys it. While she washes, she tells me about Clara and fancy parties and what my great-grandfather was like. For an old lady who couldn't put two words together a week ago, she is wearing out my ears.

The day passes quickly. Sylvia shows up for a while and hangs up clothes, then she and Trixie go home with the boys. Gram practices with her walker, and Carl spends the afternoon digging for worms. I watch them carefully. Gram is not tired and Carl is not weak.

In the morning, Gram uses her walker to get to the table and sits in a regular chair. Carl eats with his fishing hat on, ready to leave as soon as the boys arrive. He rinses his own dishes and smooths his bed. The boys still haven't come, so he pushes his wheelchair out the door and folds it up.

"They can put it in the shed. I won't be needing *that* anymore."

The boys come bumping down the road, Sylvia with them. She waves a chicken, which she bought with her own allowance.

Soon the men are ready. Frank carries the can of worms, and Ronald shoulders three fishing poles. They each offer an arm to Carl.

Nona sniffs, sounding like her old nursing-home self. "Don't hold me responsible if you fall in the river, husband," she says, and everybody laughs. "Dr. Cronin would have a heart attack if he could see you."

The three fishermen walk down the driveway and turn onto the road to the river.

I go in to pack my things. As I tuck my slippers into the duffle, I hear the clump, step, step of the walker. Gram turns and sits in her wheelchair and motions to me to sit on the bed.

"Does Clara know I'm here?"

I shake my head dumbly.

"Then where does she think I am?" Gram's voice rises.

I run my fingers over her yellow spread. "She thinks you're at Dugan's."

"How long have I been here, child?"

I look at Gram's face to see if she's lost contact, but her eyes are clear and she is solidly in the room and solidly in her right mind. "We took you out last Friday, and today is Tuesday, so it's been five days."

Gram grips the arms of her chair and looks puzzled. "Funny she didn't visit me. I remember her riding in the ambulance when I went to Dugan's. Did she ever come again?"

I grope for words that won't make Mom seem uncaring. "She did come, once. But she knew I was with you every day. She wanted to hear everything about you. Then there's the baby."

"Sue-Sue?"

"No. The new baby. The one that's not born yet."

"Oh." Gram stops to think. "Then who knows I'm here?"

I rub the ribbed bedspread hard enough to burn my finger. "No one."

"What?"

"Well, hardly anyone. Nona knows, and Ronald and Frank and the Sunshine Club and Kitty. And Carl, of course."

"For all Clara knows, I could be dying in Dugan's." Gram grows smaller, like she's taken one of Alice's "eat-me" pills and is shriveling up into nothing.

"No, no, that's not true. Mom's just busy with the urchins, and Dad's been catching up on his work. They spent a lot of time in the hospital when you were there." I swallow some tears. Nothing hurts as much as something that is very close to the truth.

Gram reaches out a hand. "Don't cry, child. You didn't leave me, you and your lovely friends, and those handsome young men."

Her hand is warm, not that dried-up fragile wing she waved from the ambulance. It has blood running through it, and flesh that has somehow thrived on canned soup and stolen fruit.

"Five days." Gram stands up and reaches for her walker. "Think I'll go tell that Sylvia what to do with that chicken. She certainly will never be a cook." Gram walks firmly out of the bedroom, and the only shaking she does is because she is laughing.

18

I hate going home. My life is now centered in that little house in the woods and I am outgrowing the stucco house. Mom and Dad are waiting for the baby, and David and Sue-Sue live in a world where they want things right now. Gram is the only one who has a part in all of life.

I drag my duffle up the front steps to the wide veranda. The house looks empty, not a toy on the porch, no movement inside.

The door crashes open. Mom stands there, her eyes red and swollen.

"Where have you been?"

"With Gram." I try to move my shaky legs inside, but Mom blocks the doorway.

"Don't lie to me." She grabs my shoulders and shakes me until my head bobs like a toy dog in the rear window of a car. I have never, never been treated this way, and almost swing at her stomach. But I don't. There's a baby swimming in there, its bones soft as poached fish.

"I thought the old folks would like some cookies. I called Dugan's this morning to see if I could bring some over to my grandmother. They said she wasn't there." Mom is hysterical. I should pour water over her head, but she won't let me pass.

"They said that she's been home this week on a visit, and they were just about to call me to see when she's coming back." Mom draws in a ragged breath. "Do you understand what I'm saying? She's not there. I called your father at work. He's coming right home. Mr. Dugan himself is coming over. And you, young lady, have a lot to answer to. Where were you this morning? Where were you last night? I called Sylvia's mother this morning, and she said you weren't there. Trixie's mother said the same thing. Where were you?" She is still talking and screaming, and now the two urchins hanging on to her knees are crying.

It's all over. My legs give way and I slide to the doorsill, hugging my duffle. Oh, Gram, it's all over.

Of course, it isn't all over. It gets worse. Mr. Dugan drives up in a big black car that looks like his hearse. Dad pulls up and screeches on the brakes just before he drives straight through the garage. Leopold, who looks like a Leopold, inches to the curb in a shiny silver sports car.

Company is company, so Mom dashes to the kitchen to splash her face with water. I still sit on the floor, duffle in arms, while David and Sue-Sue back away from me.

Everyone comes in the door at the same time and they all step over me. Dad grabs my arm and pulls me upright and into the living room.

It is the Tower of Babel all over again, no one understanding what anyone else is saying. Finally Dad uses his loudest voice, and in an instant everything is quiet.

"All right, young lady, talk."

I stare at the picture of naked bathers over the mantel. I don't know where to start. Anger and fear push at my chest and close my throat. If the words don't come out, can they force them? Pick me up and wring me until words dribble out?

"Call the police," Mr. Dugan spits out. "Those

135

people are in my care. I'm responsible for them."

"Wait." Dad holds up an immaculate hand, not a speck of dirt under any nail. He takes such good care of himself. I wonder how he'd like to be bathed by Nona. His hand holds back the forces and it is quiet again. I swallow, but there is nothing to swallow.

"Gram was dying."

"She was not, not, not." How could such a nervous pipsqueak have a neat daughter like Kitty? "She was well taken care of. I looked at her charts."

"Not her body. That wasn't dying. Not yet. Just my real Gram."

Mom is crying again. "I told you that, Jan. When she broke her hip, she changed. She did and said things she'd never done before. She was different." Mom puddles up a tissue and then shrieks, "Where is she now, Jan?"

Leopold adds his two cents. "Old people do change, young lady. Believe me, I know. It broke my heart to leave my father there."

Well, Gram, here they are. The in-betweens who take charge of the young and the old. I look up at the bathers, who, at least, have nothing to say.

"Gram and Carl are fine. They're living together."

If it was Babel in the beginning, it is bedlam now. Maybe Leopold is having a heart attack. Mom clutches her unborn baby. Dad is laughing or crying, I can't tell which. Mr. Dugan is trying to catch something slipping through his fingers.

"The Sunshine Club, that's Trixie, Sylvia, and me, found them a home. They're living in it."

"Together? My grandmother and this man's father?" I think Mom would be happier if I said Gram and Carl were dead.

I'm not sure what all the fuss is about, but I try to calm them down. "They each have a wheelchair." Mom sobs and Leopold clutches his chest.

"Your mother wants to know where they sleep," Dad says. When he says "your mother" I know he's the one who wants to know.

"Carl sleeps in the front bedroom, and Gram in the back. After all, they *are* over fifty."

Dad starts talking over Mom's sighs of relief. He looks at me as if he's never seen me before. Maybe I was adopted at birth. I just don't fit in this family.

"You still haven't answered the first question your mother asked. Where were you last night?"

When one thing comes out, it's best to empty everything else. "I was at our house last night. We take turns, and last night was my turn."

"Your mother thought you were with Sylvia."

"I wanted her to think I was with Sylvia so she wouldn't worry."

Dad spends a long time examining me, then he chuckles, the way he used to when I was his one and only. "Well, let's just go to 'your house' and see what damage you've done."

I sigh and square my shoulders. There is no way to warn anyone. No phone there, and I'm short of carrier pigeons. All I can hope is that everything is the way I left it and that Gram isn't lying in the driveway with another broken hip, and that Carl is still wearing his teeth and hasn't fallen into the river.

Leopold wants to take us in his car, and Dugan insists we go in his. Mom tries to get me to stay and babysit, but I refuse, so we end up with a caravan, our car leading the way. No one says anything until I direct them onto the dirt road; then Mom blurts out, "I knew you were up to no good that day I picked you up here. I should have asked you about it then." She sighs. "Then we wouldn't be in this mess."

The branches of the big maple almost hide the driveway, so I caution Dad to be careful. Gram might decide to take a walk. I hope she's sitting down when she sees the car or she might fall. I pray Carl isn't floating downstream. I cross my fingers and toes, but decide against crossing my eyes. Gram told me they might stick that way.

19

Dad stops at the beginning of the driveway, so the other cars have to park out in the road. David and Sue-Sue pile out as if we've just arrived at a vacation spot. My eyes mist at the sight of our lovely, warm house.

Where is everybody? Mr. Dugan and Leopold walk up the driveway and are almost bowled over by the urchins, who spin like tops and fall to the grass.

"I don't see a soul," Leopold complains.

"Well, of course not," Mom answers, quite in control of herself at last. "They're both in wheel-chairs, you know."

A little smile picks at the corners of my mouth, in spite of my whole world falling to pieces.

Sylvia walks around the side of the house. "Oh," she gasps. She thinks I broke our pact. When she gets over her shock she leads us around the corner of the house.

Gram's standing, one hand on her walker, the other hand reaching out for blueberries and dropping them, ever so gently, into one of the blueberry-patterned bowls. She has a regal look, neck stretched out, hair swept back behind her ears. At Mom's soft intake of breath Gram turns, and the warmest, broadest smile stretches her wrinkles and spreads into her eyes.

"Clara!"

Mom just forgets about that baby and runs across the grass as carelessly as Trixie runs the jumping field. Grandmother and granddaughter hug somehow, despite the walker and Mom's stomach.

"I thought you'd forgotten me." Gram is not accusing, just stating a fact.

"I'd never, never forget you. I was trying to put my life in order. I couldn't bear to see you change."

"Jan," Gram shouts with authority, "get some chairs. We'll sit in the sun and talk."

Leopold is stomping around Sylvia and demanding to see his father, so I stop and turn to Dad for help. He has a strange look on his face,

like he's been left out of a party. I tell him where
Carl is, and Dad leaves, taking Leopold and Mr.
Dugan with him. When I come out of the house
with Gram's chair and the kitchen chairs, the men
are way down the road.

"Can I get you something to eat, Clara?" Gram
is once again hostess in her own house. She sinks
into her chair and laughs. "I take that back. Food
is a problem here."

Mom is comforted by this. "As soon as I take
you back, I'll make sure you get a nice hot meal."
Not "I will cook you a meal," but you will "get"
one. She is still planning to take naughty Gram
back to Dugan's.

Gram flicks a finger at me as if getting rid of a
pesky fly. "Go play, Jan. We're talking."

I am as hot as if I'd swallowed red pepper. If
Gram goes to Dugan's, they can just send Dugan's
hearse for me. I sit under the maple tree with
Sylvia, who is in a state of shock.

"I should have known you wouldn't tell unless
you had to." She jumps up, a wild look on her
face. "If your mother called my mother and Trixie's mother, my mother doesn't know where I am,
and Trixie's in big trouble."

"Wait until the boys come. Ronald will have to
drive you home. He'll be in trouble, too."

Mom and Gram are still talking. The urchins

141

chase a butterfly. The men are still out of sight. I stretch out on the warm earth and, after all the screaming of the morning, find myself drifting into a formless cloud of nothingness. Even the bees are quiet and birds fly silently in the heavy summer air.

Voices filter in and out of my sleep and at first I think there's a radio playing. Someone turns up the volume and I hear my father's voice telling the announcer to calm down. My eyes open and I am looking up at the heavy hanging leaves.

"Calm down," Dad yells. He is not too calm himself. Frank is helping Carl into his wheelchair, which just this morning Carl had folded to put away in the shed. Ronald and Sylvia are gone and so is Ronald's car. I wonder how Trixie is making out.

Leopold is a bantam rooster next to Carl. It must be hard for a man to have his father tower over him. Right now this is not what Leopold is excited about.

"I found him right at the edge of the river. In *his* condition." Carl's condition does not look bad to me, even if he is back in his wheelchair. But a large dose of Leopold would give anyone a condition.

"All the money I've spent getting him the best of care, and for one whole week he's had no care at all. When my lawyers finish with these boys"—he waves an arm at Frank—"they'll never drive an ambulance again. They'll be in jail, they'll, they'll . . ." His voice climbs higher and I wish Nona would give him a shot, but then I realize her car is gone.

Frank puts his hands on Carl's shoulders. "Walked all the way to the river, made one of the finest casts I've ever seen, and look what he pulled out first time."

Frank shows the bucket around. There's a bass in there so big it can't stretch straight out, but lies in a curve like a half moon. "Not bad for a fellow who's been without care almost a week."

"Good," Gram says. "You boys clean it and I'll have food for everyone. Won't have to wait for Nona to come with the groceries." She claps her hand over her mouth, but too late. Mr. Dugan's ears have already picked up the name.

Carl uncurls himself from his chair and glowers down at Leopold. "A week ago I wouldn't have given this," he snaps his fingers, "for my chances. I went to Dugan's to recover from my operation. Then I found out I can't get out unless my son signs some papers. So I wait. And wait. Then these young people rescued me. In two days I was out of the wheelchair. In five days I catch the finest bass of my life. And look at her." He waves at

Gram. "She was a crazy old lady who screamed whenever anyone touched her. Now she's talking about cooking bass for all you good people."

While Carl is talking, a crowd gathers. Ronald and Sylvia, their parents, and Trixie have come in one car. Nona leaves her car on the road and runs up to join the rest of us.

Gram beckons to the tearful Sunshine Club, so we huddle at her knees where she can hug us.

Sylvia's father is a big-city lawyer, and usually we keep out of his way because he doesn't like noise or confusion. But today he makes the noise and confusion himself and looks about to tear Ronald limb from limb.

Mr. Dugan shakes a fist and yells, "You're fired," at Nona. Nona is pale, but she smiles at us.

Carl is still standing and he tells everyone to sit. Mom slides to the ground, an arm around each urchin. Sylvia's father squats on his heels, pulling our Girl Scout leader with him. Nona lowers herself on a pile of leaves. Dad sits cross-legged on the grass, Leopold next to him. The last to go down is Mr. Dugan.

Carl looks wonderful in his fishing hat. "We can go on yelling and punishing the kids and getting upset, or we can try to make sense out of what has happened."

He looks around, fixing each person with his

snapping sharp eyes. "I was dying. These three girls and these two young men saved me. Nona, and I'm sorry you got dragged into this, my dear, made sure there were no medical emergencies. Now, so far, I don't see the crime. Where I do see wrongdoing is that I was left in a place when I no longer needed to be there."

Leopold stares down at his black, businessman shoes.

"I do worry about being in this house. I have no idea who it belongs to. We're trespassers. Leopold, I want you to find the owner, whoever he is. I would like to buy this house."

We all squeeze hands, and Gram hugs us again.

"Now, as for you, Mr. Dugan"—Carl glares at the poor little man who has just lost two boarders—"you keep the money due you for this last week, but anything extra is to be turned back to me and to Jan's parents. I, personally, will pay Nona to come here every day to keep us healthy."

Carl turns to Gram and makes an elegant bow. "You are welcome to stay in my house as long as you like. I don't think it will be livable in the winter, but there is a whole summer of living to do."

Gram's hand flutters to my head and rests there lightly. "I would be delighted to live with you, Carl."

145

"But us? Are you going to leave us out?" I ask, ignoring Mom's whimper and the growl in Dad's throat.

"The whole Sunshine Club's welcome. Though aren't you getting tired of carrying water from the well?"

Leopold comes out of his volcanic gloom. "The minute you own the house, I'll have the well hooked up and a pump put in. But I've been running the business for you, and I have to know if you're coming back. And if you do, how can you run a business from this hiding place in the woods?"

"We can work things out and sign some papers. Suddenly I don't want to work anymore. I think I'll spend my summer fishing."

Nona smiles. "I refuse to clean fish, but I'll be happy to come in every day. It'll be a grand vacation, taking care of you and Mrs. Lowden. My new job doesn't start until September."

In the glorious hubbub of crisis over, everyone talks at once. Ronald about launching his boat and taking Carl fishing on the lake. Mom and Dad discuss turning the dining room into a room for Gram and making the pantry into another bathroom. The sun is dropping on the tops of trees and burning redly through the leaves. My legs hurt from sitting on the grass and my eyes burn from all the tears.

"You tired, Gram?" I look up into her eyes.

Gram blinks and nods with gray-white weariness.

"Shall I wheel you in?"

She begins to say yes. I see her set her lower jaw on the "Y," but then she shakes her head fiercely. She refuses weakness in front of all these people. "Get me my walker, child."

Gram stands and bows, as if saying good night at the end of a dinner party. "You may visit any day from two to four," the queen says to her subjects.

We all watch Gram clump, step, step, into her house.

"You told me she would never get any better," Mom says to Mr. Dugan.

"That is what my staff told me. There is never enough time for me to see every patient."

"Perhaps that's your trouble, Mr. Dugan." Carl looks as exhausted as Gram. "If you took more time to know your patients, maybe Dugan's would not laughingly be known as the 'last resort.' "

Leopold does not notice his father is tiring, but Dad does. He swoops Sue-Sue up in his arms and takes David's hand. "We're off. You included, Jan. I'll drive you back later with food. I'm sure Gram will be hungry when she wakes up."

We back out the driveway and drive past the

line of cars. Through the rear window I see Carl and Nona enter the kitchen door, and Leopold and Sylvia's father walking down the driveway, talking. "Can you call Trixie's mother and smooth things out, Mom?"

Mom shifts her stomach. "I will, Jan. At least I'll try." Poor Mom. She's had a rough day. Once again she has to face opening up the family for Gram, as well as face the new baby when it comes.

20

It is dark now. The tree frogs are singing, each one inspiring the others to sing louder, a kind of syncopated rhythm that swells and swells. June bugs hit the screen like armored tanks. Trixie and Sylvia are home, trying to settle things with their families, so it's just Gram, Carl, and me. And we are full.

"Best bass I ever ate," Carl rumbles.

"That potato salad is just like what I used to make when Clara was little."

It's not food that fills me up. It's uneasiness and sadness, and I can't understand it. Here we are, three people who love one another, in our cozy house, on the little porch with nothing surrounding us but friendly trees and comforting night sounds.

It's like Giants and Pirates, I realize. Once we had made our lists and planned everything, we usually stopped the game. It was the planning that was fun.

"We did have them fooled for a while, didn't we, girl?" Carl's laughter vibrates up from his bass-filled stomach. "Kidnapped by eleven-year-olds, placed in a stolen house, hidden away for almost a week. Not many adults could do what you've done, Jan."

Gram feels each finger on my hand as if she's trying to memorize the knuckles, the bones, the skin. "It's strange I was never frightened here, but there, with all those doctors and nurses, I was terrified. When you're scared, your mind escapes. Now my mind is back. Love did that."

My mind pictures maple leaves reddening and swirling down in the fall. The house is shut up, sleeping under a blanket of snow. I can't see where everyone has gone. "But after? I don't know—" I falter.

"Listen," Gram whispers. A bullfrog chuga-rums. "Pit, pit" sounds against the leaves.

"Rain," Carl exults. "We've been lucky. This is the first rain in our house."

150

"There'll always be a first something," Gram says. "My first steps without a walker. Carl pulling in his first bass. And you, child, your life will be full of firsts."

The rain changes from "pit, pit" to "hiss, splat," and a growing wind sprays it through the screen. Carl rises and leans to help Gram up. "It's been a long day. I'm ready to dream about leaping bass."

Gram's hands close on the walker. "Oh"—she pauses in mid step—"I left the blueberries in that lovely bowl outside."

I am feeling hollow and lonely. The secret about our house has been yanked out, leaving a gaping hole, and nothing has seeped in to fill it.

"We'll pick more in the morning," Gram says, with a firm nod of her head. "When the sun comes out."

How can she promise anything? The sun may never come out, and there may be no morning. Birds might eat the blueberries and deer smash the blueberry bowl. All we have is now. Rain against the screen, a distant flash of lightning in the sky, and the companionable breathing of three friends ready for sleep.

I unroll my sleeping bag and snuggle in. Gram's hand reaches down and takes mine. "Night, Gram." I hold on, lest she slip away.

"Tomorrow I'll teach you how to make a blueberry pie."

I hold on to that word "tomorrow" as tightly as I hold Gram's hand. The rain on our roof sings us to sleep.

ATHENS REGIONAL LIBRARY SYSTEM

3 3207 00012 1964

289469

J   DOREN

BORROWED
SUMMER

GEORGIA CHILDREN'S BOOK
AWARD NOMINEE

REGIONAL LIBRARY SERVICE

ATHENS AREA

ATHENS, GEORGIA 30601